The Naked Truth

The Naked Truth

Why Hollywood Doesn't Make
X-Rated Movies

KEVIN S. SANDLER

RUTGERS UNIVERSITY PRESS
NEW BRUNSWICK, NEW JERSEY AND LONDON

Library of Congress Cataloging-in-Publication Data

Sandler, Kevin S., 1969–
The naked truth : why Hollywood doesn't make X-rated movies / Kevin S. Sandler.
   p.   cm.
   Includes bibliographical references and index.
   ISBN-13: 978-0-8135-4088-7 (hardcover : alk. paper)
   ISBN-13: 978-0-8135-4089-4 (pbk. : alk. paper)
   1. Motion pictures—Ratings—United States. 2. Sex in motion pictures.
I. Title.
   PN1993.5.U6S23   2007
   384.'84—dc22

                                                                2006032341

A British Cataloging-in-Publication record for this book is available from the
British Library.

Manufactured in the United States of America

Contents

Acknowledgments

The genesis of this project dates back to 1990, when I attended the opening screening of the first NC-17-rated film, *Henry & June,* at the Showcase Cinemas in Ann Arbor. Drawn in and tantalized by the newly decorated X rating, I left the theater largely perplexed, wondering what all the fuss was about. My professors at the University of Michigan, particularly Stuart McDougal and Peter Bauland, had trained me soundly in textual analysis, but I could not for the life of me tell the difference between this NC-17 film and the many R-rated films I had seen in my youth: *Fast Times at Ridgemont High, 9½ Weeks,* and the long gone but not forgotten *Hot Dog . . . The Movie.*

Fast-forward several Criterion laser discs and a *Basic Instinct* later. My curiosity about the rating system evolves into graduate work at Sheffield Hallam University in Sheffield, England. I am grateful to Richard Maltby and Steve Neale for their enthusiasm and generosity in seeing through the initial stages of this book. Other people played central roles throughout this project's evolution. Their suggestions and support were invaluable, and I thank them immensely: Aaron Baker, Gregg Barak, Bryan Beckerman, Daniel Bernardi, Matthew Bernstein, David Darts, Edward Donnerstein, Tamara Falicov, Tony Grajeda, Philip Hallman, Dotty Hamilton, Lowell Harris, Heather Hendershot, Jennifer Holt, Henry Jenkins III, Dale Kunkel, Mark Langer, Peter Lehman, David Lugowski, Charlotte Pagni, Stephen Prince, Judd Ruggill, Eric Schaefer, Stephen Vaughn, Robin Wood, and Justin Wyatt. I especially want to thank my colleagues at the University of Arizona for all their support: Caren Deming, Vickki Dempsey, Mary Beth Haralovich, Nicole Koschmann, Yuri Makino, Michael Mulcahy, Patrick Roddy, Dorothy Roome, Beverly Seckinger, Barbara Selznick, Beretta Smith-Shomade, Lisanne Skyler, Albert Tucci, and Vicky Westover.

Two friends and colleagues, in particular, made a huge difference during the course of this project: Dennis Bingham and Evan Kirchhoff. Their cogent insights, keen eye for detail, and willingness to read entire chapters at a moment's notice were invaluable and so greatly appreciated. I also want to personally thank three individuals who have supported me throughout my academic career: Robert Eberwein, William Paul, and Gaylyn Studlar. I am indebted to them for their mentorship, encouragement, and advocacy. My gratitude is matched only by my respect for each of these individuals.

Support for this book came from a Fine Arts Research and Professional Development Incentive Grant, a Hanson Film Institute grant, and the Provost's Author Support Fund at the University of Arizona. Portions appeared at an earlier stage of development as "The Naked Truth: *Showgirls* and the Fate of the X/NC-17 Rating," in *Cinema Journal* 40, no. 3 (spring 2001): 69–93; and "Movie Ratings as Genre: The Incontestable R," in *Genre and Contemporary Hollywood: Formulas, Cycles, and Trends since the Late 1970s*, ed. Steve Neale (London: Routledge, 2002), 201–217.

My students, many of whom took my film censorship class at the undergraduate and graduate levels, deserve special thanks for allowing me to test my theories and presumptions on them, sometimes forcefully, sometimes unwittingly, but always with a smile. They continue to be a source of inspiration for me. I am especially grateful to Nazanin Bahkshi, Corey Becker, Rachel Boyes, Michael Burk, Jennifer Cady, Lance Christiansen, Josh Eichenstein, Ryan Fagan, Chiara Ferrari, Tana Ganeva, Tyler Gillett, Brett Gray, Robert Gudiño, Ben Herman, Justin Hultman, Henry Jenkins IV, Elisa Koehler, Kathleen Kuehn, John Laughlin, Ian Markiewicz, David McClafferty, Lanée Mellegard, Tim Morris, Stephen Parsey, Chelsea Powell, Jordan Rosenberg, Darren Rudy, Michael Schaner, Christine Scheer, Michael Shoel, Rebecca Skeels, Kyle Stine, Kristen Warner, Marissa Watson, and Matthew Witte.

A number of people in the industry agreed to share their resources, knowledge, and time with me. Among them are Paris Barclay, Wes Craven, Anthony D'Alessandro, Kirby Dick, John Fithian, Timothy Gray, Scott Hettrick, Gabriel Snyder, Michael Speier, Kenneth Turan, Christine Vachon, and John Waters. I especially want to thank Richard Heffner for making himself and his papers available to me for this project. Mary Marshall Clark, Whitney Krahn, Rosemary Newnham, Courtney Smith, and Shalini Tripathi at the Columbia University Oral History Research Office were immensely helpful in assisting me with Heffner's papers. The staff at the Margaret Herrick Library and the British Film Institute National Library were indispensable for the completion of this book.

Leslie Mitchner at Rutgers University Press has been an avid supporter of mine since my days as a master's student. She has outdone herself this time. I would put her name in caps but it is against press policy. Sincere thanks also go to Matthew Bernstein, who helped prepare this manuscript for press.

Throughout the process of researching and writing this book, my parents and siblings have stood by me. I deeply appreciate their commitment to my scholarship over the years even though I know they secretly worried about how I could build an academic career out of Bugs Bunny, *Titanic,* and X-rated movies.

Finally, this book would not have been possible without the undying support and extraordinary patience of my wife, Nadine. This is for her. Now it is time to clean the house and wash the dishes. I promise.

The Naked Truth

Introduction

*Our characters are made of wood and have no genitalia. If the puppets
did to each other what we show them doing, all they'd get is splinters.*
— Scott Rudin, producer of *Team America: World Police*

*People get shot in the head and bashed to a bloody pulp in movies all
the time, but we get an NC-17 for a glimpse of pubic hair. Why is that,
do you think?* — Wayne Kramer, director of *The Cooler*

TAKE ONE: Puppet sex. Two naked marionettes "making love." This
explicit two-minute sequence from *Team America: World Police* was given
an NC-17 (no one seventeen and under admitted) in September 2004 by the
Rating Board of the Classification and Rating Administration (CARA), the
movie rating system operated by the Motion Picture Association of America (MPAA). Contractually obligated to deliver an R-rated product (under
seventeen requires accompanying parent or adult guardian) to Paramount,
the filmmakers Trey Parker and Matt Stone—who four years earlier had a
similar ratings ruckus over *South Park: Bigger, Longer & Uncut* (1999)—
resubmitted the scene nine times with various alterations before the Rating
Board agreed to change the NC-17 to an R.[1] "They said you can't do anything but missionary position," remarked Parker, as his production team
eventually whittled down the first cut of the scene from two minutes to
forty-five seconds for theatrical release.[2] The final cut of the edited puppet-
passion sequence expunged many shots of nontraditional lovemaking practices, including moments of defecation and urination, while scenes
featuring gory bullet-ridden bodies, gruesome dismemberments, and other
forms of marionette-on-marionette violence remained untouched. For
Parker this incongruity represented CARA's hypocritical treatment of simulated sex and simulated violence. "We blow [a puppet of actress] Janeane

Garofalo's head right off. But the MPAA is more concerned with the puppets being naked."[3]

TAKE TWO: One and a half seconds of pubic hair. Thirty-six frames of
film. That is all that stood between an R and an NC-17 rating for *The Cooler*
in June 2003. The brief moment considered too explicit for an R by the Rating Board was a bedroom encounter between actors William H. Macy and
Maria Bello that revealed a glimpse of the actress's pubic region as Macy
kissed her torso. Not in question were two other moments: a shot of frank
sexuality where Bello has her hand cupped over Macy's genitals and a graphically violent scene where a hotel director, played by Alec Baldwin, whacks the
kneecaps of Macy's son with a tire iron.[4] Director Wayne Kramer contended
that the Rating Board capriciously applied the NC-17 rating to *The Cooler*,
arguing that many other R-rated films, particularly those filled with violence, were much more objectionable than *The Cooler*'s mature and honest
lovemaking scenes. "Go see *The Texas Chainsaw Massacre* [2003]," explained
Kramer. "This is an R-rated movie where somebody blows their head off, and
then the camera moves through the hole in their head and out the back of
their head again, and that's perfectly okay. Why is that so much more palat-
able than a beautiful naked body of a regular person?"[5] Macy echoed
Kramer's disgust, characterizing the R rating as a "catch-all" category for violence. "*Road to Perdition* [2002] got an R and they mowed down thirty men
in cold blood. It was just wholesome murder, a movie about vengeance. The
fact that they gave that an R rating and wouldn't give *The Cooler* an R unless
we cut two seconds of Maria Bello's pubic hair is sick."[6]

While Paramount, an MPAA-member distributor, acquiesced to the Rating Board's R specifications for *Team America*, the independent distributor
Lions Gate, a non-MPAA member, elected to appeal the NC-17 for *The Cooler*
to CARA's Appeals Board. Needing a two-thirds majority of the Appeals
Board members present to overturn the Rating Board's original rating, Lions
Gate lost by one vote, nine to six.[7] Members of the Appeals Board urged the
distributor to release the film with an NC-17, but Lions Gate went for the R,
replacing the one and a half seconds of non-hard-core imagery with alternative footage for U.S. theaters. For Lions Gate or for Paramount, the adults-
only category was never really an option.

The NC-17, like its predecessor, the X, which it replaced in 1990, carried the
stigma of pornography believed to impose too many economic barriers for
film distributors. Many TV and newspaper outlets might not advertise *Team
America* or *The Cooler*, most theater chains might refuse to book the films,
and key retailers like Wal-Mart and Blockbuster Video would not stock them,
fearing boycotts from parents, pressure groups, and politicians. Perhaps of

greater significance was that the NC-17 excluded patrons under the age of seventeen from purchasing a ticket to these films, severely cutting into their potential box office. These theatrical restrictions did not often apply, however, to the ancillary markets for these films: Paramount released an "uncensored and unrated" version of *Team America* on DVD for retailers like Best Buy, Target, and Amazon, and Lions Gate restored cut footage to *The Cooler* for its "unrated" pay-per-view airings on cable and satellite television. (Strangely, Lions Gate only offered the edited R-rated version on DVD.) Neither film generated any fuss from anyone.

The recent ratings battle over *Team America* and *The Cooler* might appear particularly absurd, illogical, or even noteworthy if the situations were not so typical. Negotiations for lower (rarely higher) ratings happen all the time between filmmakers and the Rating Board after its examiners view the initial cut of a film. All these disputes concern moments of violence, profanity, nudity, sex, drug use, and the treatment of provocative subjects and social themes that Rating Board examiners find too problematic for a particular rating category. Yet the Rating Board and the Appeals Board rarely justify their rulings to the public. As the self-regulatory system of Hollywood's two most private and powerful trade organizations, the MPAA and the National Association of Theatre Owners (NATO), CARA's methodologies, personnel, and missions have primarily been shrouded in secrecy since its creation on November 1, 1968.[8] Only since the early 1990s has CARA provided any explanation for a particular film's rating to the public.

These explanations, though, offer little insight into the organization's rating practices. For instance, *Team America* contains "graphic, crude, and sexual humor; violent images and strong language, all involving puppets," and *The Cooler* contains "sexuality, violence, language and some drug use."[9] Any further information (such as rating deliberations or cuts made to a film) is usually kept confidential; the MPAA prefers its members or signatories to keep all disagreements "in house," shielding its policies from public scrutiny. As a result, individual rating cases have been difficult to investigate and policy matters almost impossible to confirm.

Laying bare these policies, deciphering the actual boundaries between the R and NC-17—separating industry practice from Hollywood hype—is the primary goal of this book. What is most surprising, however, is that for a five-tiered rating system—G (all ages admitted), PG (parental guidance suggested), PG-13 (parents strongly cautioned), R, and NC-17—the adults-only rating is rarely used. In fact, since United Artists' *Inserts* in 1976, only two films from the MPAA signatories—Sony, Paramount, 20th Century Fox, Walt Disney, Warner Bros., and Universal (as of 2007)[10]—have seen wide release with the adults-only category: Universal's *Henry & June* (1990) and MGM/UA's *Showgirls* (1995).[11] All other MPAA-member films rated X or NC-17 during this time had been limited to small art-house releases. History clearly confirms that the MPAA signatories have almost exclusively released films categorized R or lower and that the Rating Board helps to ensure that all material that could be considered NC-17 in nature is removed from R-rated films. Yet Jack Valenti insists, time and time again, that "the rating system is *not* a censor," and CARA never commands any filmmaker to cut his or her film.[12] If this is true, why doesn't Hollywood make X or NC-17 movies?

The Naked Truth: Why Hollywood Doesn't Make X-Rated Movies argues that the collective shunning of the NC-17 by MPAA and NATO members remains a primary mechanism of industry self-regulation and self-preservation in the ratings era. By categorizing all films released by the majors and destined for mainstream theaters into R ratings (or lower), the industry ensures that its products are perceived as what I term "responsible entertainment." Under the pretense of responsible entertainment MPAA-member films are accessible by all audiences (even in the case of an R picture) and acceptable to Hollywood's various critics and detractors. CARA's Rating Board is in charge of maintaining the integrity of responsible entertainment across all rating classifications, but its most important task lies in determining the permissibility of a film's onscreen images and sounds for an R rating. CARA's arrangement of NC-17 studio product into what I call an "Incontestable R" protects the uppermost boundaries of the R rating by prohibiting controversial material, as well as by constructing cinematic representations permissible for the R category. The existence of a set of standards separating the R from the NC-17 indicates that the industry still abides by a de facto production code as a means of defense against external interference from politicians and moral reformers and against competition from independent distributors and exhibitors.

Keeping the practices of Hollywood private and confidential has always been the policy of the MPAA (known until 1945 as the Motion Picture Producers and Distributors of America [MPPDA]), dating back to the preclassification era of the Production Code (1930–1966). During and following this tenure, primary material and documentation on the MPAA/MPPDA's enforcer of the "Code"—the Studio Relations Committee (SRC, 1930–1934), the Production Code Administration (PCA, 1934–1966), and the Office of Code Administration (OCA, 1966–1968)—appeared only through individual accounts by industry members: in memoirs (MPAA president Will Hays), anecdotes (PCA examiner Jack Vizzard), oral histories (PCA chairperson Geoffrey Shurlock), and MPAA-commissioned studies (Raymond Moley).[13] Because of, or in spite of, this sequestration, 1960s and 1970s film historians

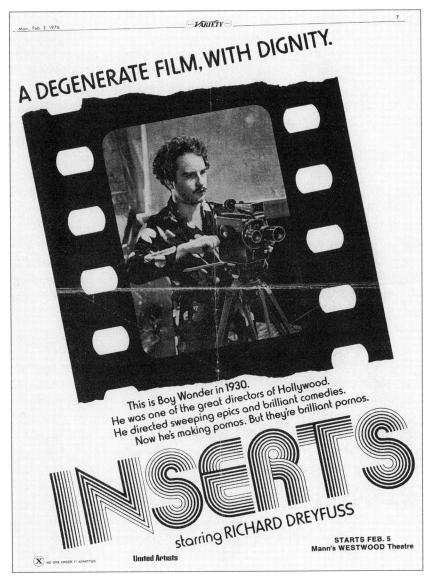

Figure 1. An ad from *Daily Variety* (Feb. 2, 1976) for one of the last X-rated films to be released by an MPAA member: Richard Dreyfuss in *Inserts* (1976).

like Garth Jowett, Robert Sklar, Richard S. Randall, and Ira Carmen concentrated their attention on the legal, political, and social dimensions of film regulation.[14] These necessarily fragmented and incomplete accounts of regulatory activities during the studio-system era persisted until 1986, almost eighteen years into CARA's regime, when MPAA president Jack Valenti released all the Production Code documents and memos to the Academy of Motion Picture Arts and Sciences' Margaret Herrick Library for scholarly research. Soon after the release of the PCA files, a deluge of scholarship filled in the noticeable, though unavoidable, gaps left by earlier researchers. Scholars (Richard Maltby, Lea Jacobs, Ruth Vasey, Gregory D. Black, and Leonard J. Leff and Jerold L. Simmons to name a few) could now fully reconstruct the processes of Hollywood self-regulation at the production level, focusing on the negotiation of individual films between filmmakers and the PCA.[15]

Like its predecessor, CARA has kept its case files classified during the time of its administration. But unlike the PCA, CARA's self-regulatory practices and history can be understood and theorized through several sources and methods unavailable to researchers of the past. Trade publications (*Variety, NATO News,* and various guild journals), national newspapers (*New York Times, Los Angeles Times*), and court transcripts, government hearings, and commission reports continue to provide some of the most valuable information on the workings of CARA. Supplementing these documents in the classification era, though, are candid, firsthand accounts of the rating process by disgruntled studio players like Trey Parker and independent filmmakers like Wayne Kramer. Unlike directors of the classical era, such filmmakers are unburdened by studio contracts and often speak frankly about their ratings battles with CARA to the broadcast, print, and online media. Additionally, these accounts can now be compared with the film texts themselves, to which scholars have almost unlimited access. With legal or bootleg copies of the same film available in differently rated or unrated versions from the United States and various foreign markets, these VHS, laser disc, and DVD versions are literal manifestations of the self-regulatory process kept secret by CARA. PCA historians must primarily rely on industry records of different cuts of a film; scholars of CARA have access to the objects themselves. Given these resources, one can authoritatively and persuasively investigate CARA during its period of operations, particularly the 1990s and beyond.

Until recently, secondary accounts and legal documents detailing CARA's practices and policies have been the principal resources for scholars such as Stephen Prince, Justin Wyatt, and Jon Lewis.[16] The second half of Lewis's book *Hollywood v. Hard Core: How the Struggle over Censorship Saved the Modern Film Industry* (2000) provided the most in-depth analysis of CARA to that date, primarily examining the organization's early years (1968–1973), when it initially struggled to protect the MPAA signatories against the liberal mind-set of the 1960s, independent distributors and exhibitors, and Hollywood filmmakers hungry to exploit the X rating. The popularity of hard- and soft-core pornography and a national standard of obscenity that rendered local censorship of obscene materials obsolete made such movies profitable and permissible. When in 1973 the Supreme Court—at that time a conservative bench as a result of four new Nixon appointees—returned content regulation to the states in *Miller v. California,* the ruling effectively eliminated the theatrical exhibition of pornography (except in a few cities) and saved Hollywood. The majors, argues Lewis, regained control of the American film industry, with CARA doing whatever it took to ensure that no MPAA films went out with an X.

Like his contemporaries, however, Lewis did not have access to any primary material of CARA's internal operations. Stephen Farber's *The Movie Rating Game* (1972), a descriptive, unauthorized account of his tumultuous six-month internship at CARA in 1970, remained the only insider's view of the organization's forty-year history for researchers.[17] This dearth of concrete information lasted until 2005, when Richard Heffner, the chairperson of CARA from 1974 to 1994, archived his papers and oral history (with film critic Charles Champlin) at Columbia University.[18] In 2006 Stephen Vaughn became the first film historian to incorporate Heffner's correspondence and recollections in his book *Freedom and Entertainment: Rating the Movies in an Age of New Media.*[19] Heffner's liberal attitudes toward a marketplace of free ideas were often at odds with Valenti's support of big business. Vaughn situates the development of the rating system around the continuous tension between the two men: their disagreements over rating sex and violence, over the integrity of the appeal process, and over the function of the X/NC-17 category. Vaughn's account of film regulation is also wide-ranging, for it considers the advent of newer distribution technologies (such as television, home video, and the V-chip) and the repercussions for copyright, the impact of special effects on the representation of violence, and the Reagan administration's war on drugs and their appearance in PG-13 films.

The Naked Truth incorporates Heffner's oral history and new interviews with the former chairperson in its analysis of the rating system. Whereas Vaughn's book provides a broader historical account of this period, I focus my attention primarily on the operations of CARA itself, particularly its Rating Board. Except when necessary, I do not examine other political, economic, and diplomatic arenas concerning the MPAA, such as film piracy, digital technology, and television ratings, all of which play an important role in *Freedom and Entertainment.* Furthermore, I examine only one set of ratings boundaries—the division between the R and the X/NC-17—as described in the snippets of puppet passion and pubic hair that began this introduction.

Only in specific cases do I account for deliberations on, contestations over, or modifications of ratings between the G, PG, PG-13, and R categories.

This is not to say that filmmakers, reform groups, politicians, and various other users of the rating system never criticize CARA publicly for what they see as hypocritical or capricious determinations made between and within these categories. For example, Robert Simonds, the producer of *Dirty Work* (1998), complained about the inconsistency and subjectivity of CARA when the film first earned an R rating for its foul language, nudity, and objectionable tone. In need of a PG-13 rating in order to reach a larger, unrestricted audience, he cut dialogue from the prison scene with the star, Norm Mac-Donald. After expressing fear about what happens to soft guys in prison, MacDonald is taken away by three hulking tattooed bikers. When he returns, he says, "You fellows have a lot of growing up to do," a line implying offscreen sodomy of MacDonald's character. "That was non-negotiable" with CARA, says Simonds. "You just can't have the star of your movie reprimanding his tormentors for being violated and still get a PG-13 rating."[20] More recently, Michael Moore publicly denounced CARA for not awarding a PG-13 to *Fahrenheit 9/11* (2004). Unwilling to cut the film, Moore released it with an R after the rating was upheld on appeal solely because of the repeated use of the word *motherfucker*.[21] Despite these instances, rating controversies over the past thirty-five years have primarily involved the boundary separating R from X and NC-17, since these debates often engage with questions of censorship, pornography, monopolization, media effects, and globalization that often do not surface together in the lower categories.

With its focus on the X/NC-17 rating, *The Naked Truth* also charts the ratings era after *Miller v. California,* the point when *Hollywood v. Hard Core* essentially ends. I particularly emphasize the period of the NC-17 rating (1990 to the present). Indeed, the most notable cases of the last fifteen years—*Basic Instinct* (1992), *Natural Born Killers* (1994), *Eyes Wide Shut* (1999), and *Kill Bill Vol. 1* (2003)—all concerned the boundary between the R and NC-17 ratings. Central to these debates are questions that have plagued CARA for years. Does CARA censor movies? Why does the MPAA need ratings in the first place? Why doesn't a rating exist between the R and NC-17 to distinguish between serious adult films and pornography? Is the rating system arbitrary and capricious? Can a film be viably marketed and released into theaters with an NC-17 rating? How can one and a half seconds of pubic hair be the difference between an R and an NC-17?

To answer these questions, *The Naked Truth* provides a history of Hollywood policy and procedure under CARA, beginning with an outline of my theoretical framework for answering the question "Does CARA censor movies?" Chapter 1 suggests that an instance of film censorship is best understood as "regulation," a negotiation between the film trade and institutions external to the film business rather than simply a prohibitory act performed by any single entity. As such, this chapter posits CARA as a strategic and constructive force similar to the PCA; its regulatory negotiations help to shape film form and narrative. The remainder of the chapter outlines this activity of what I call "boundary maintenance" by the motion picture industry during the tenure of the Production Code. It establishes that self-regulation functions as a smokescreen for larger issues of economic dominance by the MPAA and charts the erosion of its single-seal approach to Hollywood films throughout the 1950s and 1960s up to the creation of the rating system in 1968.

After this survey of the PCA, chapter 2 addresses the question, "Why does the MPAA need ratings in the first place?" I examine how classification became the new business model for the MPAA and NATO after the fall of the Production Code, a means to govern the flow of product through the production, distribution, and exhibition pipelines of the film industry. This new product—responsible entertainment—functioned much like the old standard from the Production Code—harmless entertainment—in one core respect: all CARA-rated films, even R-rated ones (as long as a child was accompanied by an adult or legal guardian), could be suitable for audiences of every age level. The industry's avoidance of the X rating and compliance with CARA's judgment on the boundary between the R and the X by the mid-1970s was central to this endeavor. Out of this collusion and cooperation emerged the Incontestable R, a social contract between Hollywood and consumers that guaranteed responsible entertainment to Hollywood's critics and audiences and, in turn, secured the long-term health of the industry from the mid-1970s onward. Case studies of *Cruising* (1980) and *Scarface* (1983) conclude the chapter, revealing the occasional challenges and obstacles to content regulation in contemporary Hollywood when an adults-only rating is at stake. These controversies make clear the ever-present instability of boundary maintenance under CARA, a series of negotiations among regulators (the Rating Board and the Appeals Board), branches (production, distribution, and exhibition), and reformers (the U.S. government, special interest groups) often at odds over the definition and management of the Incontestable R.

The legitimacy of the X category was called into question in 1990 when an array of independent filmmakers and film critics accused CARA of limiting advertising and exhibition opportunities for serious, adults-only films in the U.S. marketplace. Chapter 3 answers the question, "Why doesn't a rating exist between the R and NC-17 to distinguish between serious adult films and pornography?" Attempts to insert an A (Adult) or AO (Adults Only) rating between the two categories ultimately led to the cosmetic replacement of the X with the NC-17 for *Henry & June* (1990). As a change in name only, I argue, the NC-17 preserved industry policies governing the Incontestable R as the MPAA distributors and NATO exhibitors simply translated their no-X-rated policies into no-NC-17 policies.

The continuing avoidance of the adults-only rating also reified the formal standards established earlier with the X rating. In answering the question, "Is the rating system arbitrary and capricious?" chapter 4 demonstrates that CARA does not frivolously determine the boundaries between these two categories on a case-by-case basis as is commonly believed. By comparing the R, NC-17, and unrated versions of a single film with the media accounts of its battles with the Rating Board and the Appeals Board, I provide a set of standards regarding sex and nudity—not unlike the Production Code—that guided CARA's rating practices between 1992 and 1997. The results show that CARA was methodologically consistent with its practices and nondiscriminatory in its ratings assessments of MPAA and independently distributed films during this period before recalibrating the formal thresholds of representing masturbation and oral sex for the R rating in the late 1990s.

The various unrated and edited versions of films on video still cannot hide the fact that the NC-17 remains a stigma at the box office. Chapter 5 offers a case study of *Showgirls* (1995) to explore the question, "Can a film be viably marketed and released into theaters with an NC-17 rating?" As the only other NC-17 film besides *Henry & June* to be widely distributed by an MPAA signatory, *Showgirls* debunked long-standing industry myths that media outlets and exhibitors were hostile to adults-only pictures. MGM/UA played *Showgirls* in a large number of theaters, advertised the film in most major newspapers, and promoted it on many of the major television networks. The film's abysmal box office, however, overshadowed these inroads, reinforcing the commercial unfeasibility of the NC-17 rating. After *Showgirls,* only independent and foreign films carried the NC-17. In addition, the establishment of art-house subsidiaries by MPAA signatories and the purchase of independent distribution companies by their corporate parents since the mid-1990s marginalized the "unrated" (without a CARA rating) picture at the box office. Without the option of releasing films unrated, these subsidiaries effectively have reduced most art-house pictures to R ratings, solidifying the boundaries of the Incontestable R perhaps for years to come.

This book concludes with some brief considerations about the regulation of violence under responsible entertainment, as well as the recent movement away from the Incontestable R to the "Indisputable PG-13" after Columbine and September 11. These lines of inquiry suggest only a few of the many sub-jects and films not even discussed or mentioned in this text. *The Naked Truth* merely scratches the surface of self-regulation during the ratings era, a history aided by the Heffner papers but one that cannot be completely written until the MPAA releases all its files to the public. Until that time arrives, I hope this book serves as an appropriate hors d'oeuvre.

CHAPTER 1

Film Regulation
before the Rating System

*Markets may look like democracy, in that we are all involved in their
making, but they are fundamentally not democratic.*

—Thomas Frank, *One Market under God*

Cultural critic Thomas Frank calls the equating (or conflating) of the free
market with democracy "market populism," which for him is the defining feature of American capitalism in the last few decades of the twentieth century.
"Market populism," he suggests, "imagines individuals as fully rational economic actors, totally capable of making their needs known in the marketplace
and looking out for their interests."[1] In this view American leaders believe the
market to be infinitely diverse, perfectly expressing the will of supply and
demand, and more democratic than elections themselves.[2] This mythology,
Frank argues, may breed reverence for market forces and empowerment of
the people, but it hides the fact that markets are fundamentally not consen-
sual or democratic. "Markets are interested in profits and profits only," he
says. "The logic of business is coercion, monopoly, and the destruction of the
weak, not 'choice,' 'service,' or universal affluence" (87).

Communications scholar Robert W. McChesney connects the myths
behind market populism to the increasing privatization, deregulation, and
globalization of the culture industries by the U.S. government that allowed
the mass media to operate along noncompetitive oligopolistic lines for much
of the twentieth century.[3] Instead of a marketplace of ideas unencumbered by
governmental censorship and fueling popular and majority rule, we have a
democracy that supports private control over media communication and the
protection of corporate privilege over public service.[4] This sense of corporate
entitlement is recognized by McChesney as a new form of neoliberalism, a
phenomenon that "posits that society works best when business runs things

and there is as little possibility of government 'interference' with business as possible" (6). The corrupt nature of U.S. media policy is further exacerbated, states McChesney, because most of the vital decisions "are made behind closed doors to serve powerful special interests, with non-existent public involvement and miniscule press coverage" (xxiii). All editorial fare is subordinated to commercial values and logics with no concerns for its social implications or the will of the people.

If we accept Frank's and McChesney's arguments that market populism, privatization, and corporatization best describe the current policies and procedures of the culture industries, the notion that film classification provides the unlimited creative freedom that was denied during preclassification is ludicrous. The U.S. film industry—be it regulated by the Studio Relations Committee (SRC), the Production Code Administration (PCA), the Office of Code Administration (OCA), or the Classification and Rating Administration (CARA)—has enforced a system of entertainment whose codes, ideologies, and values have supported the economic and political interests of a handful of studios and media conglomerates since the mid-1920s. These business strategies, except for a brief period in the late 1960s and early 1970s, primarily excluded the distribution and exhibition of adults-only product. Doing so achieved, and continues to accomplish, what Ruth Vasey has called the film industry's "two most devout ambitions" in the classical era: "to please all of the people, everywhere, all—or at least most—of the time, and to displease as few people—or at least as few people who mattered—as possible."[5]

These "few people" are not the "public," which has placed its "high trust" and "confidence" in Production Code regulators, or "parents," whose children the rating system swears to protect, but *adults* likely to condemn Hollywood's products as unrepresentative or inappropriately representative of American society and culture. The press, state and national legislatures, and religious, educational, and civic groups have all expressed their opinions and exercised their authority over what they consider harmful and incorrect entertainment throughout Hollywood's history. To retain the ability to regulate its own films and reap the advantages of monopoly profit, the industry always responded to the concerns from pressure groups by deferring to the decisions made by its regulatory operations. As Richard Maltby has remarked of classical Hollywood: "The strength of the entire system of prior censorship was that it operated on the basis of a series of undefined relationships, rooted in the producers' acknowledgment that the [PCA] was a necessary intermediary to give them protection from the undesirable assaults of organizations more morally scrupulous than they themselves might care to be."[6] Negotiations between filmmakers and industry regulators for seals or ratings always reflected these external matters, and this interaction produced the permissible boundaries of Hollywood representation before, during, and after the studio era.

My argument is that content regulation under the SRC, PCA, and OCA operated along the same economic principles as CARA, despite their obvious differences: to ensure Hollywood's dominance in the U.S. marketplace and to stave off federal interference in motion picture content. I will preface my study of the Production Code by first considering *regulation* as a more fitting term than *censorship* for understanding the industry's concerns over the marketability of certain film content, then move toward a discussion of the specific aspects of content regulation during classical Hollywood, and finally, examine the industrial, legal, and social factors that led to the ineffectiveness of the Production Code and the implementation of the rating system.

Censorship versus Regulation

CARA, like its predecessors, has no legal power to prohibit anything from being produced, distributed, or exhibited in the United States. Ratings are "voluntary," a by-product of industry *self-regulation,* the term often used to describe a system by which an organization or institution deals with its own disciplinary and legal problems in private, rather than being publicly regulated by the government or any other outside force. Filmmakers or distributors can accept the designated CARA rating or reject it, instead releasing a film "unrated" or with another classification other than the copyrighted G, PG, PG-13, R, or NC-17. The creative freedom that exists under the rating system, however, is illusionary, states Stephen Farber, a journalist who wrote an insider's account of his internship with CARA called *The Movie Rating Game.* Film classification, says Farber, had the same desired effect as the Production Code: to limit "what film-makers can produce and what adult audiences—as well as children—can see."[7] For Farber censorship, classification, or whatever term one chooses to call self-regulation ultimately mean the same thing: they are all a set of repressive policies that govern film content and impede free expression.

Farber's approach to classification characterizes a substantial body of writing in media studies that conceptualizes film censorship as an act of interference. This understanding views censorship as an approach guided solely by practices of exclusion. When one applies this prohibitions model to classical Hollywood, for example, the PCA imposes controls on films by excluding certain themes, content, and images from them that it finds unacceptable for a Code seal. Raymond Moley embraced this model in his 1945 book, *The Hays*

Office, by stating that one of the main activities of industry self-regulation was "to keep morally objectionable material out of pictures."[8] Some PCA historians still shared Moley's approach after the release of the PCA case files in 1986. Gerald Gardner introduces *The Censorship Papers,* a compendium of assorted PCA files, by explaining that American film censorship was a process of "elimination" that was used to "mold and manacle the most famous films of this century."[9] And Gregory D. Black, author of *Hollywood Censored* and *The Catholic Crusade against the Movies, 1940–1975,* charts the PCA's exclusionary practices in terms of the administration's relationship to the Catholic Legion of Decency. The Legion, according to Black, walked hand in hand with the PCA, thwarting the wishes of the Hollywood studios that wished to make "more realistic and honest films" and keeping "the movies from exploring social, political, and economic issues that it believed were either immoral or a danger to the Catholic Church."[10]

While film regulation can and does operate in this fashion, the prohibitions model isolates censorship from its wider social, cultural, and historical conditions of existence. This model solely locates its practices in bodies holding claim to prohibitive power, such as the PCA or a government board. *The Naked Truth* adopts a more nuanced and multifaceted approach to regulation, one that is fully contingent on the historical context within which censorship battles are fought and products are consumed. It builds on frameworks, methods, and perspectives developed by censorship scholars, many of whom are compiled in Francis G. Couvares's *Movie Censorship and American Culture* and Matthew Bernstein's *Controlling Hollywood: Censorship and Regulation in the Studio Era.*[11] The articles in these anthologies reveal that a lot more was at stake in an instance of censorship than just the content of an individual film. Censorship constituted a battle, notes Bernstein, over "the issue and nature of cultural authority, the power to enforce it, and the various rationales that accompany it."[12]

In understanding how this "battleground" shaped and surfaced within Hollywood motion pictures themselves, the work of Annette Kuhn and Lea Jacobs has been highly influential to this new wave of censorship studies. Jacobs, in the *Velvet Light Trap* in 1989 (and two years later in her book *The Wages of Sin*), became the first to adopt Kuhn's model of censorship to the PCA and opposed it to what Kuhn in *Cinema, Censorship, and Sexuality: 1909–1925* called the "prohibition/institution" model.[13] Rather than a practice of "interference" (Moley's and Black's view) confined to a specific censoring organization (the MPAA or, in Kuhn's case, the British Board of Film Censors), Kuhn, Jacobs, Maltby, Vasey, and others viewed censorship as a process of negotiations, rivalries, and alliances between many contending powers and institutions that seek to define and control the cultural terrain. In other words, acts of censorship are historically specific series of interactions among the film trade, reform movements, religious groups, government regulatory agencies, state censor boards, and other various forces that want to impose their own values, concerns, and ideas on a film text.

By analyzing censorship as "a dynamic interplay of aims and interests" between Hollywood and the demands of external agencies, this book follows Jacobs's lead and considers self-regulation as a strategic response to social pressures that pose some threat to the industry's economic and political interests.[14] Under this model the restructuring of films does not simply entail the elimination of offending content but rather involves the anticipation of public outcry by assessing problems and arriving at compromises on a case-by-case basis. The institutionalization, repetition, and slight variations in these negotiations and policies endow Hollywood cinema with particular textual practices and configurations at certain historical moments. Such a constructive approach allows for a conceptualization of censorship not only as a practice that is done to texts but also as a motivating force that creates and shapes texts, ideologies, and meanings. In this sense, writes Kuhn, "prohibition and productivity may be regarded not as opposites, nor as mutually exclusive, but as two sides of the same coin."[15]

My book's account of censorship as an activity rather than a predefined object assumes that censorship is a necessary, normal, and constitutive element of free expression in any democracy. This position, shared by Kuhn and expressed by Sue Curry Jansen in *Censorship: The Knot That Binds Power and Knowledge,* suggests that any historical inquiry into censorship should ask not " 'Is there censorship?' but rather 'What kind of censorship?' " and "How does it work?"[16] For Curry Jansen "constituent censorship," the form one finds in the ultracapitalist and mass-consumerist culture of the United States, is no less insidious or preferable than state or religious censorship. Instead of priests or bureaucrats, she argues, industry censors control what cultural products gain access to the marketplace of ideas. They use their power to maximize profit, expand markets, and circumvent competition at the expense of democratic participation. Censorship's products, as a result, incorporate the ideologies and values that celebrate the corporate state rather than a nation's citizens.[17]

Constituent censorship is a long way from the purely prohibitive stance embraced by Moley and Black and is more in accord with Thomas Frank's and Robert McChesney's views on market populism, privatization, and conglomeration that began this chapter. The fact that American cinema has effectively been controlled, structured, and subsidized by a handful of studios and media conglomerates since the mid-1920s plays a large part in our understanding of how film censorship works in the United States. The policies of the PCA and CARA undoubtedly shape film content in a single case of self-regulation, but they also bind, as Jon Lewis notes, the various business relationships that exist between Hollywood producers, distributors, and exhibitors to ensure the long-term health of the industry. As Lewis puts it, the policing of images onscreen has everything to do with box office, "about how to make a product that won't have *problems* in the marketplace."[18]

The PCA's role in securing and solidifying these relationships through a particular set of filmic conventions and codes has been well documented. I will summarize some of these strategies in the next section. Less known are the activities of CARA. Most scholars, however, agree that 1968—the inaugural year of CARA—was the moment when the institutional activity of Hollywood censorship became dramatically altered. It is the dividing point between two different policies of regulating film content: a universal seal versus variable classification. It was the year, write Leonard J. Leff and Jerold L. Simmons, when "Old Hollywood became New Hollywood," when, says Thomas Doherty, the "Code edifice finally came crumbling down."[19]

The assumption perhaps made here, or at least made by the MPAA, is that censorship effectively came to a close when the intractable Production Code was replaced by an all-permissible rating system. It suggests that classification ushered in a new era of cinematic freedom, free of the industrial, state, and church interference that led to the enforcement of a single-seal Production Code. Indeed, the original four-tiered CARA rating system (G, M, R, and X) differs structurally—at least in theory—from a uniform-seal-for-all-films PCA approach. The X rating (and later the NC-17) enables filmmakers, distributors, and exhibitors—at least in theory—to produce and show films with few limitations. And surely, for a short period after the introduction of the rating system—approximately five years—American cinema did enjoy a freedom unlike it ever had before.

Such an understanding, however, principally endorses a prohibitive model of censorship by failing to account for self-regulation as a strategic and constructive process during the ratings era. The old mechanisms of self-regulation may have been abolished by 1968, but the nexus of self-regulation had not. Many of the same social entities that posed some threat to the industry's economic and political interests in the Production Code era still posed a threat in the ratings era. Therefore "censorship" or constraints on free expression did not disappear during classification; they just resurfaced in a different guise.

By approaching self-regulation under CARA as a series of compromises both distinct from and analogous to the operations of the SRC, PCA, and

OCA, I am suggesting that censorial pressures are always accommodated in American cinema, especially when the representations brought before CARA involve sex, violence, and certain thematic issues. Or as Richard S. Randall remarks, "The actual limits to freedom of speech in the film medium depend, in large measure, on how this accommodation takes place."[20] These acts of accommodation, what I call "boundary maintenance," are a set of policies and practices that define and enforce the boundaries of permissibility during the Production Code and classification eras. Given the difference between one seal and four (later five) categories, how does one go about understanding boundary maintenance during classification relative to the Production Code?

To address this question, I hereby adhere to Kuhn's and Jacobs's preference in referring to censorship activity as "regulation." The terms *regulation* and *boundary maintenance* provide a better theoretical framework for understanding the activities of the PCA and CARA than does the term *censorship*. This latter term does not adequately signify the continuous tensions and accommodations enacted between the PCA/CARA and various external forces during a single instance of film regulation. My framework essentially captures the "political energy" between the film trade and various agencies rather than the excision and containment of certain images and narrations by one specific industrial group.[21] The PCA and CARA might shape their entertainment differently for mass audiences, but their principles of boundary maintenance remain the same: finding the "right" regulation of representation that enable the MPAA signatories to conduct their business profitably and without interference. In this sense the foundations of responsible entertainment were laid long before CARA.

HARMLESS ENTERTAINMENT AND BOUNDARY MAINTENANCE

The film director Paul Schrader once remarked, "People have this mistaken notion that the Hollywood system has principles, morals, or values. It doesn't. It is simply a banking entity."[22] Indeed, Hollywood, past and present, is a system of business operations controlled by financial institutions. For these firms, filmmaking is a business of manufacturing, wholesaling, and retailing—or in industry parlance—the production, distribution, and exhibition of a particular product for profit. Unlike an automobile or a box of Kleenex, however, Hollywood cinema is also an art form, an aesthetic activity that echoes or reflects a message or mood for a viewer to interpret. To make a profit, Hollywood films communicate ideas and emotional experiences—what we typically refer to as "entertainment"—each with its own set of principles, morals, and values. How, then, does one resolve this conflict?

Richard Maltby's work on Hollywood cinema confronts the contradictions between the art and business of filmmaking, providing us with a model for understanding content regulation under classification. He argues that a Hollywood movie, in the first instance, must be approached as a commercial commodity in a capitalistic marketplace before its existence as a creative work, political commentary, or social document. Even so, Maltby contends, Hollywood's business strategies can never be fully separated from its aesthetic practices because the industry's products are also formally organized "to turn pleasure into a product we can buy." This premise, what Maltby calls the "commercial aesthetic," ultimately considers Hollywood film style in service to larger commercial ambitions of the industry itself.[23]

Ensuring Hollywood's commitment to American cinema as an economic enterprise since 1922 has been the industry's trade organization, originally named the Motion Picture Producers and Distributors of America (MPPDA), which was renamed the Motion Picture Association of America (MPAA) in 1945. The MPPDA was created to restore a more favorable public image for Hollywood and to prevent governmental interference in its operations. Heavily publicized scandals, antitrust charges, and the 1915 Supreme Court *Mutual* ruling that the motion picture industry was not deserving of free speech protection because it was a "business, pure and simple" led many observers to question whether Hollywood was capable of mitigating these criticisms.[24] This accountability forced the MPPDA to justify its products to Congress, moral watchdogs, state and local censorship boards, and other institutions interested in governing the content of movies. If the studios, wrote Maltby, "could be made to appear respectable in the public eye, their products would be less liable to hostile scrutiny, and hence more profitable."[25]

To undermine the efforts of reformers and to guarantee its members unrestricted and unproblematic entry into the marketplace domestically and abroad, the MPPDA established a centralized self-regulatory arm—the Studio Relations Committee (SRC, 1926–1934) and the Production Code Administration (PCA, 1934–1966)—to scrutinize theme and treatment in all Hollywood pictures. The SRC and PCA played an integrated role in film production under the studio system. Their examiners could request revisions to scripts and procure changes in film form and narrative in consultation with studio filmmakers and executives. This case-by-case evaluation of films and scripts was unique to the Production Code era and played no role during CARA except in its early years. During the years of the studio system it was an effective mechanism of boundary maintenance, a means of shaping potentially objectionable content into market-ready product. The SRC and PCA, therefore, acted as successful mediators between the artistic and business sectors of Hollywood, reconciling the short-term creative interests of studio filmmakers and executives with the profit-maximization goals of their New York financiers.

As the industry's watchdogs, the SRC and the PCA became the primary architects of Hollywood's "commercial aesthetic" and unique worldview, what Maltby has called "harmless entertainment"—movies detached from political significance, serving an affirmative cultural function, and appealing to the lowest common denominator of public taste.[26] The narrational and representational properties of harmless entertainment that developed out of these self-regulatory operations, Ruth Vasey notes, were part of the wider context of "industry policy" that gradually took shape during the 1920s and 1930s. In response to audience pressures, stateside and internationally, these policies influenced a host of issues, including depictions of sex, violence, and religion, as well as capitalism, ethnicity, and politics.[27]

These matters ultimately found their way into the document known as the Production Code, whose standards and policies can be found in earlier attempts at self-regulation during the 1920s by MPPDA president Will Hays. In 1924 Hays announced the "Formula," a vague list of instructions for scrutinizing source material such as books or plays for screen presentation. In 1927 the MPPDA published its first code of production, entitled the "Don'ts and Be Carefuls," a list of eleven things never to appear in motion pictures regardless of treatment and another twenty-six subjects to be treated with "special care." Administered by the SRC, the "Don'ts and Be Carefuls" synthesized a list of restrictions and eliminations culled from external censorship agencies that the industry could voluntarily incorporate into production instead of having such censures imposed on films upon their release. The "Formula" and the "Don'ts and Be Carefuls" were heralded by the MPPDA as indicators of its social obligations to the public, but these procedures ultimately went ungoverned and unapplied. Efforts to forestall criticism failed because these principles were mainly advisory, as the SRC had no vested authority to reject scripts or films or to impose penalties or sanctions on its members.[28]

Not until 1928, when Colonel Jason S. Joy, an MPPDA official from the New York office, arrived in Los Angeles to head the SRC, did the industry begin its adoption of a more formal system of regulation to deal with the treatment of sensitive subjects. The Production Code in 1930 modified and elaborated on the "Don'ts and Be Carefuls," attaching a moral foundation and philosophy to industry production. The "General Principles" read:

1. No picture shall be produced which will lower the moral standards of those who see it. Hence the sympathy of the audience shall never be thrown to the side of crime, wrong-doing, evil or sin.
2. Correct standards of life, subject only to the requirements of drama and entertainment, shall be presented.
3. Law, natural or human, shall not be ridiculed, nor shall sympathy be created for its violation.[29]

Following these "General Principles" were the "Particular Applications," a set of governances detailing the treatment of "crimes against the law," "sex," "vulgarity," "obscenity," "profanity," "costume," "dances," "religion," "locations," "national feelings," "titles," and "repellent subjects." By the 1960s all of these principles and applications, to some degree or another, were ignored by the industry and played no role in the crafting of the rating system in 1968 or its execution by CARA. This is not to say that contemporary Hollywood filmmakers and distributors disregarded these matters when considering the economic prospect of a film; they were just not internalized within the operations of CARA as they were with the SRC and PCA.

Although these principles and applications would provide the template for boundary maintenance during the era of harmless entertainment, their implementation was not entirely successful under the SRC stewardship of Joy or his replacement in 1932, former New York state censor James Wingate.[30] This period, commonly, though mistakenly, referred to as the "Pre-Code" era, was marked by intermittent cooperation and occasional hostility between the SRC and the MPPDA-member companies. The Catholic Church was extremely aware of the industry's failure to endorse the Production Code's principles of Christian morality during this time and in 1933 launched a national crusade called the Legion of Decency to urge its constituents to boycott films judged by Catholic officials to be indecent. This campaign was not intended to undermine the credibility of self-regulation but to outmaneuver demands for federal intervention over motion picture content and the industry's financial operations. In July 1934 the studios eventually acquiesced to the economic benefits of a stricter industry-wide enforcement of the Production Code. The SRC was renamed the Production Code Administration (PCA), with Joseph Breen as its director and a larger staff who could devote more time to policing the content of films. Industry publicity acknowledged this change as Hollywood advertised its atonement for its earlier pictures and its current commitment to manufacturing harmless entertainment. All films would have to carry a PCA seal of approval on all of its prints, and MPPDA member companies must agree not to distribute or exhibit any films without this seal. Breen's motto was, "Make them reasonably acceptable to reasonable people."[31]

In *The Wages of Sin,* a study of the fallen woman genre from the late 1920s through the 1930s, Lea Jacobs provides an exemplary account of boundary maintenance during the Production Code era.[32] She points out that under the PCA Hollywood underwent a reexamination, rather than a radical shift, of its policies. The PCA employed the same productive and prohibitive strategies over characterization, dialogue, plot, and aesthetics in films as the SRC to disarm any potential objections by the Legion of Decency, state censor boards, and other external forces in place during the production of a "fallen woman" film. Reformers believed that the sensationalization of female adultery and seduction in these films had grave social consequences for young women, threatening traditional notions of female agency and purity. In response to these concerns, Jacobs argues, regulatory strategies in the fallen woman film primarily revolved around "*structures* of narrative—the nature of endings, motivation of action, patterns of narration" (23). Individual scenes, the organization of shots, and the general narrative trajectory were "arranged" by Code officials to eliminate and work around potentially offensive material.

With the changeover to the PCA, these policies were more rigorously applied and circumspect in Hollywood films after 1934. Jacobs suggests that increased social and political pressures, as well as the threat of boycotts from the Legion of Decency, necessitated a "relatively more extensive *elaboration*" of what Breen called in the 1935 MPPDA Annual Report "compensating moral values." These included "good characters, the voice of morality, a lesson, regeneration of the transgressor, suffering, and punishment."[33] In two case studies of the fallen woman film—the SRC's *Baby Face* (1933) and the PCA's *Anna Karenina* (1935)—Jacobs demonstrates how the regulation of closure, visual style, and ellipses under two different administrations undercut or bolstered the narrative logic of sin, guilt, and redemption present in the genre. The results of these practices, states Jacobs, were "more unified and harmonious texts" under the PCA, "adjuring the double meanings, the calculated ambiguities, and the narrative disjunctures which gave the films of the early thirties their zest" (153).

First, in terms of closure, a moral and "correct" ending to a film was no longer enough to offset a fallen woman's earlier transgressions. For example, with *Baby Face* reformers believed that the heroine's fall from grace and the ending's emphasis on punishment, sacrifice, and heterosexual coupling did not adequately compensate for the film's accentuation on the heroine's rise by means of sex and exploitation. In the case of *Anna Karenina,* by contrast, marital fidelity is continually underscored by a cumulative denunciation of Anna's actions throughout the course of the story, not just her suicide at the end. In this manner Catholic morality that appeared fragmented or "tacked on" under the SRC was repeatedly integrated into films under the PCA.[34]

Second, in terms of visual detail, ideas that could not be explicitly expressed in verbal terms but could be implicitly emphasized nonverbally were more carefully scrutinized by the PCA than the SRC. In *Baby Face,* every time Lily receives a promotion, the camera tilts up a skyscraper another level, all the while accompanied by a honky-tonk rendition of "St. Louis Woman," until she arrives at the penthouse of another building. Even though we do not see Lily trading sexual favors for promotions and wealth, the visual metaphor of sexual exchange accentuated by the camera movement and music unmistakably works against the moral principles of the Production Code by dramatizing feminine aggressiveness and exploitation of men. With *Anna Karenina,* however, the condemnation of marital infidelity is rendered indirectly by nonverbal means in the garden party scene. Point-of-view shots and mise-en-scène unfavorably comment on the transgressive nature of Anna's behavior, offsetting any sympathy directed at Anna and "extending the effect of the unhappy ending throughout the course of the film."[35]

Last, in terms of ellipses the treatment of the sexual act, usually suggested in the SRC era by this indirect mode of representation, was made more ambiguous during the PCA. In *Baby Face* the unmarried heroine's seduction of an office boy still retains the suggestion of sexual activity by the use of a point-of-view shot of him watching her walk toward an empty room after an exchange of suggestive dialogue. Even though the action of the boy's following her into a vacant office door and the closing of that door were removed from the final print, Breen made it clear in 1934 that such moments immediately preceding or following the transgressive act must be omitted. With *Anna Karenina* nothing explicitly leads the spectator to believe a sexual act has taken place in three romantic scenes. Dialogue ("I know there is no hope for me"), costuming (Anna is fully clothed), and setting (the location of the scene has never been established) obscure rather than slyly suggest a sexual interpretation of the events. Spectators could still choose to read an elided scene in sexual terms, but the action or dialogue of the scene no longer confirmed (and sometimes even denied) such an interpretation.[36]

Jacobs's account of regulation in *Baby Face* and *Anna Karenina* illustrates one of the key differences of boundary maintenance in the Production Code and classification eras: the systematic activity of localizing elements in texts for narrative and formal revision. In other words, the SRC and PCA internalized social and political concerns within film representation, embedding the

affirmative cultural function of harmless entertainment within the very fab-
ric of Hollywood films themselves. CARA, as we will see, did no such thing;
regulators diffused the affirmative cultural function of "responsible entertainment" *across* rating categories, not within individual films. The resulting
industry-wide avoidance of the X/NC-17 rating led to particular formal patterns of narration regarding the R-rated treatment of sex and nudity during
certain historical junctures. CARA, however, never systematically restruc-
tured films to fit particular categories; it only guessed which rating most
American parents would find appropriate for their children and left any editing to distributors if they desired a less-restrictive rating.

The Production Code certainly may have been the most conspicuous
aspect of industry self-regulation, but the monitoring of Hollywood pictures
extended beyond simply production standards. Rules regarding antitrust,
exhibition, foreign markets, and film promotion provided a wider cooperative and collusive network for regulating harmless entertainment. The
MPPDA/MPAA also developed public-relations strategies alongside the PCA
to displace any social, political, or cultural anxieties over Hollywood's products. Mary Beth Haralovich reveals, for example, how PCA work was carried
forward by studio publicity to channel the reception of meaning toward the
realm of harmless entertainment in the proletarian woman's film *Marked
Woman* (1937).[37] Potentially explosive material like gangsterism, violence, and
prostitution in *Marked Woman,* though vetted by the PCA, was further tem-
pered by Warner Bros.' carefully prepared press book for its exhibitors. The
press book contained advertising copy, publicity stories, and consumerist dis-
courses to displace and hopefully eliminate any considerations of economic
and gender inequities taken up in the film. Warner Bros. even cautioned
exhibitors not to design their own "stunts" around *Marked Woman*'s title or
theme, assuring them that studio-designed publicity could handle any possible controversies arising from the film's narrative. Coordinated relationships such as these among management, talent, distributors, theater owners,
and the PCA ensured stability, predictability, and profitability in the movie
business throughout the 1940s.

After the onset of World War II, however, the PCA found its task of
boundary maintenance more difficult in shaping MPAA texts for public consumption. Matthew Bernstein documents such a case with *Scarlet Street*
(1945), the Fritz Lang film banned by state and local censor boards in three
different markets of the United States (the state of New York, Milwaukee,
and Atlanta).[38] The film's distributor, Universal, had to publicly and legally
defend the film's morality to state and civic leaders since the main character
goes legally unpunished for murder.[39] Bernstein ties the heated reception of

Scarlet Street to its historical moment—postwar America—as regional and local resistance to the film was informed by a wider sense of crisis in the nation:

> Americans pondered the moral and practical ramifications of the nuclear age, the incredible revelations of Nazi war crimes, and the communist menace whose dimensions were just emerging. On the home front, equally troubling issues had arisen: strikes for better wages were long past due and erupted around the country, while returning veterans and women in the workforce complicated traditional notions of how the nuclear family functioned. And at the beginning of 1946, there was considerable controversy about the role movies had played in aggravating the social ills perceived in American society, particularly in relation to the family. (161)

Bernstein speaks to a fissure in the discursive status of Hollywood entertainment that had developed in the early 1940s. The sordid depictions of sex, crime, and violence in these dystopic and often amoral city dramas (later identified by French film critics as "film noir") challenged the storytelling conventions and affirmative cultural function of harmless entertainment.

This trend toward mature subject matter eventually made it impossible for the PCA to perform boundary maintenance on Hollywood films under the existing Production Code. With the ensuing divestiture of exhibition and the granting of free speech protection to motion pictures, the PCA lost its grip on the control of film content, both domestic and foreign. The erosion of harmless entertainment and the breakdown of the PCA's authority had begun.

THE EROSION OF PCA CONTROL

The overall effectiveness of the PCA between 1934 and some variable point in the 1950s was the result of a shared collective definition of harmless entertainment between the industry, audiences, and reformers or, as Ellen Draper puts it, of "what movies were, or could be, or should be."[40] Particular representations of violence, sexuality, and other ideological matters during this period were promoted, suppressed, or arranged by the industry to conform to this consensus. Still, the years after World War II reflected a growing uncertainty and ambivalence in the consensus over what constituted harmless entertainment. This disharmony reflected changes occurring in the movie industry, movie audiences, and the medium itself, all of which threatened the established system of Hollywood self-regulation.

Alongside a transformation in the discursive nature of its products, the film industry witnessed an end to its stability and affluence in the 1950s and

1960s. The separation of exhibition from production and distribution, First Amendment protection, and competition from television and foreign films made it necessary for the PCA to modify its practices and policies of boundary maintenance. At the same time, the massive postwar shift in American leisure time, the baby boom, and the mass movement to the suburbs led to a decline in motion picture attendance. By 1962 admissions had fallen almost 75 percent from their most profitable level in 1946.[41] During this crisis the American film industry unsuccessfully searched for a new cultural and social identity apart from television and distinct from the sexual explicitness of exploitation and foreign films. Insecurity replaced solvency, commercial opportunism replaced corporate unity, and vice replaced virtue as filmmakers and exhibitors unveiled previously taboo themes, behaviors, and images to general audiences to persuade them to return to the theaters.

Prior to this economic downslide the PCA's ability to arrange the content of motion pictures into harmless entertainment concomitantly rested on the MPPDA/MPAA's ability to rule the box office, what historian Lewis Jacobs has called the most important and "controlling factor" of the movie business.[42] Ever since the mid-1920s, the motion picture industry had become dominated by vertically integrated corporations that owned each branch of the production-distribution-exhibition chain. The "Big Five" (MGM/Loew's, Paramount, Warner Bros., 20th Century–Fox, and RKO) controlled all major facets of the film business, while the "Little Three" (Columbia, United Artists, and Universal) owned no theaters but were heavily involved in production or distribution. Collectively known as the "majors," they operated together as a cartel whose control of the industry lay not in production and distribution but through the Big Five's ownership of the largest, most extravagant movie palaces in major metropolitan areas. Even though the Big Five owned no more than 15 percent of the theaters in the United States, they took in 70 percent of the total American box-office income until the mid-1950s.[43] Unaffiliated theaters clearly outnumbered the total owned by the Big Five, but independent exhibitors tended to consist of the smallest houses in less-lucrative locations.[44] At the height of its power this "studio system" also engaged in other monopolistic and collusive practices—block booking, blind bidding, and a run-zone-clearance system of distribution and exhibition—that stifled competition and inhibited fair trade. As a result of vertical integration and these restraining practices the majors, states Douglas Gomery, "were able to reduce risk, ensure continuity of operation, and almost guarantee regular profits."[45]

By distributing the most sought-after products and owning the best theaters, the majors effectively dictated the terms of what could play, where it could play, and how long it could play. Independent, non-PCA-certified films hardly screened in the large metropolitan theaters, so the MPAA could promise to Hollywood's detractors that the exhibition of all legitimate films, not only those distributed by the majors, embodied harmless entertainment. This guarantee, which effectively forestalled for many years governmental legislation and court action against the studios on antitrust grounds, finally "expired" in 1948 after a U.S. Supreme Court decision ended vertical integration of the motion picture industry. Known as the *Paramount* decision, this divestiture decree ordered the Big Five to dispose of their theaters and forbade the majors to engage in unfair trade practices like block booking.[46] Divorcement forced the majors into profiting from production and distribution alone. Their films now had to be sold to theaters on their individual merits and on a case-by-case basis. But without guaranteed outlets for its members' products, the MPAA could no longer enforce the Production Code seal in the American film industry. The result, as director Frank Capra observed in hindsight, was that "the seal became impotent because the [MPAA] could not control the theater chains. Before, if you did not have the seal, you had to play the honky-tonks. The seal is now castrated."[47]

Also leading to the castration of the PCA's authority, and, in turn, the undermining of harmless entertainment itself, was a new legal understanding of motion pictures in the United States. Justice William O. Douglas's observation in the *Paramount* case that "we have no doubt that motion pictures, like newspapers and radio, are included in the press whose freedom is guaranteed by the First Amendment," eventually led the U.S. Supreme Court to award free speech protection to the medium in 1952.[48] In the case *Burstyn v. Wilson,* better known as "the *Miracle* decision," the Court overturned the *Mutual* decision of thirty-five years earlier and ruled that "sacrilegious" was no longer a valid standard for governmental censorship of motion pictures.[49] Terms such as *indecent, harmful,* or *immoral,* once frequently used by state and municipal boards to censor Hollywood films, became unconstitutional almost overnight as the U.S. Supreme Court, without written opinion, reversed five state Supreme Court decisions.[50] Obscenity, though not yet carefully defined, became the only possible criterion for banning a film's exhibition. As a result, the Supreme Court ruling placed the MPAA in a bind: the ruling guaranteed films free-speech protection, but now the industry had to address the issue of how the PCA would self-regulate Hollywood's products in this new era of permissiveness.

The change in legal status of motion pictures reflected maturation in the medium in the late 1940s and 1950s that the PCA was unprepared for and *unable* to deal with. Prior to the *Miracle* decision Hollywood had already begun to seriously address political and social issues in films like *Gentlemen's Agreement* (1947, anti-Semitism) and *Pinky* (1949, race relations) that flirted with the boundaries of PCA acceptability. Subjects prohibited by the Code, like prostitution and drug use, also found their way into both Hollywood and independent films in attempts by distributors to differentiate their product from television. In addition, many smaller theaters filled their screen time with non-Hollywood product that did not carry a PCA seal. These art houses, as Barbara Wilinsky notes in *Sure Seaters,* sought out alternative products like independent U.S. films, documentaries, and foreign films to cater to an increasingly fragmented U.S. audience disenchanted with Hollywood products and desiring more mature treatments of sexuality on the screen.[51] These "adult" films targeted a growing young consumer base, many of whom were also responsible for the influx and popularity of foreign films in big cities and college campuses. *Open City* (1945) and *The Bicycle Thief* (1947), among others, not only exposed American audiences to the artistic and narrative possibilities of the film medium but also made it virtually impossible for the PCA to uphold the tenets of harmless entertainment in the major motion picture houses.

The PCA's single-seal approach to boundary maintenance began to crack further in the early 1950s with the release of a number of films that tested the limits of the Production Code's standards on sex and morality. Code-certified films such as *A Streetcar Named Desire* (1951), *A Place in the Sun* (1951), and *From Here to Eternity* (1953) performed well at the box office, confirming American audiences' appetite for more adult-themed material. Of these "adult" films, *The Moon Is Blue* proved to cause the most damage to the PCA's authority and legitimacy.[52] Despite knowing that Breen would reject a cinematic version of the F. Hugh Herbert play, United Artists still packaged it with major stars William Holden and David Niven, while giving director Otto Preminger complete control over the final cut, even if the PCA did not approve it. When Breen refused early on to grant a seal to *The Moon Is Blue* after reading a draft of the script, United Artists resigned from the MPAA and set up a nonaffiliated distribution company to handle its release. Despite the banning of the film by local and state censorship boards and despite Catholic opposition to it, *The Moon Is Blue* played at eleven hundred large, urban theaters and grossed $3.5 million, putting it fifteenth on the 1953 *Variety* top-fifty list.[53]

United Artists' disregard of MPAA policy, conceivable only in light of divorcement, meant that each industrial arm of the motion picture business—production, distribution, and exhibition—could literally abandon its commitment to the Production Code. Self-regulation required collusion among all the parties to work. United Artists chose to dance around the Production Code, rejoining the MPAA in 1955 to argue for a seal for the drug addiction drama *The Man with the Golden Arm* and dropping out for a second time when the seal was denied.[54] Shortly thereafter, fellow MPAA member Columbia also chose to defy the Code, distributing the French import . . . *And God Created Woman* (1956) through an art-film subsidiary, Kingsley International. Together, *The Moon Is Blue, The Man with the Golden Arm,* and . . . *And God Created Woman* proved that cooperation with the PCA could be optional for MPAA signatories, and, in turn, the Production Code could be optional as well.

Similar disagreements over the marketplace value of the MPAA imprimatur would occur during CARA's regime as well; this time, the battle took place over an R or an X/NC-17 rather than a seal or no seal. A very public controversy would ensue, and, as often was the case, the MPAA-member companies would take the R, and the independents would release a film "unrated" (without a CARA seal). The unanimity of Hollywood's acquiescence in this regard was made possible only with the stigmatization and abandonment of the adults-only category by the MPAA signatories. Just like the predivorcement days, the MPAA preserved the affirmative cultural function of Hollywood entertainment under CARA by making all its films, even R-rated ones, *potentially* available to all audiences. A rating system, in fact, may have been instituted much earlier than 1968 if not for the unwillingness of the MPAA companies to abandon their economic model of harmless entertainment for classification.

A MOVEMENT TOWARD CLASSIFICATION

Hollywood finally relented to changing economic trends and audience demographics in 1956 with the first major revision of the Production Code.[55] It was triggered by Senator Estes Kefauver's chairmanship of the Senate Subcommittee to Investigate Juvenile Delinquency in 1955, in which Kefauver implicated the movies, comic books, and television as causes of juvenile misbehavior. Films such as *The Wild One* (1954), *Blackboard Jungle* (1955), and *Rebel without a Cause* (1955) were perceived as training grounds for youth crime. The MPAA was held partially responsible for what James Gilbert called in *A Cycle of Outrage* "the impression of a mounting youth crime wave," in spite of the existence of a Production Code seal for such films.[56]

In a situation reminiscent of the SRC's ineffective strategies in the early 1930s, the PCA's failure to arrange these films successfully for the marketplace

sprang from the insolence of the MPAA signatories to the current mechanisms of self-regulation. For example, to avoid a repeat of *The Moon Is Blue*,
Breen compromised with *The Wild One* producer Stanley Kramer, allowing
him to keep intact much of the film's realistic portrayals of gang violence
and language in exchange for a prologue and speech at the end of the picture condemning the actions of the biker outlaw played by Marlon Brando.
These bookends were pointless, remarks Jon Lewis, because "Brando's
charismatic performance undermined whatever moral lesson Breen and the
PCA had in mind."[57] Clearly, Hollywood's detractors at the time found the
additions of a "correct" beginning and ending insufficient in offsetting the
sensationalistic aspects of *The Wild One*. Nevertheless, the failure to "elabo-
rate" these denunciations throughout the film's narrative marked a breakdown in PCA policy that went far beyond the corrective hand of the Breen
Office. A climate composed of companies intent on exploiting the 1950s
youth phenomenon for much-needed profit at the same time that moral
reformers were condemning youth culture in films made it impossible for
the PCA, under the existing self-regulatory system, to arrange pictures that
satisfied everybody. To rectify matters, the Senate Subcommittee concluded
in its hearings that "the proper action was to revise the code, eliminate some
of its archaic moralisms, and then enforce it firmly." The changes made by
the MPAA in 1956, mainly as a result of these investigations, now permitted
the screen presentation of discreet allowances of drug use, abortion, miscegenation, prostitution, and kidnapping, but situations involving blasphemy,
brutality, and vulgarity were still prohibited.[58] Still, these revisions were only
temporary regulatory solutions for an increasingly ineffectual system of
boundary maintenance.

In 1961 the MPAA amended its Production Code once again by liberaliz-
ing the prohibitions against sexual aberration after a series of films—most
notably *Suddenly Last Summer* (1959) and *La Dolce Vita* (1960)—further
undermined the validity and integrity of the seal and the PCA.[59] Sexual perversion could now be made acceptable if treated with "care, discretion, and
restraint," a quite difficult, if not impossible, task for the PCA since studios,
both Hollywood and independent ones, were determined to continually
violate the moral firmament of the Code. These sexual perversion allowances
were already quite necessary as a series of upcoming films with homosexuality as an overarching theme—*The Children's Hour* (1961), *Advise and
Consent* (1962), and *The Best Man* (1964)—would certainly (and did) encounter Production Code difficulties. Since these films would be released by
major Hollywood distributors, the MPAA had no choice but to revise the
Code to meet the needs of its members.

Despite the increasing liberalization of PCA policy to adapt to the rapidly changing lifestyles of American youth, Hollywood was still reluctant to isolate and classify its products into age groups. As Garth Jowett states about this tumultuous period, "While nothing was certain in the movie business, there was enough enormous box-office and critical 'hits' to suggest the continued existence of a large potential audience waiting for the 'right' film."[60] The industry's adversity to classification, however, ran counter to the opinions of those outside the film trade. The most important religious, educational, and civic groups had favored the practice since the mid-to-late 1950s. These organizations, especially the Catholic Legion of Decency,[61] recognized that age classifications, not Code amendments, were the best ways to protect children from exposure to films containing drug use, sexual aberration, and other illicit representations.

Unlike the MPAA, the Legion had always classified Hollywood's products, establishing a clear distinction between films suitable for adults only, films suitable for children, and films unsuitable for anybody. Since 1936 its rating categories—"A1" (Unobjectionable for general patronage), "A2" (Unobjectionable for adults), "B" (Objectionable in part), and "C" (Condemned)—existed alongside the PCA seal, often harmoniously, sometimes uneasily, and with increasing divisiveness, especially after the *Miracle* decision in 1952. For example, the Legion "condemned" *The Moon Is Blue* (the PCA refused to grant a seal), awarded a "B" to *The Man with the Golden Arm* (the PCA refused a seal as well), and "condemned" *Baby Doll* (1956) (the PCA passed it). To adjust to the cultural and social changes of the 1950s and 1960s, the Legion also revised its classification system (shortly after the first round of revisions to the Production Code) to accommodate (and keep pace with) Hollywood's transition to more adult themes. In 1958 "A2" was redefined as "morally acceptable for adults and adolescents," and "A3" was added as "morally acceptable for adults." Four years later the Legion added the "A4" for "morally acceptable for adults with reservations" to further accommodate more permissive content in American films. Despite these changes, however, the power of the Legion, like the PCA, withered in the 1950s with its inability to exact concessions from filmmakers on once-taboo subjects.

To salvage its dwindling influence over its constituents' movie choices, the Legion in 1962 unsuccessfully lobbied MPAA president Eric Johnston (who replaced Will Hays in 1945) to abandon the Production Code and endorse a classificatory scheme similar to its own. Johnston repeatedly vetoed such requests, preferring to revise the Code rather than dismantle it since the MPAA-member companies still feared governmental censorship. In fact, Johnston went as far as to argue to Congress that Hollywood was

actually fighting censorship in its defiance of classification, that a rating system actually was undemocratic since it superseded parental authority and
decision making.[62] Production Code scholars Leonard Leff and Jerold L.
Simmons precisely recognized the driving force behind the industry's obsti-
nacy. "Beneath such golden platitudes," they said, "was base metal: the
industry found classification far less unconstitutional than uneconomi-
cal."[63] This sentiment was also shared by *New York Times* columnist Murray
Schumach, who wrote one of the earlier books on film and television regulation in 1964, called *The Face on the Cutting Room Floor*. At that time he
referred to the industry's fight against self-classification as a major-league
"hoax," a method of "perverting freedom of the cinema art in its lust for
cash."[64]

Surprisingly, however, the MPAA's view of classification was not shared by
PCA administrators, including chairperson Geoffrey Shurlock (a Code examiner who succeeded Joseph Breen in 1954). Shurlock staunchly believed that
revisions to the Production Code actually made it easier for children to see
adults-only films than would have been possible under classification.[65] Shurlock and his PCA staff also clearly realized that the Code was becoming
increasingly toothless and antiquated. "We're tired of playing nursemaid to
the industry," Code administrator Jack Vizzard reported Johnston as saying.
"It's keeping pictures adolescent."[66]

Despite this internal strife and the dwindling authority of the PCA, the
MPAA still publicly defended the Production Code into the 1960s. The association did not stand alone. The independent Theater Owners Association of
America—who together with the Allied States Association of Motion Picture
Exhibitors comprised ten thousand of the nation's thirteen thousand theaters
by the mid-1960s—also publicly rejected any form of self-classification but
for an entirely different reason.[67] For the Theater Owners Association of
America, classification would shift the burden of enforcing a code of self-regulation away from the MPAA onto the box office, a responsibility that had
increasingly become a hardship to exhibitors. Even though a newly deregu-
lated theatrical marketplace enabled exhibitors to show any film with any
subject they wanted—regardless of whether it had a Code seal, First Amendment protection for motion pictures did not necessarily mean public acceptance of this philosophy.[68] To this day, film culture in the United States rests
on the notion of motion pictures as entertainment, a condition, like it or not,
the MPAA must always contend with.

As the Production Code gradually weakened, it was the theater owners,
not the MPAA, who regularly found themselves the target of local regulatory
boards. Ironically, local protests of Hollywood films were the very thing the

MPPDA tried to avoid with self-regulation in the 1920s and 1930s. Now, as Jon Lewis explains, that was no longer the case:

> As the PCA increasingly lost its ability to control the studio product, censorship of film content was left to grassroots organizations and local censorship boards. These organizations and boards knew that taking on the studios was a difficult and expensive project. But taking on a local, independent theater owner was another matter entirely. The shift in public pressure from production to exhibition was good news for the studios. They produced more and more adult-themed pictures and then stood by as restrictive actions against exhibitors escalated. From 1962 to 1965, censorial action—including prosecutions, arrests, confiscations, license revocations, and local boycotts—increased tenfold. By 1965 roughly 60 percent of the films in general release were met by some sort of local censorship action, all of it targeted at the nation's exhibitors.[69]

On one hand, the MPAA could remain steadfast in its position vis-à-vis classification because drop-offs in movie attendance (partly the result of greater permissiveness and alternative forms of pleasure like television) were offset by higher rental prices, decreased film production, and corporate investments in television production. On the other hand, exhibitors were the ones vulnerable to arrest and boycott by local officials for showing films—usually ones of a sexual nature—that offended their communities. Since the MPAA had policies not to intervene in local censorship cases, the Production Code seemed the lesser of two evils in the eyes of exhibitors who still relied primarily on Hollywood product to fill their screens.[70]

Thus, an uneasy and contentious alliance emerged between the MPAA and the nation's exhibitors during the downfall of the Production Code. As an industry they were still publicly opposed to classification and committed to the appearance of harmless entertainment. But as separate entities they recognized that Code guidelines, in spite of the revisions, made it extremely difficult to market films to a more diversified, selective audience. Boundary maintenance—once originating in-house with the studios, formalized by the PCA, then supported by theater owners—now progressively got ignored at the production, distribution, and exhibition levels. For example, to compete with foreign film imports distributed by many independent companies, the MPAA-member distributors started to classify movies themselves in an attempt to capitalize on the adult market forsaken by the Code. *Elmer Gantry* (1960), *Lolita* (1962), and *Irma la Douce* (1963) were advertised by their distributors as strictly being for "adults only," even though the PCA granted them an all-ages seal. Exhibitors also took classification into their

Figure 2. A breakdown of the Production Code at the site of exhibition: Leslie
Caron and Maurice Chevalier in *Fanny* (1961). Courtesy of the Academy of Motion
Picture Arts and Sciences.

own hands, refusing to sell tickets to children without an adult guardian
whenever they believed a movie was too "adult." These de facto attempts at
voluntary classification by distributors and exhibitors nevertheless cut profits for everyone in the industry: "adult" films often played only a downtown
run; neighborhood theaters rarely booked them because of community criticism; exhibitors scratched them from double bills; and concession stands
sold less candy. In the case of the "adult" film *Fanny* (1961), theater owners
preempted matinees for the film and then refused to pay Warner Bros. for
the performances, even though they had contractually booked the film for the
entire weekend.[71]

With the various branches of the industry performing their own brand of
boundary maintenance, the PCA could no longer safeguard harmless entertainment. The linchpin of self-regulation, then and now, has always lain with
the collusive support of the major distributors and exhibitors. Without their
shared commitment to Code standards and deference to a single-seal enterprise, reformers and politicians began calling for a new system of content reg-

ulation to deal with the influx of sex, violence, and mature themes on U.S. screens. An overhaul of the Production Code was not only necessary for the industry; it was inevitable.

THE 1966 CODE OF SELF-REGULATION AND THE SMA TAG

[It] would be a very good thing if we would classify our pictures voluntarily and by ourselves. By classify I mean, first of all, that we should inform the public honestly in our advertising, in our publicity, what the picture is about, what theme the picture has, so that people who want to bring up their children a certain way and do not want their children to see pictures that handle certain themes should have a chance to prevent them from seeing them.
                              —Otto Preminger, quoted in the *New York Post* (1961)

By the mid 1960s, Hollywood's system of self-regulation was largely ineffective and painstakingly anachronistic, unable to adapt to changing industry wants or to audience compositions and tastes. The absence of a classification system placed the PCA in an awkward position: it had to deal with the MPAA signatories' making fewer films suitable for the "family" audience, while adhering to an outdated and inflexible set of standards designed for harmless entertainment. At one time the PCA could set policy for all films distributed and exhibited by MPAA members in the United States. Before the *Paramount* decree 95 percent of all films shown in this country had an MPAA seal. By 1966 that number had shrunk to 59 percent. Furthermore, between 1963 and 1965, thirty-nine films by MPAA-member companies were either not submitted to the PCA or were released through subsidiaries after being denied a seal by the PCA.[72] For distributors suffering from a two-decade-long decline in box-office revenues, short-term self-interest and profit often outweighed any long-term concern for the industry's welfare. The studios clearly had given up adhering to moral strictures of the PCA, weakening public confidence in the integrity of industry self-regulation.

In September 1966 the MPAA instituted a new production code, a prototype that two years later would morph into a classification system. As early as 1963 the organization had actively sought a new form of boundary maintenance after its president, Eric Johnston, suddenly died that year in August, two months after entering the hospital. The association's executive secretary, Ralph Hetzel, temporarily replaced Johnston as president while the MPAA searched for a successor. This period also saw the deaths of two other old guards of the Production Code: Joe Breen and Code cofounder Martin Quigley in 1964. During this time the MPAA courted as possible successor to

Johnston a key adviser to John F. Kennedy, attorney Louis Nizer (who eventually became the organization's special counsel), and Lyndon Johnson aide Jack Valenti, who became the organization's president in May 1966.[73]

Unlike his predecessors, Valenti did not fear motion picture classification as two films, *The Pawnbroker* (1965) and *Who's Afraid of Virginia Woolf?* (1966), greatly accelerated its implementation. Both featured the last remaining prohibitions in the Code—nudity, profanity, and blasphemy—and both eventually had PCA denials overturned on appeal. The distributor of *The Pawnbroker,* Allied Artists—then a member of the MPAA, but an independent outfit—threatened to release the film through a subsidiary, like so many distributors before it, if the PCA forced it to cut some nude footage. Rather than further erode or, more likely, futilely comply with the Production Code, Geoffrey Shurlock granted a "special exemption" to *The Pawnbroker,* making it the first PCA-certified film to feature bare female breasts.[74]

Valenti, after assuming leadership of the MPAA, handed down a similar concession to Warner Bros. for *Who's Afraid of Virginia Woolf?* This prestige picture, based on the controversial Edward Albee stage play, was granted a special exemption for Code-forbidden language like "son of a bitch" and "goddamn." The studio, in return, agreed to label the film "for adults only." *Who's Afraid of Virginia Woolf?* served as a test case, wrote Jon Lewis, for the industry, its Code exemption offering an opportunity to see if an age-based system, enforced not by the distributors but by exhibitors, could work and whether a narrowly targeted film could make money.[75] The film ranked third for that year's box office, suggesting that "adult" films could be financially lucrative. Theater owners, however, were not in agreement over now having the responsibility to enforce the box office themselves. They also still feared classification would further reduce the number of lucrative general audience pictures and box-office admissions. In fact, during second runs of *Who's Afraid of Virginia Woolf?* some exhibitors relaxed the film's stipulation, even dropping its age restrictions altogether.[76] Despite these concerns, the ability of Valenti to marshal through the system a mature, expensive, studio-produced hit like *Who's Afraid of Virginia Woolf?* signaled a shift in industry acceptance toward the distribution of more adult-themed pictures.

Only a few months after the *Who's Afraid of Virginia Woolf?* case, the MPAA formally instituted classification, replacing the single-seal Production Code with a two-tiered Code of Self-Regulation. The era of harmless entertainment, very much in decline already, now officially ended as the revised Code of Self-Regulation dismantled the industry's system of boundary maintenance that had been in operation for the last thirty-six years. Under the Code of Self-Regulation the newly named Office of Code Administration

Figure 3. The end of the Production Code: Elizabeth Taylor in *Who's Afraid of Virginia Woolf?* (1966).

(OCA, headed by Shurlock) could identify certain pictures as Suggested for Mature Audiences (SMA), an outright admission to the public that some OCA-certified films may no longer be appropriate for all audiences. The decision of whether a particular picture was unsuitable for children (because of treatment, content, and/or theme) passed from the OCA to the parent, who now became the arbiter of appropriate Hollywood entertainment. "Look, Mr.

Parent," Valenti explained to the *New York Post* at the SMA's onset, "This may be a picture that your child should or should not see. We don't know. You make the judgment. Don't just go willy-nilly into this picture."[77] Relinquishing its claims to the harmlessness and wholesomeness of its products quickly became industry policy, a discursive strategy the MPAA maintains to this day under CARA.

This abnegation manifests itself in many of the new Code of Self-Regulation's "Standards for Production," a loosely worded, sometimes vague, set of standards righteous enough to placate any detractors and oblique enough for its administrators to give a seal to almost any film. Left over from the Production Code (but in far less detail) were the following ten moral postures:

1. The basic dignity and value of human life shall be respected and upheld. Restraint shall be exercised in portraying the taking of life.
2. Evil, sin, crime, and wrong-doing shall not be justified.
3. Special restraint shall be exercised in portraying criminal or anti-social activities in which minors participate or are involved.
4. Detailed and protracted acts of brutality, cruelty, physical violence, torture and abuse shall not be presented.
5. Indecent or undue exposure of the human body shall not be presented.
6. Illicit sex relationships shall not be justified. Intimate sex scenes violating common standards of decency shall not be portrayed. Restraint and care shall be exercised in presentations dealing with sex aberrations.
7. Obscene speech, gestures or movements shall not be presented. Undue profanity shall not be permitted.
8. Religion shall not be demeaned.
9. Words or symbols contemptuous of racial, religious or national groups, shall not be used so as to incite bigotry or hatred.
10. Excessive cruelty to animals shall not be portrayed and animals shall not be treated inhumanely.[78]

None of these standards, however, which were actually carried over into CARA documentation until the late 1970s, were ever systematically upheld. First Amendment protection, the rise of independent production houses, the major Hollywood studios' primarily acting as distributors, and the dissolution of most local and state censorship boards no longer made it possible (or even necessary) for the MPAA to regulate content at the point of production. Rules and constraints, once localized and internalized within film form and narrative under the PCA, were merely lip service under the new regime. The

SMA label just alerted viewers to the potential "adult" nature of a film; it did not generate new aesthetic principles for regulating films with that tag.

Nevertheless, Hollywood still served an affirmative cultural function in the minds of politicians, reformers, and spectators, even without the mechanisms of harmless entertainment in place. The Code of Self-Regulation took this function into account, for it was the OCA's job, just like its predecessors the SRC and PCA, to protect MPAA-member films from public scrutiny. Written into the revised Code of Self-Regulation was a new declaration of boundary maintenance in accord with contemporary mores and one that provides the framework for responsible entertainment in the classification era. I will discuss these objectives in the next chapter since the 1968 Code—the rating system—is almost an exact replica of the 1966 Code (except for the SMA's being replaced with four rating categories).

The 1966 Code of Self-Regulation and its SMA provision gave the OCA more discretion in determining the acceptability of motion picture content for U.S. audiences, but it still failed to restore public confidence and industry cooperation in content regulation. The public spectacle of the *Virginia Woolf* case and the increased frequency of calls for governmental classification forced the MPAA to unveil some new kind of self-regulatory system, whether or not it addressed many of the industry's box-office problems and public-relations issues. The longtime Production Code and classification adminis-trator Albert Van Schmus testifies to the Code's status as a temporary solution, calling the SMA "simply an advertising effort" on the road to classi-fication and not the "complete answer."[79] First of all, the SMA tag was solely an advisory label with little binding power. It appeared only in advertising, with no pledge by independent distributors to adopt it and no arrangement with exhibitors to enforce it at the box office. Second, without such support the SMA could not adequately address growing community and court con-cerns about children's access to films containing adult subject matter. The designation accommodated an increasing number of films—many distrib-uted by MPAA signatories—that featured sexual themes, frank language, and graphic violence, without safeguards to protect children.[80] Last, the new sys-tem failed to address the practice of MPAA-member companies releasing films under a wholly owned subsidiary after being denied a Code seal.[81] Together, these apprehensions cast strong doubt on the integrity of the new Code of Self-Regulation and the affirmative cultural function of Hollywood entertainment.

The irrelevancy and ineffectiveness of the 1966 Code of Self-Regulation was most pronounced over the controversy surrounding the U.S. release of Michelangelo Antonioni's critically acclaimed film *Blow-Up* (1966). Shurlock, with the support of Valenti, demanded that several nude scenes be cut from the MGM film in order to earn a seal. Antonioni, who had final cut approval, refused, and MGM, an MPAA member, released the film uncut through a one-time subsidary, Premier, because of the film's box-office potential. The repercussions of this loophole did not go unnoticed by the *New York Times* after Warner Bros. similarly released the lesbian-themed *The Fox* through Claridge Pictures, a foreign subsidiary, in 1968: "It is a devious ploy and the code becomes toothless while the company retains its simon-pure status as a member of the association."[82] *Blow-Up* proved to be a hit in its initial urban run, and once-hesitant exhibitors booked the film nationwide, ignoring its absence of an MPAA seal.

A bill introduced by Senator Margaret Chase Smith in 1967 to establish a federal Committee on Film Classification strongly implied that unrestricted distribution and unregulated exhibition in the United States could no longer continue. Between November 1967 and November 1968 the U.S. film market had become inundated with more "adult" films than at any point in Hollywood's history; only 160 of the 350 feature-length films shown in the United States that year had a seal, and almost 60 percent of those pictures with seals had an SMA tag.[83] The success of *The Graduate* (1967) and *Bonnie and Clyde* (1967) proved that American films could also amplify the level of sex and violence for box-office profit. The SMA may have freed the screen for filmmakers, but it did so without industry accountability for the protection of children. A voluntary plan for a rating system was drawn up by the MPAA in 1968 and given to the National Association of Theatre Owners (NATO)—the result of a 1965 merger between Allied States and Theater Owners of America. Julian Rifkin, president of NATO, told his members in July that immediate action was necessary to stave off outside legislation: "The responsible elements in the industry must respond immediately to the crescendo of demand for affirmative action, or others less qualified will act for us. Already statutory classification, obscenity law, and rating systems are springing up all over the United States."[84]

Rifkin was responding specifically to two recent Supreme Court cases that greatly accelerated the industry's adoption of classification. Both cases hinged on the concept of "variable obscenity," which upheld the constitutional power of states and cities to regulate sexually explicit material. *Ginsberg v. New York* decreed that the government could deny minors access to sexually explicit material that was available to adults. *Interstate Circuit v. Dallas* found the city's age-based film classification system too "vague" to enforce but suggested that, with proper wording, the city ordinance could deny children access to films that could be viewed by adults.[85] In the MPAA's *A Year in*

Review report for 1968 Valenti considered the temporary defeat of the Dallas classification system as a victory for the First Amendment. However, at the same time he acknowledged there were limits to free expression in a democratic society, boundaries: "As we see it, there is a dual responsibility: we in motion pictures have an obligation to observe reasonable standards in films; the public has an obligation to select movie entertainment with foreknowledge and discretion. These dual obligations haven't yet joined but they are coming closer and the Code furnishes a bridge."[86]

A few months later, before any state or municipal government could pass any classification bills, Valenti dropped the ineffectual SMA label and on November 1, 1968, instituted a rating system. It was labeled the Code and Rating Administration (CARA), a partnership among the MPAA, NATO, and IFIDA (International Film Importers and Distributors of America).[87] With standards and objectives borrowed from the 1966 Code, Valenti promised a new form of Hollywood entertainment—what I call "responsible entertainment"—that balanced artistic freedom with restraint. Responsible entertainment, with the addition and then later abandonment of the X rating, clearly established boundaries of acceptability for motion pictures aimed at children sixteen and under. Little did Valenti know, however, it would establish the boundaries for the nature of Hollywood cinema itself for the next forty years.

In looking at the history of U.S. film regulation up to the rating system, we can better observe how the external forces that shaped the policies of harmless entertainment will similarly shape the policies of responsible entertainment. While the mechanisms of boundary maintenance might differ between the PCA and CARA, they both still respond to the same political and economic pressures affecting the MPAA: the legal establishment, outside censor boards, social reformers, and politicians. At one time or another these authorities, separately or in partnership, exercise their power over what they believe should be the function of Hollywood entertainment. During its tenure the PCA responded to their concerns, constructing film form and narrative under a protocol of harmless entertainment. An outmoded Code without distributor and exhibitor support led to its demise. For CARA enforcement to succeed, it needed to repair a lot of broken relationships in order for the MPAA to be trusted again.

CHAPTER 2

CARA and the Emergence of Responsible Entertainment

When Al Van Schmus—the last of the Breen Boys—retired, the
Classification and Rating Administration lost all resemblance to
the Production Code Administration. Or did it?
        —Leonard J. Leff and Jerold L. Simmons, *The Dame in the Kimono*

A regulatory facelift could not have come at a better time when the MPAA established the Code and Rating Administration (CARA—changed to Classification and Rating Administration in 1977) on November 1, 1968; the motion picture business in the United States was in shambles. Declining attendance, shifting cultural mores, cinematic free expression, and independent and foreign film competition led producers, distributors, and exhibitors to discard long-standing codes of industry conduct and cooperation for short-term personal gain. These abandoned "gentleman rules," as Jon Lewis calls them, dissolved a business arrangement between the three branches of the motion picture business that guaranteed the appearance of harmless entertainment to Hollywood's various audiences and detractors.[1] The standards and practices of the industry's centralized process of self-regulation were impotent amidst this undoing, unable to endow Hollywood entertainment with an affirmative cultural function so systematically accomplished in the past. The MPAA had to reconceptualize its products whether it wanted to or not.

Despite these obstacles, the rating system prevailed, surpassing the tenure of the Production Code Administration (1930–1966) as it celebrated its thirty-ninth year in 2007. Instead of a uniform PCA seal, CARA currently assigns one of five age-based rating categories to a film: G (suggested for general audiences); PG (parental guidance suggested); PG-13 (parents strongly cautioned); R (persons under 17 not admitted, unless accompanied by parent or adult guardian); and NC-17 (no one 17 and under admitted). Since the inception of a rating system, the MPAA and its longtime president, Jack Valenti (who retired in 2004 and was replaced by Dan Glickman, who served as secretary of agriculture under Bill Clinton), have repeatedly differentiated the self-regulatory policies and procedures of CARA from its predecessors: "a voluntary rating plan" that "assures freedom of the screen," announced a 1968 press release; "a totally new approach," declared Valenti for *Daily Variety* in 1975, that "would no longer 'approve or disapprove' the content of a film"; a replacement for "a stern, forbidding catalogue of 'Dos and Don'ts' [that had] the odious smell of censorship," wrote Valenti in a 1991 industry pamphlet. And in 1998 an MPAA press release proclaimed that the voluntary rating system replaced "an absurd manifesto called the Hays Code."[2] These accounts indicate that the MPAA always wanted consumers to believe that CARA and the PCA were entirely separate regimes, distinctive markers of censorious "Classical Hollywood" and liberated "New Hollywood." Valenti frequently expressed this sentiment of CARA being a more modernized system, one that allowed the filmmaker "to tell his story in his way without anyone thwarting him."[3]

Valenti's words seem initially plausible. First, different age categories gave filmmakers greater creative leeway than a single-seal-for-all-audiences approach. Content and themes previously forbidden by the PCA were now more permissible under a classification system. Second, moral absolutism, once the backbone of the Production Code, gave way to a world of moral relativism under classification. Film ratings were a determination of the possible suitability of a film for children and were not grounded in Catholic doctrine. Last, CARA regulated films only after their completion. Unlike the PCA, CARA did not actively shape film narrative and form during the production process in order to ensure mass distribution and exhibition of Hollywood's products. Classification, it would appear then, enabled and permitted freer expression in Hollywood films than self-regulation under the Production Code.

Freer expression? Indeed. Free expression? Definitely not. This chapter will demonstrate that CARA functioned similarly to the PCA in one key respect: to control entryway and participation into the legitimate theatrical marketplace. I will first argue that classification reestablished a system by which the MPAA could govern the flow of product through the production, distribution, and exhibition sectors of the Hollywood film industry. Together with the full cooperation of the National Association of Theatre Owners (NATO) by 1973, the MPAA, through CARA, was able to construct a new model of entertainment, what I call "responsible entertainment," an industry standard that functioned much like "harmless entertainment" during the

Production Code. Responsible entertainment required, above all, a collective adherence and commitment by the major distributors and exhibitors to completely abandon the use of the X/NC-17-rating product line. By regulating all Hollywood films into R categories or lower—what I call the Incontestable R—the industry could ensure the suitability and respectability of Hollywood's products in the eyes of audiences. Hollywood, in other words, updated its business practices (a rating system enabling free expression) without changing its business model (entertainment for all ages). The remainder of the chapter will focus on the mid-1970s to 1990, a period of notable rating cases when filmmakers and opportunistic distributors challenged the boundaries of the Incontestable R, causing a momentary rupture in the guise of responsible entertainment. Moments like these were few, I argue, but they highlighted the fact that the rating system, while enabling greater creative freedom than the Production Code, still is a virtual synonym, in the words of Bruce A. Austin, for both "self-preservation" and self-interest," the same ideals that have motivated the MPAA for more than eighty years.[4]

Responsible Entertainment and a New Code of Self-Regulation

In his 1990 *American Film* article "What Will H. Hays Begat: Fifty Years of the Production Code," film critic and historian Charles Champlin correctly asserts that the Production Code never truly ended; it was momentarily sidetracked, then gradually transformed into a classification system, another "voluntary and self-regulating way of heading off more imposed censorship."[5] This new "way" of self-regulation not only served once again as a buttress against federal legislation, but it also helped to reestablish the commercial efficiency of the Hollywood film industry under the guise of responsible entertainment.

In beginning to understand CARA as a reformulation of the MPAA's business practices rather than an overhaul of its operations, it is important to realize that the rating system was actually always intended to be a "production code" for the major Hollywood distributors just like its predecessor. On the surface there were many points of continuity between the two administrations. CARA originally stood for the Code and Rating Administration, and many PCA administrators moved over to CARA (which also occupied the same Hollywood offices for a time). Eugene Dougherty, the senior member of the Production Code staff who served under Joseph Breen and Geoffrey Shurlock, became CARA's first chairperson. Shurlock himself remained as a consultant. Also retained was Richard R. Mathison, a PCA staff member since 1965, and longtime examiner Albert E. Van Schmus, who continued in his role as a senior examiner until his retirement in 1982.[6] The CARA seals maintained the numerical sequence set by the PCA seals.

To be sure, the Production Code was definitely a more determining and constrictive force in the constitution of Hollywood-produced films from 1930 to 1966. Van Schmus admits that its single-seal-for-all-audiences standard was undoubtedly censorship of free expression: "I always looked upon myself as a censor. I admit it. That's what I was there for, to try to talk somebody out of doing something in their script."[7] The rating system liberalized the Code, allowing filmmakers to theoretically address any and all subjects across various age categories. CARA examiners looked at a film's theme, content, and treatment of subject matter to determine its appropriateness for children. In the early years a rating of G, M (later GP then PG), or R was then assigned to those films that all or some parents may find acceptable viewing for their children. An X rating was awarded to films off-limits to children under sixteen (later under eighteen). In any case CARA, unlike the PCA, guaranteed a rating "category" to each applicant and nearly unlimited cinematic expression to all.

Yet an examination of the official 1968 Code of Self-Regulation reveals a less altruistic side to the MPAA, one that supports a claim made by outgoing PCA head Geoffrey Shurlock at the time of CARA's creation: "We'll use the same standards that we've used for 30 years in applying the code."[8] In fact, the 1968 Code was practically a carbon copy of the 1966 Code (which itself was based on the 1930 Production Code), with one key difference: a four-tiered rating system replaced the Suggested for Mature Audiences tag. Even the "Declaration of Principles" and "Standards of Production" were lifted directly from the 1966 Code of Self-Regulation to guide administrators about matters of sex, violence, and other wrongdoings in considering motion pictures for ratings approval. These replications confirm Van Schmus's pronouncement that the 1966 Code of Self-Regulation was merely an "advertising effort" in preparation for classification.

Even so, contained in the language of the 1966 and 1968 Code documents lies the foundation of boundary maintenance under CARA, what I have previously referred to as "responsible entertainment." The word *responsible* is stated four times throughout both Codes, and none of these four is more important than the one employed in the "Declaration of Principles": "To encourage artistic expression by expanding creative freedom," and "To assure that the freedom which encourages the artist remains *responsible* and sensitive to the standards of the larger society."[9] Valenti elaborated more on these tenets in a section entitled "Censorship and Classification-by-Law Are Wrong" from a "Personal Statement" released in connection with the announcement of CARA and the 1968 Code:

> We will oppose these intrusions into a communications art-form shielded and protected by the First Amendment. We believe the screen should be as free for film-makers as it is for those who write books, produce television material, publish newspapers and magazines, compose music and create paintings and sculptures.
>
> At the same time I have urged film creators to remember that freedom without discipline is license, and that's wrong, too. I have, in the many meetings I have had with creative people in film, suggested that the freedom which is rightly theirs ought to be a *responsible* freedom and each individual film-maker must judge his work in that sensible light. I'm cheered by the response to my suggestions.[10]

The balance between artistic expression and cultural sensitivity, what Valenti delineated here as "responsible freedom," is essentially the philosophy behind "responsible entertainment" in the classification era. A process for determining the upper threshold of responsible entertainment and CARA's strategies for effectively enforcing this boundary was never outlined in the 1968 Code. At CARA's inception, though, a policy to negotiate these concerns can be found in the new Code's proclamation, "Freedom of expression does not mean toleration of license." Often repeated by Valenti throughout his tenure, this phrase points to the strategies the MPAA envisioned for responsible entertainment at that time and the ones it currently upholds now.

How, then, did the MPAA reconcile two contradictory objectives in the Code of Self-Regulation, one in which creative freedom could flourish as long as it was balanced by a sense of self-restraint and social responsibility? Or as Valenti succinctly put it again: "Every filmmaker ought to be able to tell a story the way he wants to. But that kind of freedom ought to be harnessed."[11] The MPAA did so by having it both ways, by perpetuating the belief that CARA supports free expression of filmmakers while at the same time actively discouraging the use of the X rating among its membership. In this manner the MPAA could subscribe to a framework of creative license but still function according to an affirmative cultural model of entertainment. As a result, the MPAA could manage the flow of product through every sector of the film industry under its own terms of boundary maintenance—responsible entertainment—while also publicly denying its role as a censor.

Before this could happen, Valenti needed the industry to adhere to the standards of responsible entertainment not only in theory but in practice.

The success of CARA depended on the collusive support of its judgments by the members of the MPAA and NATO. What responsible entertainment might look like or feel like or taste like was anybody's guess at the time. But Valenti knew early on that the menu did not include the X rating.

THE MPAA AND THE X RATING

In a 1977 hearing on Capitol Hill Jack Valenti outlined the principles that led to the success of the MPAA rating system:

> Let me tell you that the linchpin of this rating system was the interlinking of essential ingredients. First, the system must have integrity, must have probity. It must be proof against pressure from all sides, majors and independents, from anyone who has a personal economic stake, or anyone who may assume they have an economic stake, in the outcome of the ratings. . . . Second, we had to have a partnership of everybody involved in films, the retailer, the theaterowner who exhibits the film, the independent director and producer, and the major director and producer. . . . Third, a policy mechanism had to be created so that if someone felt aggrieved by a rating, he had a place to go. You can't have a czar or a dictator saying, "That is it, and no more." Four, and this is the crux of the system, it really had to perform a service for parents. Otherwise, the ratings had no meaning. Those were the four indispensable elements that formed the recipe for the rating system.[12]

When the MPAA established CARA in 1968, these four elements were effectively set in place. Lending initial integrity to the system was the creation of the X rating, which barred those under sixteen and quieted concerns about children's access to sexually explicit material. I will examine the advent of the X in terms of two of the three major partners in CARA: the MPAA (the seven "majors" minus RKO, which had its assets stripped by Howard Hughes in 1955, plus two new independent distributors: Allied Artists and Avco Embassy) and NATO (which represented most of the major exhibition chains). The third partner in CARA was the International Film Importers and Distributors of America (IFIDA), a trade organization representing a mass of independent companies, which played little role in the rating system.[13] If any distributor disagreed with an assigned rating from CARA's Rating Board, one had the opportunity to appeal the original rating to CARA's Appeals Board. And written into the principles of the Code of Self-Regulation was a commitment to parents to help them "determine whether a particular picture is one which children should see at the discretion of the parent; or only when accompanied by a parent; or should not see."[14]

An industry-wide commitment to these goals was necessary to lay the foundation of responsible entertainment. The MPAA needed protection from moral reformers and politicians. NATO was bound by the courts to keep sexually explicit material away from children. And Valenti, wanting no part of any of them, wished to keep the industry, in the words of Jon Lewis, "out of the dirty movie business."[15] It was not until 1973, however, that the members of the MPAA and NATO collectively abandoned the use of the X rating, a category that had quickly become synonymous with "the dirty movie business" shortly after the inception of CARA.

"The stigma of the X," Justin Wyatt explains, was the result of the rating's widespread and pronounced use as a marketing tool in the late 1960s and early 1970s to tap into a market segment of adult viewers previously ignored by Hollywood. Mainstream filmmakers, distributors, and exhibitors took advantage of the creative freedom and notoriety provided by an adults-only category, as did exploitation filmmakers and pornographers. This inter-industry practice, Wyatt notes, created initial confusion over the meaning of the X rating, dividing the adult-film marketplace into three distinct areas: serious "adult dramas," like *A Clockwork Orange* (1971), primarily distributed by the MPAA signatories and incorporating graphic, though simulated, sex scenes and/or adult subject matter; "soft-core" exploitation (*Cherry, Harry & Raquel* [1969]); and "hard-core" pornography (*Deep Throat* [1972]), the domain of the independents and marked by differences in sexual content, exhibition, and pricing.[16] As a result of the category's appropriation by members of the legitimate and the nonlegitimate film industry for exploitative purposes, the X quickly became associated with pornography, providing little chance for serious artistic filmmakers to adopt the rating. It became clear that if filmmakers wanted to make responsible Hollywood entertainment in the classification era, they had to make it with an R rating or go outside the legitimate theatrical marketplace.

The fact that independent distributors could self-impose the X was the result of the MPAA's never copyrighting the category, unlike the other ratings. I am uncertain, though, if this omission was a legal maneuver on the part of Valenti or a Machiavellian scheme of his to force filmmakers to use their creative freedom "responsibly." In the case of the former, Valenti stated in a 1975 MPAA press release that his original intent was to have only three ratings—G, M, and R—because it was his view that parents should have the right to take their children to any film they choose. He said, however, that NATO urged him to create the X category out of fear of legal redress under

Ginsberg, the 1968 Supreme Court case that ruled that material could be considered obscene for children but not for adults.[17] He supplements this legal explanation in a 1990 interview, claiming that the X rating was not copyrighted because the MPAA charged a fee for its rating service. The X "had to be open-ended," he said, "so that if somebody doesn't want to submit a picture [to the MPAA], they can use the X. Otherwise, we could be challenged on First Amendment grounds."[18] As for the Machiavellian rationale, it is hard to believe that Valenti did not anticipate the appropriation of the uncopyrighted X by soft- and hard-core pornographers. The X permitted any and all representations of sex and violence to be subsumed under its category. The basic principle of responsible entertainment—"freedom of expression does not mean toleration of license"—could never be contained within a no-limits classification. Even if there is some truth to Valenti's legal justifications for not copyrighting the X, the excuses peculiarly support a system of boundary maintenance dependent on that rating's stigmatization and abandonment.

Whatever the reason(s) may be for failing to copyright the X, the MPAA pretty much avoided the "dirty movie business" for both serious adult works and soft-core features from the very beginning of CARA. The number of X-rated films released by the MPAA signatories (Columbia, MGM, Paramount, 20th Century–Fox, United Artists, Universal, and Warner Bros.) between November 1, 1968, and October 8, 1973, totaled only twenty-five pictures (1968: 4; 1969: 8; 1970: 7; 1971: 5; 1972: 0; and 1973: 1).[19] Many of these films were foreign produced, including adult dramas (*The Damned* [1969]; *The Devils* [1971]), soft-core sexual comedies (*The Best House in London* [1969]), and a documentary (*The Body* [1971]). Only a small proportion was U.S. produced, including serious-minded films like *Medium Cool* (1969),[20] *Midnight Cowboy* (1969), and *Last of the Mobile Hot-shots* (1971), as well as sexual farces like *Can Hieronymus Merkin Ever Forget Mercy Humppe and Find True Happiness?* (1969) and *Beyond the Valley of the Dolls* (1970). The shrinking year-to-year number of legitimate X pictures produced stateside and released by the majors reflected the rating's instant cultural stigma and especially its economic liabilities: the category's age restrictions prevented a large portion of the potential audience from ever purchasing tickets.

When some MPAA signatories did exploit the notoriety provided by the X rating and its suggestion of "uncensored spectacle," as did Warner Bros. with *Girl on a Motorcycle* (1968), for example, they met with a harsh reception. One unnamed Warner Bros. executive said, "[The Code staff] asked us to make some cuts, but we decided to go ahead and take the X rating and make some money."[21] But after *Girl on a Motorcycle*'s disastrous performance at the box

Figure 4. Rereleasing an X-rated picture with an R rating: Alain Delon and
Marianne Faithfull in *Girl on a Motorcycle* (1968). Courtesy of the Academy of
Motion Picture Arts and Sciences.

office, Warner Bros. rereleased the film with an R rating and a new name
(*Naked under Leather*) after removing an erotic lovemaking scene and Marianne Faithfull's masturbation scene. Paramount's *if . . .* (1968) and the independent Sigma III film *Greetings* (1968) were also released in edited R
versions after their initial X runs.[22]

The rereleasing of *Girl on a Motorcycle, Greetings,* and *if . . .* with R ratings
in 1969 suggests that both MPAA and independent distributors became
quickly disenchanted with the box-office potential of serious-minded X-
rated pictures. Their initial eagerness to take advantage of the adults-only rating gave way almost immediately to its cultural stigmatization. By July 1969
certain newspapers had begun to reject advertisements for X-rated films, and
many TV and radio stations established policies refusing to run trailers for
them. Some stations would not even run ads for M-rated films before 10
p.m.[23] Moreover, difficulties in promoting X-rated films exposed the rating's
inherent economic limitations to the MPAA signatories: the age restrictions
simply made them a poor financial investment. If an R could play to a mass

audience, so the executives thought—albeit one that required adult supervision for children—why not cut a film to fit the lower category's requirements? In fact, the *New York Times,* on the very day of CARA's formation, reported that MPAA members were already editing their films down from an X rating before they were even officially rated. The newspaper stated that Paramount had removed some obscene dialogue from a prison film, *Riot* (1969), to get an R;[24] the *Times* also reported that Michelangelo Antonioni would excise a four-letter word for copulation in the script for MGM's *Zabriskie Point* (1970) if its inclusion meant an X. "The general view" in the industry, wrote *Newsweek* four months later, in February 1969, was "that, while nobody quite knows what draws an X rating, it is something to avoid."[25]

Even the commercial and artistic success of *Midnight Cowboy* (1969) failed to establish a trend in X-rated film production. *Midnight Cowboy's* triumph, suggests Jon Lewis, had more to do with its kinship with prestige adults-only pictures like *Bonnie and Clyde* (1967) rather than with soft- or hard-core features like *I Am Curious (Yellow)* (1967) and *3 in the Attic* (1968), two other X-rated films in the top-twenty box office for 1969.[26] By the end of the decade, too many "dirty" movies had already damaged beyond repair the adults-only rating's commercial viability. In his 1972 book, *The Movie Rating Game,* former CARA intern Stephen Farber confirms the widespread avoidance of the X by 1970: "By now the X has lost whatever chance it might have had to achieve respectability," he said. "Several studios have made it a policy to produce *no* X films, and most studio contracts with directors stipulate that the director must win an R or less restrictive rating on the finished film." The X may even keep some films from being made at all. Farber identifies already-completed films like *Joe* (1970), *Hi, Mom!* (1970), and *Straw Dogs* (1971) as being cut by their distributors so they could be awarded an R.[27]

At the same time that the MPAA signatories put policies in place to abolish the X rating as a business strategy, CARA further protected MPAA interests by instituting a new policy of its own to assure that more films could be awarded R ratings. In 1970 CARA raised the R and X age limits from sixteen to seventeen in order to absorb previous X-rated content into the R category. This bump, in the words of CARA chairperson Eugene Dougherty, was intended so that "no serious film-makers would want to go beyond the limits of the R."[28] The term *serious* appears to be CARA's (or, at the very least, Dougherty's) synonym for self-restraint, the responsible kind of entertainment Valenti envisioned for the Hollywood film industry. Indeed, no U.S.-produced, MPAA-distributed films actually did go beyond the boundaries of the R for a long time after 1970. Only auteur-driven foreign productions distributed by the majors carried the badge—Stanley Kubrick's

A Clockwork Orange, Pier Paolo Pasolini's *Decameron* (1971), Ken Russell's
The Devils (1971), Bernardo Bertolucci's *Last Tango in Paris* (1973)—as did a
few soft-core features: *Emmanuelle* (1974) and *Inserts* (1976).

The near-abandonment of the X rating and the expansion of the age range
for R pictures in 1970 also caught the attention of *Variety* at the time. The
trade paper described 1970 as the year of the "wandering X and R," because of
the number of films seemingly of X caliber that drifted over into R and,
strangely, even into GP territory.[29] Films like *Women in Love* (male frontal
nudity) and *The Boys in the Band* (homosexuality) earned R ratings, whereas
a year earlier they may have been given X ratings. Statistics support these
claims. R ratings accounted for only 23 percent of films from 1968 to 1969 but
rose to 37 percent from 1969 to 1970 and gradually increased through the early
part of the decade, reaching a plateau of 48 percent from 1974 to 1975.[30] As a
result of these changes to MPAA and CARA policies, Valenti redesigned a
system that was more inclusive of MPAA product while simultaneously promoting Hollywood as a responsible industry committed to making mass-
audience films. The R rating became the tag that signified Hollywood, and
the X became associated with U.S. independent and foreign art fare, as well as
soft- and hard-core pornographic films. Writing in the *Journal of the University Film Association* in 1971, Julian C. Burroughs Jr. foresaw this strategy by
the MPAA as a means of reducing criticism of its projects and staving off federal legislation. "The major motion picture companies which are represented
by the MPAA," he said, "will have to decide how far they are willing to follow
the 'anything/everything goes' trend. To put it another way, as long as the
majors—and others who would aspire to general public favor—allow good
taste to play a significant role in their productions and promotions, they are
not likely to lose the support of the majority of Americans."[31]

The following year, the Associated Press reported in April 1971 that "the
day of the X rated film appears to be over" for the MPAA signatories. In
this story Columbia Pictures reiterated its stance against releasing X-rated
pictures, and James Aubrey, president of MGM, explained why his company no longer was in the business of making X films: "Everybody was
caught in the newfound freedom. The industry wallowed in it. But while
permissive films might have been successful six months ago, they aren't now."
20th Century–Fox also abandoned X-film production after the back-to-back
box-office bombs of the soft-core *Myra Breckenridge* and *Beyond the Valley of
the Dolls* in 1970. "The board of directors decided then never again," said a Fox
studio source, "not for all the money in the world." Even smaller, semilegiti-
mate, independent distributors were abandoning the rating. Samuel Z.
Arkoff, chairman of American International Pictures, remarked in May 1971:

"It's good business sense today to make only Gs and GPs," and independent distributor Donald S. Rugoff admitted, "I never bought a film before with ratings in mind but I do now. The hassle just isn't worth it."[32] How quickly the X became an oddity for MPAA signatories is summed up by a *Variety* headline in July 1971: "WB acceptance of X for 'The Devils' a Rarity Nowadays for Major Film."

Even with MPAA-member unity over the branding of the X, Hollywood's new form of boundary maintenance could only succeed with the joint cooperation of NATO. Exhibiting adults-only pictures in legitimate first-run houses still gave the public impression that the MPAA sanctioned all these films, even if they were not reviewed and awarded an "official" X by CARA. The infiltration of adult-themed films, however, came at an inopportune time for the industry. As Justin Wyatt notes, in 1969 the majors suffered more than $200 million in losses, weekly attendance was almost one-sixth of its 1946 high, and "the youth 'revolution' served to feed the increasing freedom in terms of subject matter, further enhancing the marketability of the adult/porno feature."[33] Abandoning the X might have been the last thing on the minds of NATO exhibitors at a time of floundering box-office receipts.

NATO and the X

On the day of the inauguration of CARA in 1968, *New York Times* film critic Vincent Canby reported that proponents of the rating system saw two possible reasons why it could fail, both related to the X: first, X-rated films would prove so successful that they would stimulate more production; and second, as a result, exhibitors might loosen their enforcement of the rating, inviting new calls for governmental censorship and putting pressure on the Rating Board to place limits on the number of X films released.[34] He was right on both accounts. The X rating did prove to be a successful marketing category for distributors in the early years of CARA, and exhibitors were negligent in their handling of the adults-only category, igniting criticism and calls for reform of the rating system. To give rise to the era of responsible entertainment, the MPAA abandoned the product line altogether. NATO needed to recalibrate its box-office policy as well.

A new working relationship between the MPAA and NATO was absolutely mandatory after the Production Code since enforcement of the Code of Self-Regulation no longer fell on the shoulders of the distributors but on the theater owners themselves. In 1968 NATO made clear in the *NATO News,* a monthly bulletin available only to its members, that it shared responsibility with the MPAA for the system's success: "The local box office is the crucial point at which the rating system will succeed or fail. No amount of publicity or church support can guarantee the plan unless exhibitors themselves understand it, enforce it at their theatres, and work to create favorable public opinion in their communities. A lack of support on the part of theatre owners can only serve to create the circumstances which encourage hard feelings and, ultimately, censorship."[35] Enforcement would include checking IDs for X-rated films, ensuring that children were accompanied by a parent for R-rated films, patrolling theaters for children jumping screens, refraining from playing an R- or X-rated trailer in front of a G- or M-rated feature, being aware that the severest rating prevailed on a double feature, running the rating trailer before each film, and educating theater staff on the differences between the ratings.

Some of the criticism of the rating system in its first few years can be attributed to NATO's failure to carefully implement these obligations, many of which unsurprisingly centered on the X rating. Newspapers reported that neighborhood theaters neglected to police the box office. For example, the *New York Sunday News* found in July 1969 that underage children were being admitted to X-rated films and that exhibition policies sometimes allowed X trailers to accompany R films. The article reported the horror of one woman who took her fourteen-year-old son to see the R-rated *Goodbye Columbus* only to view the coming attraction of the X-rated *I, a Woman II*.[36] In other instances inattentive exhibitors showed X-rated trailers with G-rated films. It certainly did not help that opportunistic distributors took advantage of the new system at NATO's expense by releasing films with two ratings—with and without restrictive footage—to play for different audiences and theaters across the country.[37] The problems the X rating immediately posed to local theater owners led to a plea in July 1969 by the *Motion Picture Herald*'s Charlie Poorman to exhibitors to forgo X-rated features altogether. "While it is true that a powerful segment of the populace will patronize the maximum in perversion," he said, "there is no industrial future in this." He believed that the X rating "doesn't represent our best cinematic efforts" and suggested that theater owners replay older films in lieu of "unsuitable" ones.[38]

Two months later, a survey conducted by Young NATO, a committee of second- and third-generation exhibitors in the organization, reported that 47 percent of its respondents—who accounted for 89 percent of the nation's thirteen thousand theaters—automatically excluded X-rated films already from potential engagements for their theaters. The survey also supported claims that theaters carelessly enforced rating restrictions, with 30 percent of those NATO theaters playing X pictures to underage patrons.[39] For at least half of NATO's members, banning X films avoided the expense of modifying prints and trailers for local censor boards (most of which would cease their operations by the mid-1970s). These costs, partially if not entirely, would fall on the individual theaters. It also helped exhibitors to avoid community pressure, especially if they could not properly promote an X film in the local newspaper. Justin Wyatt viewed this split reaction to the economic opportunity of adult film in NATO's membership as reflecting a division along urban and rural lines. Ever since the *Miracle* decision forced the MPAA to divorce itself from exhibition and created numerous independent theater owners and chains, small-town exhibitors were more reluctant to play adult pictures than their big-city counterparts because of a lack of support from their communities.[40] These policies corresponded with the growing number of newspapers in small cities that refused to accept advertising for X films. While the newspaper chains in urban centers (New York, Philadelphia, Chicago, Los Angeles, and San Francisco) did not turn away advertisements, dailies in smaller cities (Birmingham, Chattanooga, Miami, Milwaukee, San Diego, Wichita) banned X-rated ads to conform to the standards of their respective communities.[41] In November 1969 the MPAA listed twenty-three such newspapers that would not take ads for X-rated films, a number that jumped to thirty-four newspapers by July 1972 and included major metropolitan city newspapers such as the *Detroit News, Cleveland Plain-Dealer, Cincinnati Enquirer,* and the *Boston Herald-Traveler.*[42]

Community grievances, inconsistent exhibitor policies, and media bans such as these fueled public concerns over the availability of obscenity to minors and renewed calls for federal censorship of motion pictures. On January 28, 1970, just prior to the release of the report of the President's Commission on Obscenity and Pornography, Valenti appeared before a subcommittee of the Committee on the Judiciary in the House of Representatives to oppose an impending bill to regulate local exhibition of theatrical motion pictures. He reassured Congress that NATO overwhelmingly supported the rating system and that voluntary self-regulation on the part of the film industry was the best course of action. Drawing from results of the Young NATO survey, as well as the MPAA's own recent study conducted by the Opinion Research Corporation (a survey of CARA's awareness and usefulness to parents that has been conducted every year since), Valenti announced two principal revisions to the Code of self-regulation to clarify the rating system to politicians, parents, and patrons at the box office. Mentioned earlier in this chapter, these revisions included the replacement of the M, supposedly the least understood of the four categories, with the GP (all ages admitted but parental guidance suggested) and the raising of the age limit for the R and X categories from sixteen to seventeen.

Throughout his tenure Valenti would often make such cosmetic adjustments to the system of boundary maintenance, changes that were honest enough to placate Hollywood's detractors but inconsequential enough not to endanger the economic and political interests of the MPAA. At this crossroads Valenti's diversionary tactics obfuscated the MPAA's overwhelming reliance on NATO for CARA's success and effectiveness. He used the occasion not to criticize exhibitors, who were the linchpins of the rating system, but to lend his unwavering support for the medium's First Amendment protection while also criticizing those "smut pushers," "salacious pornographers," and "fastbuck peddlers of garbage" who infringed on the privilege of creative freedom for others. The fact that these "fastbuck peddlers of garbage" found homes for their films at NATO theaters went unmentioned as Valenti's closing remark at this hearing reified the rating system's main objectives and its blueprint of responsible entertainment—"freedom of expression does not mean toleration of license":

> Too often, it appears to me, the public does not differentiate between the responsible filmmaker and the irresponsible. There is a difference, a decisively important one. . . .
>
> The responsible leaders in the motion picture industry will not permit this medium to be tarnished. Personally I shall never cease, whatever the cost, to fight for self-regulation and self-restraint. I shall condemn obvious and gratuitous trash no matter where it comes from or who cashes in on it.[43]

While Valenti could ensure that the MPAA carried out this responsibility through the self-regulatory operations of CARA, he still needed NATO theater owners to abandon any and all exhibition of X-rated pictures, many of which made more money than some legitimate Hollywood releases at the time.

That very same day, in the pages of a safer, less-public form—*Variety*—Valenti attacked Loews for eroding faith in the rating system. In this unprecedented criticism of a major theater circuit, he chastised the exhibition chain for booking the Danish sex film *Without a Stitch* (1970) in State I and Cine, two Manhattan first-run theaters. In no uncertain terms he made it clear to NATO that its members could not simultaneously be serving the needs of both sex voyeurs and a responsible community enterprise:

> I told the chief executive of [Loews] that if other large, responsible theater operators decide to play this kind of film, then we are going to be witness to the death of quality exhibition in this country. The theater cannot have it both ways. The theater cannot be half quality and half smut. . . .
>
> If there is a proliferation of the quasi-porn film playing in first-class houses to the exclusion of product of wider appeal, we are in trouble.[44]

Following Valenti's tirade, Tonlyn Productions, the independent distributor of *Without a Stitch,* filed a $30-million damage suit against the MPAA. The company claimed that Paramount head, Charles G. Bludhorn, told Loews that it would withhold its products from the chain if it continued to book X films from non-MPAA members. At the same time these bullying and perhaps illegal anticompetitive practices took place, 175 bills calling for film censorship or punitive actions against exhibitors were pending in state legislatures. Proposals ranged, for example, from official state film classification and bans on R and X trailers to taxes of five cents per G admission up to fifty cents per X admission.[45] Although many of these bills were later found to be unconstitutional, they pointed to the X rating's growing association with bawdiness and pornography by many legislators around the country. This, in effect, convinced more NATO members to abandon its use.

Valenti's remarks to the U.S. House of Representatives and in *Variety* spelled out the MPAA's commercial strategy in the age of classification: only CARA-certified films rated R or lower should play in NATO theaters. Films officially rated X (with or without serious artistic pretensions) and especially those without an MPAA rating ("unrated") were greatly discouraged, since the outermost rating category and its unrated stepchild would always imply a violation of CARA's responsibility to the "standards of the larger society." The wedge driven between "quality" adults-only films and pornography, be they X or unrated, would forever distort the rating system, particularly for independent distributors. If they wanted access to the legitimate marketplace, they would have to play by the MPAA's rules under the MPAA's rating system in mainly NATO-owned theaters. In CARA's first few years many independents had rated their films X for surefire booking. But rapid changes in public acceptance and taste toward the adults-only rating and "soft-core" compelled them to work with, rather than against, the rating system. As a result, more and more independent distributors started to comply with CARA, submitting their products for classification so they could secure bookings in better, more lucrative, houses.

Like the Production Code, the rating system eventually became a gateway to the legitimate film marketplace: a code of production, distribution, and exhibition serving the major players in the industry. In 1972 domestic theater admissions rose roughly 20 percent over the previous year, primarily because of *The Godfather,* halting a seven-year slide, while total box-office revenues surged from $1 billion to $1.64 billion.[46] At the same time that Hollywood rediscovered how to make money, the R rating solidified itself as a marker of responsible entertainment in the New Hollywood.

THE INCONTESTABLE R

In 1972 Valenti's repeated warnings to the MPAA signatories against producing and distributing soft-core films or irresponsible entertainment finally had
an effect: Hollywood did not release any X-rated pictures that year.[47] The
abandonment of the adults-only product line certainly had an effect on the
industry's image. *Variety,* in its annual overview of CARA, noted that Hollywood's sudden shift away from X-rated material effectively helped to reduce
public criticism of the standards for its other categories.[48] Obviously, the
MPAA could never totally eliminate criticism of its members' practices, but
acceding to CARA the authority to excise potentially problematic material
from "serious" adults-only films to accommodate an R rating accomplished
two important things: it gave the appearance that the film industry was
responsible and ensured that Hollywood's products were available to audiences of all ages, R-rated guardian or no guardian. The development and
maintenance of this practice created what I call the "Incontestable R," an aesthetic and discursive framework that guaranteed all R-rated films to Hollywood's audience as responsible entertainment.

Exhibitor cooperation was essential to the R's incontestability, and many
NATO members, particularly small-city exhibitors, pledged their allegiance
to the rating system and the abandonment of the X. Still, certain NATO members continued to exhibit soft- and hard-core films with MPAA X ratings or
self-applied X ratings until the middle of 1973. During that time hard-core
films like *Deep Throat, The Devil in Miss Jones,* and *Behind the Green Door*
were quite successful in the marketplace, outgrossing many Hollywood films.
What finally secured an industry-wide commitment to responsible entertainment were a series of obscenity rulings handed down on June 21, 1973, by
the U.S. Supreme Court under the leadership of conservative chief justice
Warren Burger, appointed by Richard Nixon in 1969.

In the two cases most relevant to the film industry—*Miller v. California*
and *Paris Adult Theater I v. Slaton*—the Court reaffirmed that obscene material—defined as the depiction or description of hard-core sexual content—
had no protection under the First Amendment. In the five-to-four *Miller v.
California* opinion the Court rejected the idea of the Warren Court's
national standard for defining obscenity, as well as its test for obscenity:
"utterly without redeeming social value." Instead, it gave power to the states
to determine what constitutes obscene material under local, rather than
national, community standards. A specifically defined state offense, wrote
the Court, would be "limited to works which taken as a whole, appeal to the
prurient interest in sex, which portray sexual conduct in a patently offensive

way, and which, taken as a whole, do not have serious literary, artistic, or political value."[49]

In *Paris Adult Theater I v. Slaton* the Court upheld (again five to four) the rights of states to regulate exhibition of obscene material to consenting adults, even those theaters with restrictive admission policies for minors. It also ruled that constitutional doctrines of privacy in the home did not protect obscene matter in public places like adult theaters. These reinterpretations of obscenity law in relation to the First Amendment elaborated on the standards given back to the states in *Miller v. California,* leaving content regulation open to prosecutors in individual communities.

Local and state authorities quickly took advantage of these rulings, seeing them as an opportunity to legally attack serious, artistic pictures given *Miller's* vague guidelines of what constituted obscenity. Most notorious was a ruling by the Georgia Supreme Court declaring the R-rated *Carnal Knowledge* (1973) to be obscene, even though it only contained brief nudity, some salty language, and no hard-core—real or simulated—sexual conduct. The U.S. Supreme Court, however, in a unanimous decision in *Jenkins v. Georgia* in June 1974, argued that the film "did not depict sexual conduct in a patently offensive way" and made it clear that under the *Miller* standards obscene material had to be "hard-core" sexual conduct.[50] Despite this clarification, local district attorneys were already and would continue to be quite successful in winning legal injunctions against screenings of *Deep Throat* in various cities, such as Atlanta, Baltimore, and Memphis.[51] Injunctions such as these effectively sealed the fate for hard-core film exhibition and the X rating in all but a few selected urban markets.

Thanks to the U.S. Supreme Court, the MPAA had almost exclusive control over the legitimate theatrical marketplace. Previously uncooperative NATO exhibitors, now completely vulnerable to this new obscenity standard, had no choice but to acquiesce completely to the rating system, whose MPAA-member distributors by this time had given up on the X rating. For both the MPAA and NATO the R rating would prove to be an incontestable bulwark in the absence of the X, serving as a seal of approval for responsible entertainment in the classification era. The birth of the Incontestable R, in effect, was the death of the Hollywood X.

Despite the *Carnal Knowledge* victory, proponents of free expression—especially critics and filmmakers—were not happy with the results of the *Miller* ruling or the MPAA's response to it. A *New York Times* story in December 1973 echoed many disparagements directed at the MPAA during this time. Stephen Farber (who at that time regularly wrote articles about the rating system) and Estelle Changas (who interned with him at CARA) criticized the

MPAA for its reluctance to openly challenge *Miller*'s supposed infringement of the First Amendment, its readiness to avoid adult material, and its willingness to trim films down from an X to an R rating. They described a series of projects that either had been cancelled or altered in light of the Court's decision. For example, a major distributor backed out of financing Arthur Hiller's film of Hubert Selby Jr.'s violent street novel *Last Exit to Brooklyn* (later made in 1989) because of its financial risk factor. Additionally, Universal vice president Ned Tanen, Columbia producer Larry Gordon, and director Robert Altman all had rejected or considered rejecting scripts containing potentially controversial elements. "I was just reading a script that has a sexual scene with a young man and a prostitute—a comic scene," Altman recounts. "And without even wanting to, I found myself thinking, 'This is going to be a problem. How am I going to do it? Is it really necessary, and should it be done in a very explicit, funny way? But if I do it that way, I don't know if it can be shown.'" For *Alice Doesn't Live Here Anymore* (1974) Martin Scorsese received a five-page memo from Warner Bros. detailing strategies for rewriting dialogue and for protection shots in case of objection by CARA, local communities, or television stations. One admonition read: "Love scenes must show 'taste' and not show lovers." Such aesthetic and economic concessions to obscenity regulation, stated Farber and Changas, were "incompatible" with artistic freedom and according to Altman "actually spawned the acceptance of censorship" by the Hollywood community.[52]

Valenti's series of editorials and articles after the *Miller* decision clearly demonstrate the MPAA's position regarding accusations of censorship in the rating era. Valenti would articulate a realistic stance condemning governmental infringement on the First Amendment, except in cases of hard-core pornography, while categorically denying that classification was a form of censorship. In a same-day response to the Farber and Changas piece Valenti lamented the Court's decision on obscenity law ("We may curse it, defy, theorize it, but there it is. It won't go away."), but he called for action to assure that "serious, entertaining works of drama and comedy are not hauled into court" under an overly broad obscenity statute. He also assertively pronounced that the "MPAA rating board is not a censor," that "[it] does not command (nor could it if it tried) any filmmaker to edit one millimeter of film." Any decision to take a lesser rating to reach a larger audience, he believed, lies with the individual filmmaker, not with CARA, whose "sole objective is to give information to parents about the content of films so that parents can make decisions about their children's moviegoing." To Valenti industry self-regulation enabled creative expression, whereas the alternative—governmental classification—would quash it.[53]

If critics like Farber and Changas overestimate the power that CARA wielded in regulating X-rated MPAA films almost out of existence in 1973, Valenti underemphasized the role that he, the MPAA, and CARA play in shaping the Incontestable R practice. In the eyes of Valenti, and there is no reason to doubt this, the X rating was a legitimate category. "[It] does not mean 'obscene' or 'dirty,'" he frequently said. "X simply means unsuitable for viewing by children."[54] Valenti, though, never publicly condemned the industry's avoidance of the X rating or endorsed its practice of the Incontestable R. The fact remains that he, as the president of the MPAA and overseer of CARA, was paid by the major film distributors to protect their economic and political interests. If responsible entertainment is the standard by which this is safeguarded, and if it is not inclusive of the X rating, so be it.

The MPAA was never a trade organization to defend artists' rights or to ensure competitive markets anyway. The MPAA staved off classification for many years with an ineffective Production Code despite the awarding of First Amendment protection to motion pictures in the *Miracle* case. In addition, the MPAA also reintegrated distribution and exhibition through a collusive arrangement with NATO in the rating system twenty years after the *Paramount* decree. The abandonment of the X rating preserves this arrangement with CARA, its trusty knave of responsible entertainment. When Ralph Bakshi, director of the animated X-rated (though independently released) *Fritz the Cat* (1972) and *Human Traffic* (1973), claims he doesn't "know of a single director who hasn't been told not to make an X film," he expresses the view that it is not necessarily the muscle of CARA that dictates the rules but rather the might of the MPAA signatories.

With the MPAA's and NATO's virtual abandonment of the X by 1973, it became the primary responsibility of CARA's Rating Board to guarantee that all R-rated products—be they MPAA or independently distributed films— were free of X-rated residue before getting released in theaters. Some of the criticisms aimed at CARA during this time, however, were due to its inconsistent and unreliable policies for the X rating, as well as its other categories. Much blame has been assigned to chairperson Aaron Stern, a former rating consultant and psychiatrist on the faculty of Columbia University's College of Physicians and Surgeons, who replaced Eugene Dougherty as head of CARA in July 1970. In *Freedom and Entertainment* Stephen Vaughn characterized Stern as "too judgmental, intolerant of dissent, and eager to please the Catholic Church." Farber and Changas found him to be a "psychological crusader" against the "youth culture" of the time, handing out harsher ratings to movies if they contained "immaturity," "rebelliousness," or "liberal attitudes toward sex." Stern also seemed mesmerized by his power as chair, helping to edit films after their submission to CARA and frequently talking to the press about the rating system. It was this last point that particularly incensed Valenti, who wanted CARA to have only one voice: his own.[55]

Stern's interest in the educative potential of the cinematic form, however, did not translate into a similar protection of the economic and political interests of the MPAA, the rationale for CARA's existence in the first place. His public assaults against the X rating—against responsible entertainment— during his time in office must have been a major reason for his dismissal by Valenti at the end of 1973. In 1972, Stern told the *Los Angeles Herald Examiner* that "My strategy is to design a rating system in such a way that the only way you can have a more intrusive system is by defeating not only the constitutionality of the United States but the spirit of the government. If the rating system were called upon to defend itself as a noncensoring action, it could not defend itself. The fact that we keep somebody out of the theater is literally not defendable. I'm absolutely opposed to the X rating."[56] Unlike the U.S. Supreme Court, Stern believed children should not be denied access to films intended for adults, and unlike the MPAA signatories, Stern deplored the bargaining of shots or line of dialogue between producers and the Rating Board to get a particular rating. Given such comments, it is not surprising that Valenti later admitted he made a mistake in putting a behavioral psychiatrist in charge of CARA. "There were a lot of things we didn't agree on," Valenti said. "Nothing personal. It was his views on movies in general, demeanor, the ratings system, how he viewed certain things, the stance he was taking in the press, which was not consonant with the motives of the ratings system."[57]

To restore harmony in the rating system, Valenti replaced Stern with Rutgers University communication professor Richard Heffner in July 1974, who remained the chair of CARA until the end of June 1994. Heffner's personal disposition and approach to rating films could not be more different from his predecessor's. Under his administration ratings were assigned to films by a majority vote of the Rating Board, who based their decisions not on moral or psychological precepts but on contemporary parental attitudes toward film content. And unlike the PCA or CARA before it, Heffner's Rating Board did not assist in the editing of the films themselves; that task fell on the shoulders of filmmakers and distributors. It would appear that Valenti had found in Heffner a loyal and obedient chairperson, especially since the two lasted twenty years together. Their relationship, however, was often marked by disagreement and animosity, particularly involving the appeals process. The history of the Incontestable R through 1994 can be viewed, I believe, as a history of Rating Board decisions and Appeals Board reversals, of parental surrogacy and studio favoritism, of Heffner and Valenti. When the X was at stake, these contentions sometimes damaged, but never fully toppled, the bastion of responsible entertainment.

THE CASE OF *CRUISING*

When Heffner became chair of CARA in 1974, the era of the Incontestable R had officially begun. *Variety* announced in its November year-end report that "traditional film suppliers now avoid the X rating like the plague."[58] To be sure, none of the major Hollywood distributors released any X films in 1974. The rating was only self-imposed by pornographers or self-applied by independent distributors. Instead, all films from MPAA-member companies were geared to an R rating or less. This guaranteed all Hollywood products were once again permissible for an all-ages audience, stabilizing the rating system, which encountered little or no controversy until 1980 with *Cruising*.

Signaling a shift away from the X rating were certain industrial, cultural, and social changes that occurred in the mid-1970s. During this period of the "New Hollywood," wrote Thomas Schatz, the art cinema movement that dealt with politically subversive, sexually graphic, or explicitly violent material—such as the auteur-driven, X-rated works *The Devils, A Clockwork Orange,* and *Last Tango in Paris*—ceased to be an economic force. Demographically, viewers were becoming younger and lacked the cinema literacy these adult films presupposed. The surge of mall-based theaters led to widespread policies prohibiting X-rated pictures. And the sudden success of *Jaws* (1975) "recalibrated the profit potential of the Hollywood hit," ushering in an era of PG-rated high-concept blockbusters like *Star Wars* (1977) and *Superman* (1978).[59]

After Columbia's *Emmanuelle* in 1974 and United Artists' *Inserts* in 1976, the MPAA signatories released only two X-rated films until 1990's *Henry & June:* United Artists Classics' *Arabian Nights* (1975) and *The Canterbury Tales* (1972), both directed by Pier Paolo Pasolini and both released in the United States in 1979.[60] During these intervening years CARA actively arranged all MPAA-member films into the R category; however, it did not necessarily arrange all these films into Incontestable Rs. These notorious cases could be described as "limit texts," Lea Jacobs's term for those films approved and released by the PCA that were subsequently condemned by external groups like state censors or the Catholic Legion of Decency.[61] In the age of CARA these limit texts were R films "that felt like" X/NC-17 films (or PG-13 films "that felt like" R films, and so on) and were subsequently met with harsh reproach by filmmakers, distributors, and exhibitors, as well as special interest groups, moral reformers, and politicians.

To be sure, lapses in content regulation can be attributed in part to the Rating Board, the board chaired by Heffner (and others) and assigned to rate all motion pictures submitted to CARA. Since the process of categorizing films is inherently subjective and can never fully account for audience response, the Rating Board could and sometimes did misrate a film. Controversies over a film's rating were oftentimes manufactured, though, by angry filmmakers and distributors for marketing purposes when no such controversy might have existed in the first place. These occurrences, not surprisingly, were especially pronounced around the R/X or R/NC-17 boundary. On most occasions negotiations were private and congenial between the Rating Board and filmmakers—most of whom were contractually obligated to deliver an R—and distributors—many of whom were unwilling to release an X/NC-17 or unrated picture. Eventually, an R-rated cut emerged after one or more resubmissions of the film to the Rating Board or a successful appeal to the Appeals Board of CARA. The more public and confrontational cases followed the same pathway but not before becoming limit texts to some degree and damaging the integrity of the Rating Board.

Limit texts involving the X/NC-17 rating lay bare the collusive and collective framework of responsible entertainment, one that requires industry-wide allegiance to the Incontestable R. The Rating Board is just one component, albeit the most conspicuous, of a larger system of self-regulation that primarily benefits the economic and political interests of the MPAA signatories. This marketplace practice is monopolistic rather than competitive, coercive rather than democratic, private rather than public. Yet Heffner's records and personal recollections, articulated both to me and to Stephen Vaughn, reveal an administration in constant tension with MPAA company executives and MPAA president Jack Valenti. Heffner's commitment to reason, fairness, and a marketplace of ideas often collided with the immediate economic interests of the MPAA. Instead of lining the purses of corporations, he believed the Rating Board's function was "to reflect parental attitudes just enough that the public wouldn't get angry enough with the content of films" to demand state or federal censorship. Heffner also made changes to CARA over time—but not without struggle—so the rating system served the public in a more open and honest manner. Some of these changes included reconstituting the Rating Board with non-industry-affiliated parents rather than industry personnel, periodically replacing Rating Board examiners in order to better reflect changing public attitudes, and providing detailed rating descriptions for films. Heffner also repeatedly refused to alter a rating for an MPAA-member film upon Valenti's request and refused to sign any documents prohibiting him from writing about his experiences at CARA. His philosophy of self-regulation unceasingly irritated Valenti, who Heffner believed "felt his power came not from dialogue with the public but from telling the public something, conning it, not from trying to inform it."[62]

The Rating Board, in fact, could be considered the least self-serving mechanism of industry self-regulation during the CARA regime under Heffner. In cases of the most publicized, rancorous, limit texts the fault lay not with the Rating Board but with the industry itself for one of two reasons. First, the MPAA signatories, who now acted mainly as financiers and distributors for individual production houses, deliberately bankrolled or picked up a controversial film whose theme or tone, regardless of cutting, still crossed the line of the Incontestable R. Since the majors will not release a picture without a rating (per their agreement with the MPAA) or release an X picture (because of the rating's stigma), the Rating Board (which ultimately serves the interests of the MPAA) must eventually accept a submitted cut of the film, awarding it an unjustified R rating. Second, the Appeals Board (headed by Valenti and comprising industry executives, mainly from the MPAA and NATO) overturns an X granted to a film by the Rating Board (comprising the chairperson and examiners, mostly parents unaffiliated with the industry) by a two-thirds-majority vote. These reversals often pertain to films distributed by the MPAA signatories themselves, who, as members of the Appeals Board, apply economic criteria to the contested film ("How much money is at stake?") instead of the Rating Board's parental criteria ("Do most parents feel this would be an X?"). Both of these instances represent failures of self-regulation, giving credence to the perennial charges that the industry's system of boundary maintenance can be hypocritical, arbitrary, and discriminatory.

The Rating Board's impotence in the face of overwhelming MPAA self-interest is best illustrated with United Artists' *Cruising* (1980), William Friedkin's R-rated adaptation of Gerald Walker's 1970 novel about a cop trying to catch a killer in New York's gay community. The film's violation of the standards of responsible entertainment represented a rare synergistic breakdown of the industry as both the MPAA and NATO undermined the validity of the Incontestable R. Because of its combination of two elements often problematic in terms of responsible entertainment—tabooed sexual practices and graphic violence—*Cruising* was still considered to be an X-rated picture by critics, gay rights groups, and exhibitors. *Los Angeles Times* film reporter Dale Pollock called *Cruising* a "deep crack" in the rating system, and film critic Jack Garner believed it was "easily the most graphic and vivid sex-and-violence film ever to escape an X rating."[63] The harshest words came from James Harwood of *Variety*: "If this is an R, then the only X left is hardcore. . . . To put it bluntly, if an R allows the showing of one man greasing

Figure 5. "If this is an R, then the only X left is hardcore": Al Pacino in *Cruising* (1980). Courtesy of the Academy of Motion Picture Arts and Sciences.

his fist followed by the rising ecstasy of a second man held in chains by others, then there's only one close-up left for the X."[64] The only two people who thought otherwise, said Heffner, were Charles Champlin and, of course, Valenti.[65]

For United Artists *Cruising* certainly contained market exploitation value. It starred Al Pacino in a mystery tale probing the S&M underworld of gay sexuality, a subculture rarely explored in such realistic, detailed fashion in a Hollywood film. The film's negative and insulting stereotyping of homosexuality, however, galvanized a nationwide protest by the gay community (spearheaded by the National Gay Task Force, an organization that achieved increased visibility and power throughout the 1970s).[66] Cofounder Martin Bell got a copy of an early draft of the screenplay and, after reading it, wrote a scathing column in the *Village Voice* on the notion of Hollywood profiting from portrayals of homosexual psychopaths:

> [William Friedkin's] film promises to be the most oppressive, ugly, bigoted look at homosexuality ever presented on the screen, the worst possible nightmare of the most uptight straight and a validation of Anita Bryant's

hate campaign. It will negate years of positive movement work and may well send gays running back into the closet and precipitate heavy violence against homosexuals. I implore readers—gay, straight, liberal, radical, atheist, communist, or whatever—to give Friedkin and his production crew a terrible time if you spot them in your neighborhood. . . . Owners of gay establishments would do well to tell Friedkin to fuck off when he comes around to film and exploit.[67]

During production, activists denounced the film, disrupted the location shooting, and made a failed attempt to persuade Mayor Ed Koch to withdraw the film's production permit.[68] Despite the rallies, marches, and press conferences, Friedkin finished *Cruising* without altering the script. The end product, historian Vito Russo notes in *The Celluloid Closet,* leaves audiences "with the message that homosexuality is not only contagious but inescapably brutal."[69]

NATO exhibitors also directed outrage at *Cruising* after seeing a cut of the film prior to its national release on February 15, 1980. The unprecedented extent of exhibitor dissatisfaction over *Cruising*'s R rating was like none other during the classification era: theater owners broke from CARA's designation and asserted their own opinion on the film's rating and qualification for exhibition. General Cinema Corporation (GCC)—the largest chain in the United States at the time—cancelled the film's thirty-three engagements two weeks before the film's opening. The chain issued a statement explaining its decision: "General Cinema Corporation policy is to refuse to play X rated pictures or pictures which in our judgment should be X rated."[70] GCC's defiance of CARA authority, aided by United Artists' disregard of responsible entertainment standards, threatened to undermine the entire rating system, according to Stephen Prince:

> GCC's actions threatened the validity of the whole ratings enterprise, which, lacking the force of law, depended on mutual cooperation and observance of the codes by all sectors of the movie industry. If MPAA ratings could be so questioned, then the agency's protective authority would be weakened. The organization operated as a buffer, shielding the majors from outside efforts to regulate its products and lobbying Washington to promote issues and bills favorable to business. If the ratings system were undermined or its authority impeded, as it had been by the GCC decision, the industry could be more vulnerable to charges from outside groups that its films were unwholesome, unhealthy, or otherwise deserving of censure.[71]

The relative "wholesomeness" and "healthiness" expected out of Hollywood by GCC executives was tellingly characterized by executive vice president Mel

Whitman, who offered this additional explanation for *Cruising* after the company stood by its cancellation of the picture even after a second viewing: "An R rating permits an adult to bring an 8-year-old child to *Cruising*. The theme, the extreme violence, and the abnormal sexual aspects make the movie unsuitable for children."[72]

Whitman's words, together with the corporation's public statement, support the argument of the Incontestable R's being an unrestricted "adult" category. General Cinema's assumptions that an R film can be clearly distinguished from an X film, and that an R film should be suitable for children, personifies the unspoken industry policy of responsible entertainment in the classification era: anyone—regardless of age—-should feel "comfortable" watching an R picture.

To some extent, GCC's boycott of *Cruising* resulted from fears of community backlash and the possibility of violence at theaters showing the film. Yet the chain's concerns were also fiscal in nature, as it, like other exhibitors, put up nonrefundable guarantees of as much as $65,000 on a blind-bid basis (booking the film in advance before seeing it, a practice the U.S. Supreme Court had ordered to cease but had not made illegal in the 1948 *Paramount* decree).[73] United Artists Theaters (no relation to United Artists, the distribution company), who also blind-bid the film, did not cancel its bookings like GCC had but took it upon itself to prevent unescorted *and* escorted children from attending *Cruising*.[74] It posted signs at its theaters advising patrons, "In the opinion of management this picture should be rated X. No one under 18 will be admitted."[75] Another exhibitor, Mid-America Cinema, personally asked United Artists to release it from its *Cruising* contract, but the distributor refused. In place of a *Cruising* poster in three of its theaters' lobbies, Mid-America displayed the following letter, dissociating itself from United Artists:

> *Cruising* is a picture we sincerely wish we did not have to show. Had we been afforded an opportunity to preview this picture ahead of purchase, you would not see it on our screen today. However, because of a system called "blind bidding" wherein future movies are offered for bid months before we can view them, our hands are tied. We are now obligated to play *Cruising*. Our request to be released from this contract was denied. It's play or face possible lawsuit. The management of Mid-America Cinema offers its apology to patrons and suggests all comments be addressed to: United Artists, 729 7th Ave., New York, N.Y. 10019.[76]

Audiences, while initially intrigued by the controversy, eventually lost interest in *Cruising*, an $8-million film costing at least $5 million to promote. The combined total of its third and fourth weeks was less than the $5 million the film earned in its first five days, putting its total amount in film rentals from the United States and Canada at an unimpressive number between $12 million and $15 million.[77]

Although viewers rapidly lost interest in *Cruising,* theater owners had already abandoned faith in the movie as a work of responsible entertainment. Blind-bidding practices presuppose the delivery of an Incontestable R from CARA. Yet, United Artists had to justify its R rating, attaching to the beginning of *Cruising* its own statement: "This film is not intended as an indictment of the homosexual world. It is set in one small segment of that world, which is not meant to be representative of the whole." This disclaimer, when viewed alongside exhibitors' disavowal of the film, was more or less an apology for *Cruising*'s R rating masquerading as mass entertainment—an apology being something Hollywood should never have to do for its products.

The eventual awarding of an R to *Cruising* "was the worst thing that ever happened to the rating system," said Heffner, but the Rating Board had little choice. United Artists is an MPAA member, CARA is a division of the MPAA, and Jerry Weintraub, the producer of *Cruising,* insisted to Valenti that the film *had* to have an R. Heffner and the Rating Board, however, did not relent easily, despite Valenti's support for the film and his pleas to let Weintraub have his way. For it was not a single shot or scene that should have earned the film an X but what Heffner described as the "intensity of the whole sado-masochistic thrust of the film"; it was not the theme of homosexuality but the "treatment" of it. In most cases the cuts necessitated for an R entail the excision of shots of soft-core or hard-core sex, the elimination of frames to reduce the impact of a violent act, or the blurring of an image to obscure an offending moment. What happens though, when the problematic footage extends beyond the individual shot or scene to subsume the entire work, like with *Cruising?* It then becomes quite challenging, if not impossible, to "edit the X out" without destroying the film. Heffner has said, "We were never *not* going to give a film an R if the editing enabled us to do so *responsibly.*"[78] To be sure, reshaping a film's mood, spirit, or attitude—the "treatment" of its themes to use Heffner's words, more commonly referred to as "tone"—is difficult. *Cruising*'s lurid subject matter, eroticized violence, and overall unpleasantness—in other words, its *tone*—still proved to be insurmountable for the Rating Board to sufficiently arrange into a responsible product for general distribution.

In an embellished though revealing account in 1998, director William Friedkin reported that Heffner found *Cruising* unreleasable in any form ever since the CARA chairperson viewed an early cut of the film in Weintraub's house. Friedkin describes Heffner's reaction with flourish: "This is the worst movie ever made!!" "How could you do this!! How could you make this film!" "There's not enough Xs in the alphabet! I would have to go and find Xs from some other alphabet. This is a 59,000 X rating is what the rating is!"[79] Heffner denies such an unhinged response and describes his visit—it being a favor to Valenti and certainly not CARA policy—as one in which he clearly identified to Weintraub and Friedkin the problematic moments and scenes involving sexuality and violence that earned an X from the Rating Board. After refusing to edit the film with Friedkin as Aaron Stern did with the director's previous films, Heffner suggested they secure Stern's services to help gain an R rating.[80] This unusual and perhaps unprecedented move points to the delicacy of the predicament that CARA found itself in with *Cruising:* a major Hollywood production so "adult" and "irresponsible" in tone that any ordinary degree of cutting would fail to render the movie acceptable for an Incontestable R.

A day after *Cruising's* release in February, Heffner performed damage control on the film. His comments to the *New York Times* are noteworthy, not only for their acknowledgment of the Rating Board's problem with the tone of the film but also for Heffner's defense of the integrity of the film's R rating, a designation most everyone perceived to be wrong:

> No picture has given us so much anguish as *Cruising.* Because the theme is so incredibly unpleasant we knew that people would want us to punish the film. People are angry. They want to be saved from this film. But it's not the job of the ratings system to punish movies for moral or esthetic reasons.
>
> There was only one thing we could have done that was worse than giving the film an R rating. That was to give it an X to save our own necks. It would have been easier to give the movie an X. We'd have been heroes. Homosexuals would love us. But we wouldn't have been correct. The question we had to answer in order to give it an X was whether every parent of a 17-year-old in New York City had to be prohibited from bringing his child to the movie. We didn't think so.[81]

Heffner's staunch denials of any weakening in the standards of the Incontestable R camouflaged wrongdoings that would not be publicly revealed until May 1980: Friedkin and Weintraub had not made the agreed-upon, R-rated cuts for the version of *Cruising* currently in theatrical distribution. The Rating Board had not seen the final print before its release but provided a good-faith certification in early January to the filmmakers in exchange for their word that the editing would be completed according to specifications laid out between *Cruising* editor Bud Smith and Heffner.[82] After several months of battle to revoke the film's original R rating, CARA got the "unrated" *Cruising* withdrawn from theaters after the completion of its initial run and rereleased in a reedited R version in June, a seeming acknowledgment, said Stephen Prince, "that the first version of *Cruising* was what its detractors had claimed all along, an X-rated picture."[83] Valenti, to whom all specific inquiries about the film were now referred as a result of the embattlement with United Artists, denied this was the case. He made the specious argument, as he often did, that the system was not perfect. "You can't see every version [of a film]. Now in 12 years of the rating system if we only have two or three pictures that blatantly lie, that's a very good record. . . . You are dealing with a flawed system."[84]

The relative absence since 1973 of such flaws with the X rating can be explained not only by the existence of trust and cooperation among producers, the MPAA, NATO, and CARA but also by the formal consistency of the Rating Board's standards for the Incontestable R. Precisely identifying the Rating Board's codes of operation at given historical junctures would not be possible to assess until the simultaneous release of uncut and R-rated versions of the same film in the 1990s. In the case of *Cruising,* however, evidence strongly suggests that Heffner and his staff carefully, if not dutifully, followed the same regulatory protocols for sex and violence as other R-rated films of its time. Heffner often remarked that the Rating Board made every respectful effort to accommodate its *procedural modes* to assure filmmakers that they received a fair rating for their films. But in doing so, he says, the Rating Board never deviated from adhering to the *content* and *principles* of its ratings. The standards for an R rating with *Cruising* were no different.[85]

Various firsthand accounts from other parties involved in the editing of *Cruising* testify to the Rating Board's meticulousness in detail for the film's Incontestable R. In its final R-rated form the film was nowhere near as graphic as the first cut—which, according to editor Bud Smith, contained a golden shower scene, blow jobs, and fist-fucking. Four sequences were also heavily edited: two gay bar scenes and the killings in the apartment and the peep show. The hard-core images were excised, darkened, and/or obscured using a traveling matte. To tone down the violence, the filmmakers eliminated repeated stabbing motions, squirting blood, and a knife being pulled out of a victim's body. Audio edits included sound effects of murder and a whip across someone's back. In total, the film was resubmitted five or six times to the Rating Board with nearly three minutes excised from its original version.[86]

What delayed the Rating Board's certification (besides Friedkin and Weintraub) were *Cruising*'s intangibles—its sordid tone, its nasty spirit, its unpleasantness "not necessarily because of its subject matter," wrote Vincent Canby in his *New York Times* review, "but because [the film] makes no attempt to comprehend [the subject matter]." The Heffner Rating Board, however, does not function like the PCA; it does not "comprehend" a film's subject matter based on morality or media effects when determining a film's rating. Responsible entertainment in the classification era primarily involves shots and images, content that can be added or deleted across rating categories. Since CARA only regulates film after completion, it can only handle extreme cases of sex and violence, of their treatment *onscreen*. As Heffner remarked about *Cruising,* "We can't give the movie an X rating because the audience thinks it sees something that isn't there."[87]

Valenti defended CARA on similar grounds with Friedkin's earlier film *The Exorcist* when the Rating Board passed it uncut with an R in 1973:

> Consider what is in *The Exorcist* and what is not, because the Rating Board can rate only what is on the screen. Ratings come from what viewers see, not what they imagine they see. In *The Exorcist,* there is no overt sex. There is no excessive violence. There is some strong language, but it is rationally related to the film's theme and is kept to a minimum. . . . Much of what might concern some people is not on the screen: it is in the mind and imagination of the viewer. A film cannot be punished for what people think because all people do not think alike.[88]

Equally sensationalist and lurid for its time, *The Exorcist*'s combination of perverse sexuality, blood and violence, and demonic possession generated the opposite response to *Cruising*'s: critics' ten-best lists, ten Academy Award nominations (winning two for Adapted Screenplay and Sound), and $89.3 million in film rentals, making it one of the most successful films of the decade. Perhaps the film's acclaim, best-selling novel pedigree, Roman Catholic religiosity (Jesuit priests were consultants), and failed efforts to ban the film made *The Exorcist* appear more legitimate, moral, and incontestable than *Cruising*.[89] Or maybe it was a better or more entertaining film for consumers.

The *Cruising* situation demonstrates that the treatment of themes, not the themes themselves alone, generate limit texts in the classification era. Would the film have been just as controversial had United Artists released the R-rated version certified by the Rating Board? Probably not. Nevertheless, *Cruising* violated the tenets of the Incontestable R in every branch of the industry: debasement in production, deceitfulness in distribution, and disloyalty in exhibition. No other films would reverberate across the contingencies of responsible entertainment like this ever again. It only takes one facet of the film business to jeopardize the Incontestable R, however, especially if you have an outspoken, bankable, director of sex and violence. Enter Brian De Palma.

DE PALMA VERSUS THE RATING BOARD

Media people always ask how I can make movies like this [Scarface]. *This is what's in my brain. I don't have to justify it to anyone. Studio heads are only interested if a movie makes money. And out of 15 movies I've made, I've justified my existence to them on at least ten of them.*

—Brian De Palma, *Playboy* (1985)

Allegiance to the rating system requires cooperation not only from the MPAA and NATO but also from filmmakers working within this industrial framework. Despite the outrage felt by film critics, reform groups, and exhibitors over the R rating given to *Cruising* and the disagreement over the cut approved by CARA for general release, William Friedkin himself never once during this controversy publicly criticized the Rating Board or its policies in the press. Sure, his film probably exceeded the boundaries of the Incontestable R, and yes, he and Weintraub released an X-rated cut as an R-rated film. Still, they privately worked with the Rating Board to arrange a version they believed might be suitable for the R rating (which did not happen). The alternative option was to take the film to the Appeals Board, the internal course of review at CARA where filmmakers who were dissatisfied with their rating from the Rating Board could challenge the classification. By 1980 the Appeals Board was hearing appeals seven or eight times a year and had a reversal rate of a little more than 15 percent. Friedkin and Weintraub chose not to use this option, preferring to keep everything in-house in fear that an appeal would draw negative publicity to *Cruising* because of the stigmatization of the X.[90]

And then there are those like Brian De Palma, who, in the words of Heffner, liked "having his rating cake and eat[ing] it, too."[91] In the first half of the 1980s he repeatedly fought the Rating Board in the press to maximize the publicity for *Dressed to Kill* (1980), *Scarface* (1983), and *Body Double* (1984), despite being contractually obligated to deliver an R rating on all three films. De Palma criticized the Rating Board for tentatively giving an X to each film, with *Scarface* the only one officially adopting the rating in order to appeal it. To be sure, De Palma certainly pushed the boundary limits of responsible entertainment; his use of graphic violence in *Scarface* combined with erotic sexuality in *Dressed to Kill* and *Body Double* forced audiences, in the words of Laurence F. Knapp, "to confront situations and impulses that tested the ideological boundaries of good taste."[92] De Palma's public disparagements of CARA, however, fueled by mass advertising campaigns from the MPAA and independent distributors of his films, turned what may have been ordinary, or ordinarily received, products into limit texts. Protests only magnified the

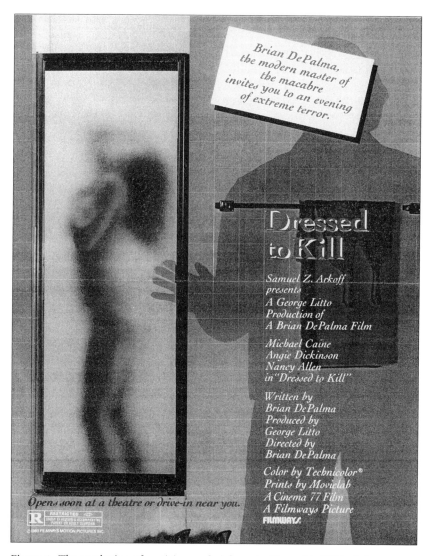

Figure 6. The marketing of eroticism and violence in *Dressed to Kill* (1980).

controversies over these films as De Palma manifested the industry's opportunistic nature, as well as its potential self-destructiveness.

The notoriety of *Dressed to Kill* can be attributed in large part to the marketing strategies of its MPAA-member distributor, Filmways Pictures, a television and film production company that had merged with American
International Pictures (AIP) in 1979 and went out of business in 1982. According to Jon Lewis, AIP chairperson Samuel Z. Arkoff developed and coordi-

Figure 7. The marketing of eroticism and violence in *Dressed to Kill* (1980).

nated the promotion of the film using exploitation methods proven successful to work for such films as *The Trip* (1967) and *3 in the Attic*. The lurid
advertising campaign for *Dressed to Kill* cost almost as much as the film ($6
million compared to $6.5 million) and highlighted De Palma's unique autho-
rial style ("the modern master of the macabre invites you to an evening of
extreme terror") while also foreshadowing the film's erotic and violent nature
(a woman peeling off her stocking as a man lurks in the distance).[93]

To further market *Dressed to Kill,* Arkoff likely contacted the *New York Times* to request that the paper publish an article about the film. The paper obliged with an article by Peter Wood titled "'Dressed to Kill'—How a Film Changes from 'X' to 'R.'" Printed only a few days before the film's national release on July 25, 1980, the piece is significant not only for being the first of many smear campaigns orchestrated by De Palma against the Rating Board but also for the inaccuracies reported about the rating system by the press itself. In the article De Palma accuses the Rating Board of censorship and of using more repressive standards in the wake of the *Cruising* uproar six months earlier. "Why should I suffer," he says, "for something Billy Friedkin did not do?"[94] Because the film was "too strong," De Palma claims he had to make certain strategic cuts and dialogue dubs—involving razor slashes, pubic hair, and harsh language—to finally earn *Dressed to Kill* an R rating on its third submission.[95] Supporting these accusations were Wood's misconceived notions about the rating system. For instance, Wood incorrectly states that ratings are "based entirely on what [the Rating Board's] seven members believe the American public finds acceptable at that particular moment in history" and that the X rating is simply designated for "hard-core pornography and extreme violence."

Such faulty perceptions of CARA were no doubt fueled by the private nature of its operations and the constant battle between Valenti and Heffner over talking to the press. Valenti, who insisted that his name be the only one associated with the rating system, often spread misinformation about its operations (which he knew little about) and perpetuated a more conservative outlook on artist rights (his motto again: "freedom of expression does not mean toleration of license"). In the Wood article, for instance, he chides creative people for "still living in the world of revolution" and blames television for making "filmmakers feel they have to go one better." Heffner, on the other hand, always supported a more open policy with the public and encouraged the adoption of the X by filmmakers. Much to Valenti's chagrin, he believed CARA should always correct errors in the public record, and in the case of the *Dressed to Kill* piece in the *New York Times,* he wrote a letter to the editor to uphold the integrity of the rating system. He corrects some of Wood's (never Valenti's) misinformation, stating that the Rating Board's "singular responsibility" is to help parents decide the moviegoing patterns of their children and not to tell filmmakers how to edit their films.[96]

The *New York Times* published Heffner's response nearly one month after De Palma's attack on the rating system and the premiere of *Dressed to Kill.* During that time the film received critical praise and did respectable box office, delivering on its advertised promise: graphic violence against its female

Figure 8. Brian De Palma directing Angie Dickinson and Michael Caine in the elevator murder scene of *Dressed to Kill* (1980). Courtesy of the Academy of Motion Picture Arts and Sciences.

characters (either through rape, murder, or attempted murder) after moments of sexual pleasure. Much has been written about the demonstrations accompanying *Dressed to Kill* in the wake of this fanfare by antipornography feminist groups protesting the film's misogynistic treatment of women and its eroticization of violence.[97] Although these rallies were not directly aimed at CARA, they did intensify the debate over the nature of responsible entertainment and Hollywood's perpetuation of violence against women in recent slasher films like *Friday the 13th* (1980). Unlike Friedkin, De Palma did much to inflame this environment, hiding behind the First Amendment and ridiculing those groups who failed to see the satire in his films. He told *Newsday*'s Judy Stone, "I think you should be able to make a film about anything. Should we get into censorship because we have movies that are going to upset some part of the community?" The fact that these protests enhanced the box-office appeal of *Dressed to Kill*, much to the lament of feminist groups, encouraged De Palma and his distributors to use such tactics for his next two films, *Scarface* and *Body Double*.[98]

Unlike the medium-budgeted *Dressed to Kill*, *Scarface* was Universal's Christmas picture in 1983, costing upward of $25 million, running almost three hours, and opening in wide release in almost one thousand theaters.

Universal and NATO exhibitors, who had already booked the film for the holiday season, expected *Scarface* to earn a lot of money. An X rating was certainly out of the question, especially since De Palma was contractually obligated to deliver an R rating to Universal. This time De Palma and his distributor chose to appeal the X rather than continuing to cut *Scarface* to meet the R-rated criteria of the Rating Board. The subsequent, decisive overturning of the X by the Appeals Board reveals one of the least-known aspects of self-regulation in the classification era and potentially the most destructive: the capacity of the Appeals Board to undermine the policies of the Rating Board and, in turn, responsible entertainment.

Almost eighteen months before its opening on December 9, 1983, *Scarface* had already acquired some notoriety among the Cuban community in Miami for its potential negative portrayals of Latinos. To avoid demonstrations and production stoppages, producer Martin Bregman relocated filming to Los Angeles, returning to Miami only to shoot exteriors.[99] Controversy over stereotypes, however, eventually got overshadowed by negotiations for an R rating between Universal and the Rating Board, a situation that the distributor leaked to the press in late October 1983. A very public ratings dispute ensued with every party involved in the battle—De Palma, Bregman, Valenti, Heffner, and Universal president Robert Rehme—either condemning or validating the industry's system of self-regulation.

At issue, once again, was an X rating for an MPAA-member film. On *Cruising* Weintraub threatened Heffner in an attempt to get an R rating for the picture and then subsequently embarrassed the Rating Board in the media when the chairperson stood his ground. Bregman, said Heffner, acted no different with him on *Scarface,* telling him, "We're going to fix you and we're going to ruin you and we're going to do it in the press." The attack on the Rating Board subsequently came from all sides. Rehme stated that the rating implied pornography and that "there is no way this company would send *Scarface* out in an X-rated version." De Palma used the occasion to continue his war against the rating system and to bait Heffner, who he claimed—in a widely repeated allegation—had a "personal vendetta" against him: "I feel that I'm being singled out here because I went to the newspapers and accused Richard Heffner of being a censor when I was forced to take things out of *Dressed To Kill.*" Bregman perpetuated this lie as well: "This is not a porno film and it's not a mindless violence-exploitation film. It's a serious film and we were shocked that it got an X-rating. The only reason I can think of why it originally got an X-rating, is that ratings board chairman Richard Heffner has a vendetta against us." Exploiting the situation even further, De Palma and Bregman complained about the X rating on a segment of the syndicated

TV series *Entertainment Tonight* and arranged for special screenings of *Scarface* for reporters and critics so they could write about the film.[100]

De Palma reported that *Scarface* earned an X for being "excessively and cumulatively violent," a reason Heffner does not deny: "The accumulation of violence and language was too much," he said. "We consider ourselves responsible to parents, and we didn't think many parents would cheer us for giving this film an R rating." Additionally, Pacino's ad nauseam use of the word *fuck*—reportedly 183 times—also contributed to the film's initial X, a rating agreed on by Heffner and all but one of his six examiners.[101] De Palma, who said he "had been very careful to avoid the uses of explicit violence," submitted four versions of the film to the Rating Board until he refused to cut his film any further. He eventually told Universal, "Look, you guys are going to have to fire me, and you can finish the process yourselves. I think we are affecting the effectiveness of this film, and I won't work and I don't care anymore."[102]

Up to this point *Scarface* was a typical rating controversy: angry filmmaker and producer, attacks on the Rating Board, unsuccessful resubmissions. Universal, however, chose to appeal the rating, says Heffner, for one simple reason: the "fix" was in. When diplomacy failed between an MPAA signatory and the Rating Board—especially when a lot of money was at stake—Valenti sometimes "fixed" the appeals process to ensure a two-thirds-majority vote to overturn the original rating. Up to that time Valenti had intervened in the appeals for Warner Bros.' *All the President's Men* (1976) and MGM/United Artists' *Poltergeist* (1982) to obtain lower ratings.[103] With *Scarface* Valenti presided over the Appeals Board and secured votes from its MPAA and NATO members before the hearing. All that was needed was their attendance at the appeal, and Valenti ensured a large number of his co-conspirators showed up. Universal even brought in the first cut of *Scarface* (minus one twelve-frame shot of an arm that had been chain-sawed off) to the New York Appeals Board hearing because the distributor knew they were going to win.[104] And to give the corrupt proceedings an air of credibility and forthrightness, expert witnesses accompanied De Palma, Bregman, and Rehme, including film critics Jay Cocks of *Time* magazine; Major Nick Novarro, commander of the Sheriff's Organized Crime Division in Broward County, Florida (who testified to the film's authenticity and antidrug message); and two psychiatrists. Heffner, as he always did, argued for the Rating Board unaccompanied.[105] As anticipated, the Appeals Board vote was seventeen to three to overturn the X for *Scarface*. Mickey Mayer, who represented the now-defunct IFIDA—one of the three forming partners of CARA that represented the independents—likely voted to support the X and told Heffner after the appeal: "I hereby declare the X for violence dead because when the

Figure 9. MPAA favoritism and the Appeals Board: Al Pacino in *Scarface* (1983).

Appeals Board can overturn, by vote of seventeen to three, this X, when is there ever going to be an X again, for violence?"[106]

The dirty dealings behind the Appeals Board's decision to reclassify *Scarface* may have protected Universal's immense investment in the film, but they also undermined the very principles of the industry's classification system and the Incontestable R. Accusations of hypocrisy and discrimination that have followed CARA during its entire administration can often be linked to the egregious abuses of power by Valenti, the MPAA, and NATO in the appeals process. The task of the Appeals Board is supposedly the same task as the Rating Board: to estimate what rating most American parents would find most appropriate for their children. The members of the Appeals Board, however—made up primarily of representatives of the MPAA and NATO— regularly vote along the lines of what rating it believes best serves the economic and political interests of its constituency, not the concerns of parents.

Heffner often commented privately about such favoritism and the irrevocable damage it had on the integrity of the rating system. Speaking for the Rating Board, he explicitly brought these issues up (as well as the shenanigans that accompanied them) in his appeal statement at the *Scarface* hearing:

> We're concerned, too, with fairness and equality for the little guys in the industry to whom $30,000 or $300,000 looms just as large as $30 million, and who just as frantically seek special treatment, though *they* tend to use entreaty and cajolery rather than threats, intimidation and public slander as the means to get what they want, whatever the consequences to the public, to the rating system, and to the industry. We haven't ever given *them* the wrong R instead of the right X; and we won't do so here. For it is most important of *all* that we give precisely the same substantive treatment, extend precisely the *same* courtesy, to *all* companies, large and small.[107]

Heffner's appeals statement reveals a classification policy with standards inconsistently and inequitably applied between the Rating Board and the Appeals Board. These inequities surely continued unabated, but one would never know this from the public record. Heffner's oral history and papers reveal that press coverage of these conflicts (and many more about the rating system) have been full of misinformation and lies. Valenti and Heffner, the MPAA and CARA, the Rating Board and the Appeals Board are often discussed collectively as if they had the same missions, responsibilities, and functions. These misconceptions have no doubt been sustained by Valenti's cloak of secrecy over the entire classification system but also by Heffner himself, who refused to publicly criticize the operations of CARA during his tenure in office. Following the *Scarface* hearing, Heffner's response to a press inquiry that the Appeals Board was biased toward the MPAA was profoundly statesmanlike: "The fact is that we have rated about 3,500 films in just under 10 years that I have done this job, and in that time only 55 have gone to the appeal board," he said. "Out of that 55, only 12 occasions—including *Scarface*—has the vote gone the other way. So I think that sinks that argument."[108] While this remark is patently untrue, it does not derive from blind loyalty to Valenti. Instead, Heffner always sought to initiate reform of CARA from within, rather than airing its dirty laundry in a public forum, because he truly believed that industry self-regulation was always preferable to government censorship.[109]

As it turned out, *Scarface* did not become the automatic blockbuster it was anticipated to be, earning $45 million domestically and another $20 million overseas before becoming a cult hit. *Body Double* fared much worse financially (less than $9 million domestically), despite De Palma's attempt to market its controversial nature shortly after *Scarface*: "I'm going to go out and make an X-rated suspense porn picture. I'm sick of being censored. *Dressed to Kill* was going to get an X rating and I had to cut a lot. So if they want an X, they'll get a *real* X. They wanna see suspense, they wanna see terror, they wanna see SEX—I'm the person for the job."[110] The Rating Board saw the violent erotic thriller centered on the world of pornographic filmmaking that way—for "sexuality of a 'porno level'" and profanity said Heffner—and gave *Body Double* an X rating.[111] Most observers, however, did not play De Palma's game this time around. Critics did not write publicity pieces about the film's eroticization of violence, and feminist groups aimed their efforts at rewriting pornography laws rather than helping to publicize films like *Body Double* through their complaints.[112] Without any hype or protests De Palma quietly edited the film in order to get an R, and the film never became a limit text like his earlier pictures.

Body Double, like the majority of films rated R by CARA, barely raised a fuss. After a wobbly initial period, CARA, with a few exceptions, had the R/X distinction well in hand. As long as Hollywood filmmakers, MPAA distributors, and NATO exhibitors respected the authority of the Rating Board in helping them prepare X-rated films for an R-rated market, the industry's system of boundary maintenance would encounter little resistance surrounding the uppermost categories. *Cruising, Dressed to Kill,* and *Scarface,* however, dodged many important issues involving the Incontestable R. First, what would be the industrial ramifications if an MPAA signatory released an X picture? Second, does responsible entertainment—a system principally based on the Rating Board's assessment of what *most American parents* might feel a rating should be for a given film—automatically favor the product of Hollywood distributors and exhibitors over the independents? Third, what is the formal difference, if any, between an R and an X rating? And last, why does the Rating Board lack a rating that could distinguish serious adult fare from pornography? Each one of these concerns would become central to discussions surrounding the creation of the NC-17 in 1990.

CHAPTER 3

From X to NC-17

*The ratings board makes no judgment of quality. It's what you see on
the screen, period. They cannot make distinctions between artistic
versus non-artistic films. Once they start doing that, the entire rating
system will collapse.* —Jack Valenti, *Variety*, June 20, 1990

Not a single mainstream film was released with an X throughout the 1980s.
The conscious abandonment of this product line by the MPAA and NATO
solidified the R rating—the Incontestable R—as a seal of responsible entertainment for the Hollywood film industry. The X, in turn, fortified itself as a
marker of obscenity, artistic worthlessness, and anything other than responsible entertainment for the moviegoing public. With the X rating's stigma left
over from the 1970s, most NATO exhibitors refused to play X-rated films,
many newspapers prohibited ads for them, and pay cable networks like HBO
refused to air them. Hard-core filmmakers still appropriated the X as well,
permanently cementing the category's association with pornography. Any
filmmakers wanting to explore adult content were forced to cut their films
down to an R category if they wanted access to the majority of motion picture houses.

Many groups, however, did not celebrate Hollywood's abandonment of
the adults-only rating. In 1990 calls for a new category to be inserted between
the R and the X were reignited to differentiate serious films from pornographic ones. Petitions for such a rating—commonly identified as AO
(Adults Only) or A (Adult)—were nothing new; they had been circulating in
the industry since the dawn of CARA. Numerous players with some economic or artistic stake in the rating system had called for the A category.
Filmmakers desired creative freedom. Distributors wanted to exploit its marketing potential. Exhibitors needed protection from protest groups. Reformers aimed to control movie content. And critics demanded artistic works for
consenting adults. Different motives may have justified their dissatisfaction

with the current classification arrangement at one time or another, but one thing they always agreed on: the rating system was broken.

Criticism of the X did not radiate from reform groups, the source of protests against Hollywood films such as *Year of the Dragon* (1985) and *The Last Temptation of Christ* (1988) during the "culture wars" of the 1980s.[1] Instead, disapproval emerged from independent producers and distributors, who led the charge of the long-standing accusation that CARA's policies prevented serious adult films from being made. They blamed CARA for the limited advertising and exhibition opportunities for X-rated films in the marketplace, citing the system's failure to distinguish between art and exploitation in assigning ratings. Soon thereafter, the National Society of Film Critics, motion picture directors, and other groups demanded an "A" rating to differentiate between intense adult product and pornography, similar to the British system of self-regulation on which CARA was originally based.[2] These concerns and demands reflected and fueled the perennial debate over the legitimacy of the entire rating system by the nation's film critics. Echoing objections made by the media in regard to the ineffectual PCA in the 1960s, Jack Mathews of the *Los Angeles Times* called the rating system "antiquated and narrow-minded," and Charles Champlin of the same newspaper believed the X had "outlived whatever usefulness it ever had."[3]

Amidst this rating debate, Valenti restated in the *New York Times* the same rhetoric he had used for more than twenty-one years in defending his rating administration from the nation's critics: (1) *CARA, unlike the PCA, does not rate films based on qualitative factors.* You can't have two ratings, "one for 'serious' slasher movies and one for 'pornographic' slasher movies," because people could sue you for placing their film in the "leper" category. "Sometimes," he said, "the distinctions . . . between 'erotic' and 'porn' are not that easy to judge." (2) *The system is merely voluntary.* CARA cannot be held responsible for the limited distribution of X-rated films. "Whatever [the film-maker or distributor] does on an economic basis is up to him. . . . The strength of the current system is voluntarism. It's survived several lawsuits because it is not government-sanctioned and because no one has to submit to it." (3) *Complaints of censorship always help sell a film.* Attacking CARA is a wonderful marketing tool for a distributor who receives an X, Valenti said. "A good publicity man complains about censorship and gets a lot of publicity" for his film. (4) *Why fix what is not broken?* CARA serves the parents of America and not producers, distributors, or film critics, he remarked. "More than 450 films a year come up for a rating, on average, and why should we change this rating system, which is working, because of one or two or three films a year where this is a problem? . . . We are getting no letters from parents demanding that we end the rating system. And our opinion polls for years have shown that 70 to 73 percent of parents find it useful."[4]

Valenti's remarks belie, as they so often do, the fundamental truth of CARA's existence: to serve the economic and political interests of the MPAA signatories by categorizing all their products into responsible, non-X-rated entertainment. Such platitudes of free expression, parental rights, and volunteerism, in conjunction with industry cooperation and collusion, often protected CARA in the past from reformers and the politicians that had demanded greater restrictions on cinematic content. Now, these very same platitudes were being turned against CARA by a large number of filmmakers and critics who desired greater cinematic freedom in motion pictures.

Opponents of the X got their wish on September 27, 1990, as the MPAA replaced the stigmatized X rating with the NC-17 ("No children under 17 allowed," later changed to "No one 17 and under admitted"). In spite of the hope that serious, nonpornographic films for adults would at last be widely distributed and exhibited in the United States, this reclassification turned out to be merely cosmetic. The MPAA and NATO conducted business as usual, continuing to abandon the adults-only category, as did video store chains, by now a well-established lucrative ancillary market for theatrical films.

This chapter will explain how responsible entertainment remained the cornerstone of the rating system even with the introduction of a new adults-only category. Like previous rating revisions, the NC-17 was a ploy, a means of preserving the economic and political interests of the MPAA while appearing to respond to criticisms of its mechanisms for boundary maintenance. I will begin by briefly examining early attempts by film critics during the 1970s and 1980s to reform the X. Although unsuccessful in creating an A rating, their outcries (together with others) about the level of violence and sex in the PG category in the early 1980s led to the institution of the PG-13 (Parents strongly cautioned: Some material may be inappropriate for children under 13). It too, was a ruse; an all-ages rating that actually broadened rather than restricted the level of sex and violence available to children by providing greater classification flexibility to CARA. The A rating, however, called for greater elasticity at the outermost boundaries of responsible entertainment, a license the MPAA fought successfully to eliminate by the mid-1970s with its abandonment of the X rating. My next section will discuss the MPAA's attempts to preserve its Incontestable R in 1990 as independent distributors and Hollywood filmmakers joined critics in calling for reforms in the rating system. Ultimately, the cluster of X-rated independent films, the *Tie Me Up! Tie Me Down!* (1990) court case, and the *Henry & June* (1990) controversy forced the MPAA to change its adult classification. Finally, I will argue that the NC-17 was merely a face-lift of the X, a category no less stigmatized than its predecessor and one the MPAA never intended to use in the first place.

PG-13 AND RATING REFORM IN THE 1980S

The impetus for the NC-17 rating originated from film critics. Ever since soft- and hard-core pornographers began to exploit the X rating soon after the establishment of CARA, film critics have actively berated the MPAA for abandoning its use and for failing to adopt any designation between what Midwest NATO members in 1970 identified as pictures of "adult and quality nature" from those "of far lesser quality and low moral values."[5] Exhibitors at the time rationalized the need for this distinction to stave off what could have been official municipal classification in their respective states. The standards of local classification boards in Chicago and Dallas had been declared constitutional in the aftermath of *Interstate Circuit v. Dallas,* but few others followed their lead, a response, I believe, to the success of the Incontestable R and responsible entertainment.[6] Film critics, however, took a different stance. Sometimes they took the position of civil libertarians, against "censorship" of any kind for adults; more often, however, these critics defended the creative freedom of serious nonpornographic filmmakers, arguing for a rating, as *Look* and future *Today Show* critic Gene Shalit did in 1970, that established "quality" guidelines for adults-only films. "There is the artistic film and there is smut," he said. "To hang them on the same X is an injustice to the artist, an insult to the intelligent people, and a financial windfall for the spewers of stag reels."[7]

   The first formidable demand by the nation's critics for an A rating occurred in May 1972 when the New York Film Critics Circle passed a resolution urging "drastic revision or abolition" of the MPAA rating system because it was "causing confusion and actions harmful to the interests of filmmakers and the film-going public."[8] Their declaration was triggered by the adoption of policies by many major newspapers (the *Detroit News,* the *Cleveland Plain Dealer,* the *Cincinnati Enquirer,* and the *Boston Herald-Traveler*) to exclude display advertising for all films with an X rating or not carrying a rating at all.[9] Valenti's metaphorical answer to these charges—"Your arrow is aimed at the wrong target. . . . The clear and tragic fact is that the media which are doing the censorship are responsible and no one else is"[10]—insulted many film critics, including the *Hollywood Reporter*'s Arthur Knight, who singularly blamed Valenti for the stigmatization of the X:

Closer to the heart of the present matter, however, is the MPAA's total failure to comprehend that the general public—which would seem to include
newspaper publishers as well—is not prepared to draw fine distinctions
between a movie that has received an X from the Code and Rating Administration, and an independently produced sexploitation picture that has
gotten its X by default. . . . In the eyes of the general public, a movie is a
movie, and all movies emanate from a single source, called variously
"Hollywood" or "the industry." Today, all X-rated movies are being tarred
with the same brush. And whether Valenti likes it or not, his organization
invented that brush.[11]

New York magazine film critic Judith Crist responded to Valenti's misunderstanding of the New York Film Critics Circle's resolution in a personal letter
to the president of the MPAA:

Like all who attempt to "legislate" morality, you have succeeded only in
elevating the lowest and denigrating the finest. That films like *Midnight
Cowboy* and *A Clockwork Orange* are lumped together by X ratings with the
shoddiest of sexploitation films is the doing of the MPAA: you have forced
upon established filmmakers a marketplace level of bargaining, interfering
with their creative concepts when, for sheer survival, they must cut their
films to get an "R" rather than "X." . . . You who have justified the censorial
rating code as self-censorship and an alternative to government censorship
have now brought public censorship upon your industry. And within that
industry, the ratings have reduced movie quality to a debate on how many
pubic hairs can flutter on the edge of a frame.[12]

Despite the pointing out of these issues time and time again by the
nation's film critics (self-censorship of filmmakers, the unintentional stigma
of the X, appropriation of the X by pornographers), they wielded little power
on their own to change the self-regulatory apparatus of CARA. In fact,
Warner Bros. turned a blind eye to their concerns only a few months after the
Crist letter when Stanley Kubrick agreed to cut thirty seconds from the X-
rated *A Clockwork Orange*—primarily from the ménage à trois scene—to
earn a less restrictive R for wider release.[13] After the *Miller* decision gave
power to the states to determine obscenity standards the following year, the
A rating lost whatever traction it had with the MPAA and NATO for a very
long time. By the end of 1975, *Variety* noted, "film ratings . . . ha[d] become
simply a part of American and Hollywood life disturbed only by an occasional outburst."[14]

As I noted in chapter 2, debates surrounding the X rating resurfaced with a vengeance during the controversy over *Cruising* in 1980. The uproar, however, centered on the picture's being "misrated" rather than on the need for an additional classification between the R and X. Ironically, the only person publicly raising the idea of additional ratings was CARA chairperson Richard Heffner, who declared, "What *Cruising* does show is the need for refinement in the rating system, the need to differentiate between R pictures that are almost PG and those that are almost X."[15] Heffner would soon get his wish, but only for the former, and not for the kind of middle-ground categorization he had been advocating for many years to Valenti. The PG-13, like the NC-17, was simply another tactic of self-interest, an illusionary amendment of self-regulation driven by the economic and political motives of the MPAA.

Heffner had always sought a more open and honest process of boundary maintenance than had Valenti. Unlike his predecessors, Eugene Dougherty and Aaron Stern, who had to juggle four ratings at a time of industrial instability, Heffner arrived at the onset of responsible entertainment, needing to worry about two categories only, the PG and the R.[16] With the Incontestable R serving as guarantor on one end of the scale, Heffner quickly aimed at improving CARA's approval rating for the PG, which had already gone through two permutations (M and GP) because of confusion over its meaning. First, violence that was once ensconced in the PG category was increasingly awarded an R under the Heffner Rating Board, and nudity was treated less stringently. "*Barry Lyndon* (1975) and *Lies My Father Told Me* (1975) had the kind of nudity that had always automatically gotten an R," he told the *New York Times* in 1978. "But we felt that, in the context of those pictures, parents wouldn't feel their brief nudity deserved an R."[17] Second, Heffner altered the composition of the Rating Board in 1978 to make all its categories more flexible and responsive to parental concerns. Replacing some of its members with industry ties (dating back to the PCA) were nonindustry-affiliated parents, who, after a six-month trial period, could serve only three years at the most. "We are trying in our ratings, to represent a changing parental population," Heffner said.[18] Third, he spearheaded the attrition of an existing automatic R rating for pictures containing the word *fuck* or other "harsher sexually derived words" (slang expressions for lovemaking or genitalia). The longstanding automatic language rule was overturned on appeal fifty-five consecutive times under his watch, beginning with *All the President's Men* (1976) and including *The Front* (1976), *A Bridge Too Far* (1977), and *The Last Waltz* (1978). Steven Vaughn observed that Heffner soon regretted this development, feeling a share of responsibility for the accumulation of bad language in motion pictures by filmmakers exploiting the rating system.[19]

Motivating these changes for Heffner was his belief that film classification could forestall federal censorship as long as it effectively served private *and* public interests, particularly the needs of parents to make more informed decisions about their children's moviegoing. As he told the *New York Times* in 1975: "We're not competent to judge whether children will be harmed by watching a particular film. To be frank, after listening to experts disagree, I don't think anyone else is either. I happen to believe that a parent can not escape responsibility for saying 'This is good for my children' or 'That is bad.' But parents need reliable information if they're going to exercise their responsibility. CARA was set up to provide this information."[20] To assist parental decision making and to stem the escalating language problems of the PG category, Heffner urged Valenti to convince the MPAA and NATO to adopt a rating between the PG and the R in a series of memos and discussions dating back to 1976, shortly after the *All the President's Men* incident.

Two points of contention permeate these exchanges, highlighting the differences between the two men and their respective approaches to boundary maintenance under CARA. First, Valenti disliked change, perceiving it as admittance, perhaps, that the system—his creation—was broken. He often quoted Lyndon Johnson ("If change isn't necessary it isn't necessary to change"). Heffner, however, embraced change under articles of reason and referenced Abraham Lincoln ("When new views become true views I shall adopt them").[21] Second, Valenti wanted to insert between PG and R a category called PG-Mature, an all-ages rating with particular caution for children under thirteen; Heffner, however, preferred an R-13, a restrictive rating like the R that required preteens to be accompanied by a parent. The issue at hand was money versus accountability. Valenti wanted no restrictions at the box office that might hurt sales or prove unworkable at the point of sale. Heffner wanted parental needs met more effectively. He also felt strongly that a PG-Mature would diminish the credibility of CARA by appearing to "loosen up" the rating system, allowing once R-rated content into an all-ages category.[22]

For a time Valenti resisted any rating additions despite Heffner's periodic submission of materials estimating which past PG and R films would have likely received a PG-Mature or R-13 classification.[23] The *Cruising* incident, however, severely damaged the integrity of CARA inside and outside the industry. As a result, Valenti felt pressure from the MPAA and NATO—much coming from Heffner's lobbying efforts of powerful Hollywood executives such as Paramount's Barry Diller and MCA's (Universal) Lew Wasserman—to pursue implementation of a rating between PG and R and to provide descriptive language tags explaining the reasons behind rating decisions to the public.[24] In January 1981 NATO chairperson Richard Orear wrote Valenti, asking for these very changes on behalf of his exhibitors *as well as* for a restrictive but not prohibitive category—either an RR or VR (Very Restricted)—between an R and X to distinguish between nonpornographic and pornographic material.[25] Valenti rejected calls for all three modifications.[26] However, in March—after much forestalling with exhibitors—he agreed to conduct an experiment in Missouri and Kansas in which rating explanations were listed in advertising and publicized in theaters.[27] The study discontinued in January 1982 after NATO concluded from an MPAA survey that only a small part of the public used the explanations that exhibitors themselves believed were too brief to accurately describe the content of a film.[28] Heffner, who believed the Missouri/Kansas theater owners found the reasons immensely helpful, attributed the experiment's failure to Valenti, whose research man conducted the tests and interpreted the results in a negative fashion to purposely kill the enterprise. Both Valenti and the MPAA's Advertising Administration head, Bethlyn Hand, Heffner thought, were "scared to death" that rating reasons would get them in trouble with the MPAA signatories.[29]

Even with Valenti's and Hand's best efforts to avoid making a change, the PG/R problem just would not go away. In the early 1980s a series of successful R-rated films starring teenagers but banned for teenage viewing (unless viewers were accompanied by a parent or adult guardian) fueled demands for rating reform. *The Blue Lagoon* (Brooke Shields), *Little Darlings* (Tatum O'Neal, Kristy McNichol), *Foxes* (Jodie Foster, Scott Baio), and *Fame* drew a large teenage audience in 1980, many of whom bought tickets or sneaked into theaters.[30] Also, a genre of films primarily centered on high school or college life—what William Paul terms "animal comedies"[31]—emerged in the wake of *Porky's* (1981), including *Fast Times at Ridgemont High* (1982), *Spring Break* (1983), *Valley Girl* (1983), and *Risky Business* (1983). This surge in production of R-rated entertainment with teenage appeal led to increased complaints from critics about increasingly lax admission policies and from exhibitors increasingly frustrated by the difficulty of policing teenage patrons at the growing number of multiplexes.[32]

It was, however, the violence in several high-profile, PG-rated Hollywood blockbusters, many directed or produced by Steven Spielberg, that ultimately signaled to Valenti the necessity for a rating between PG and R. As early as Universal's *Jaws* (1975)—which received a special PG disclaimer, "some material may be too intense for younger viewers"[33]—Spielberg exercised great leverage over the rating system's representation of violence because of the political clout of Wasserman at MCA and Diller, who would release *Raiders of the Lost Ark* (1981) a few years later at Paramount. MGM's *Poltergeist* (1982), directed by Tobe Hooper and coproduced and cowritten by Spielberg, won its rating on appeal—twenty to four in support of the PG—despite Heffner's insistence that the level of "terror" (made even more troubling by Dolby sound) warranted an R. It was another reminder, said Heffner, that the "[rating] system was set up to allow the people who really knew the [economic] stakes to have final say on a rating" at the appeals hearing.[34]

Nevertheless, the fallout after the *Poltergeist* reversal started a chain reaction that led to the institution of the PG-13. Shortly after the appeal, William Nix, CARA's counsel, told Valenti that the participation and voting by the recently merged MGM/United Artists at the hearing violated CARA rules. It created a conflict of interests that could (or already did) expose CARA to charges of discrimination and unfair dealings by the independents. The National Council of Churches' James M. Wall, who Valenti let sit in but never vote on Appeals Board hearings, also found the PG for *Poltergeist* egregious and called for the implementation of an R-13 in the pages of *Christian Century*.[35] And Spielberg himself promised Heffner an intermediate rating between PG and R to avoid problems like *Poltergeist* in the future. "I'll get that for you. This mustn't happen again," Heffner recalls the director telling him.[36]

Spielberg's "assurance" for an "intermediate rating" would nevertheless take two more years to materialize. In 1984 a number of R films won PGs on appeal—*Beat Street, Sixteen Candles, Hard to Hold*—making more explicit films available to children, as well as undermining CARA's authority.[37] Ironically, none were as damaging that year as the Spielberg executive-produced *Gremlins* and Spielberg-directed *Indiana Jones and the Temple of Doom*.[38] One sequence from each film caused a controversy: the sequence in which gremlins terrorize a woman in a kitchen before she ends up blenderizing and microwaving two of them; and the sequence when Indiana Jones witnesses a ritual sacrifice in which a man's still-beating heart is ripped out of his chest. Barry Diller, perhaps self-servingly but tellingly, in a widely publicized remark, stated he would put his hands over a ten-year-old child's eyes rather than let the child see the twenty-minute dungeon scene in *Temple of Doom*.[39] After getting the support of all the MPAA distributors and NATO exhibitors, Valenti created the PG-13 category on July 1, 1984. The automatic language rule now applied to the PG-13 rating instead of the R; one use of a single sexual expletive would place a film in the new category, two or more would earn it an R. Two years later, CARA decided that any reference to the use of an illegal drug was automatic PG-13 material as well.[40]

The PG-13 category, however, was neither the restrictive category Heffner had privately discussed with the industry for the past ten years nor the one

Valenti contracted with the MPAA and NATO less than a month before the rating's official announcement ("PG-13: Young children under 13 years must be accompanied by a parent or adult guardian," read the June 7, 1984, draft press release).[41] Instead, the PG-13 was an unrestrictive "cautionary" category under the same parameters, a substantial modification that Valenti revealed to Heffner only a week before the new rating took effect. It was the "practical equivalent of restriction," Valenti explained to him, without actual restrictions at the box office.[42] NATO, in fact, had pressured Valenti to revise the classification because it was already difficult to enforce the R rating restrictions at the box office; two would be unwieldy.[43] What appeared to be a change in the rating system and a response to public opinion, said Heffner, was, in fact, window-dressing for the MPAA and NATO: better returns for Valenti's companies, easier enforcement for theater owners.[44]

Creating the PG-13 preserved the industry's commitment to responsible entertainment with a minimum of effort. To this end the MPAA and NATO introduced a new product line for Hollywood without really addressing the nature of Hollywood's line of products. Although the new category provided CARA greater flexibility in classification, the PG-13 evaded concerns about rising levels of sex and violence in the movies, sidestepped the installment of more specific information on all ratings to the public, and diverted discussion from negligent rating enforcement at many theaters. Initially reform groups, mostly religious coalitions, were angry over the industry's flip-flop, considering the R-13 discussions two years earlier after the *Poltergeist* case. They believed, like Heffner at the time, that a cautionary-only PG-13 was a dumping ground for R-rated material without box-office restrictions.[45] Indeed, the PG-13 was just that, a reflection of the economic might of the MPAA and NATO, the powerlessness of religious groups in the CARA era, and the inability of Heffner to effect any substantial change in the rating system.

Similar tactics of circumvention would occur six years later in 1990 with the replacement of the X with the NC-17, an illusory amendment to disguise the industry's core principle of responsible entertainment: "free expression does not mean toleration of license." Until that year only a few films received notoriety for their original X rating, but most of these films—such as Ken Russell's *Crimes of Passion* (1984), Adrian Lyne's *9½ Weeks* (1986), and Paul Verhoeven's *RoboCop* (1987)—were cut down to an R with little fanfare. Generating greater box-office success and renewed calls for an A rating was Alan Parker's *Angel Heart,* which initially received an X from the Rating Board in February 1987. The well-publicized controversy dwelled on the sexually violent love scene between Mickey Rourke and Lisa Bonet, in which they are drenched by rainwater that turns into blood. Tri-Star, a division of Columbia

Figure 10. Edited to an Incontestable R by excising an NC-17 shot of "bobbing buttocks": Mickey Rourke and Lisa Bonet in *Angel Heart* (1987). Courtesy of the Academy of Motion Picture Arts and Sciences.

(an MPAA signatory), and Parker, who signed a standard studio contract guaranteeing delivery of an R film, appealed the decision. Since the vote was only six to five in favor of reclassifying *Angel Heart,* the filmmakers did not receive the necessary two-thirds majority to overturn the Appeals Board's judgment.[46] The close vote, however, enabled them to receive a new hearing, which ended with another insufficient majority vote of eight to six.[47] Declaring "commercial blackmail,"[48] Parker trimmed ten seconds from the sex scene featuring what Andrew Sarris called Rourke's "bobbing buttocks" in order to earn an R.[49] These fourteen feet of film, along with six additional minutes for *Crimes of Passion,* would eventually be restored on video that year, making them some of the earliest unrated and unedited versions of Hollywood and independent films released in the ancillary markets.[50]

At that time, however, most critics believed that *Angel Heart,* unlike *Cruising, Scarface,* or *Crimes of Passion,* did not warrant the X. Something so trivial as "bobbing buttocks" provided them with the material they needed to attack the Rating Board for what they believed to be its arbitrary and subjective policies. Roger Ebert and Jack Mathews, like most critics, found nothing violent or erotic in *Angel Heart* that had not been shown numerous times in other R films such as the *Nightmare on Elm Street* series.[51] They reiterated the common complaint that the X had evolved into a skull and crossbones for legitimate filmmakers because distributors would not release pictures with that rating, media outlets would not advertise them, and exhibitors would not play them. Both critics proposed an A rating be inserted between the R and X for films that were adult but nonpornographic. Ebert and Gene Siskel suggested this idea on their syndicated television show, *Siskel and Ebert and the Movies,* in a special episode devoted to ratings reform. Mathews did so in a series of articles in the *Los Angeles Times.*

Heffner often blamed Ebert, Mathews, and reporter Aljean Harmetz of the *New York Times* for overgeneralizing rating controversies, perpetuating irrational and untrue accounts of the Rating Board's operations. Yet who could blame them? All public comments on CARA came from Valenti, who continued to restrain Heffner from correcting any inaccuracies or discussing the rating system with reporters. Valenti remained the primary voice of CARA in the 1980s and until his retirement, but generally his colorful remarks fueled greater misunderstandings of the rating system. In a response to Mathews in 1981, Valenti rightfully stated that CARA had no "residence" in judging the pornographic or obscene, that the rating system was supported by the courts because of its "non-discriminatory" practices.[52] A week later, however, in an interview with Harmetz Valenti denounced the X, stigmatizing its usage even further and rekindling accusations that CARA was a "censorship" board. "I don't care if you call it 'AO' for adults only, or Chopped Liver or Father Goose," Valenti said. "[An X-rated] movie will still have the stigma of being in a category that's going to be inhabited by the very worst of pictures."[53]

Three years later, Valenti's words proved prescient. Arguments for an A rating resurfaced when a slew of pictures—many distributed by a then relatively unknown independent company called Miramax—received the X. With less riding financially on a movie, and even less on the integrity of the rating system, the battles between the independent distributors and CARA differed quite markedly from those with the MPAA signatories. Creative freedom, not responsible entertainment, was their very loud and very public rallying cry.

Miramax and the X

The designation of a series of independent films as X-rated in 1990 reignited the debate over the adults-only classification that the MPAA failed to copyright almost twenty-two years earlier. As we saw in chapter 2, pornographers

opportunistically adopted the X for their own in 1968, as did the MPAA signatories who, until 1973, ventured into soft-core distribution and soft- and
hard-core exhibition. As a result, the X became irreversibly tainted; few filmmakers, distributors, exhibitors, newspapers, or television stations would
touch the rating now associated with smut and obscenity.

Those non-MPAA members—the independent filmmakers and distributors—given an X by CARA had two choices: (1) release a film unrated—
something the MPAA signatories would not do—in the hope that theater
chains and newspapers would consider the film on the basis of its individual
merit rather than ban it outright, or (2) cut a film down to R specifications
so it could be potentially released in a large number of theaters. For the latter
the Incontestable R rating and the parameters of responsible entertainment
often made it quite difficult to edit a film without sacrificing artistic integrity
or compromising those elements that could make an independent film stand
out in the marketplace: explicit sex, graphic violence, or harsh language, for
example. These and other potentially controversial elements played a large
role in the ten independent films initially awarded an X by the Rating Board
in 1990: Circle Releasing's *The Killer* and *Dark Obsession;* New Line's *King of
New York;* Shapiro-Glickenhaus's *Frankenhooker;* Omega Entertainment's *In
the Cold of the Night;* Silverlight Entertainment's *Life Is Cheap . . . but Toilet
Paper Is Expensive;* Miramax Films' *Hardware* (under the company's Millimeter Films banner), *Tie Me Up! Tie Me Down!* and *The Cook, the Thief, His
Wife, and Her Lover;* and Greycat Films' *Henry: Portrait of a Serial Killer.*[54] The
public battles that led to the creation of the NC-17 centered prominently on
the last three of these independent films.

"You're seeing a caliber of aberrational behavior on the screen that just
wasn't extant before," Jack Valenti told *Premiere* in January 1991 to describe
the kind of films now facing CARA.[55] One of those hotly debated films,
Henry: Portrait of a Serial Killer, an unrelenting documentary-style feature on
the life of serial killer Henry Lee Lucas, actually earned its X a couple of years
earlier. The film, produced by Maljack Productions in 1995 for only $100,000,
became a cause célèbre among critics after languishing on the shelf for five
years. *Henry's* first two distributors, Vestron and Atlantic, had withdrawn
their support of the film. The latter did so in 1988, after the Rating Board
unanimously gave the film an X rating and then the Appeals Board rejected
Maljack's appeal with a six-to-one vote.[56] *Henry's* breakthrough came when
documentarian Errol Morris, guest director of the Telluride Film Festival in
September 1989, chose it as one of his two "picks" at the event. The critical
attention and controversy generated by this disturbing melodrama at Telluride finally landed the film a distribution deal with Greycat Films, which

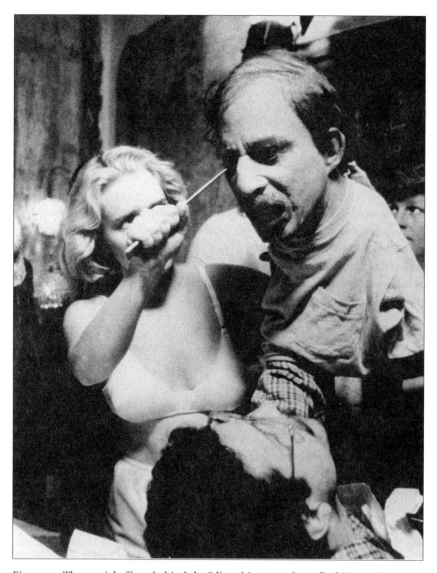

Figure 11. The special effects behind the "disturbing moral tone" of *Henry: Portrait of a Serial Killer* (1986). Courtesy of the Academy of Motion Picture Arts and Sciences.

released the film unrated. It soon reappeared on the top-ten lists of publications such as *Time, USA Today,* and the *Chicago Tribune* in 1990.[57]

Director John McNaughton told the press that his film received an X for excessive violence and a "disturbing moral tone," a lie, says Richard Heffner, to

generate publicity for the film like so many filmmakers before him. According to Heffner, specifics on four scenes had been given to McNaughton, who
refused to cut any of them: "Fat TV salesman stabbed repeatedly. TV jammed
on head. Blood pours. He is electrocuted. Shooting of the man in the stom-
ach and the head. Brother rapes sister, Henry kills brother, saws brother up in
bathtub."[58] Heffner would also state unequivocally that it was the "treatment"
of themes involving sex and/or violence that earned *Henry* an X, not a "disturbing moral tone."[59] I believe, however, the difference between the two has
to do with mere accumulation: one scene may just be disturbing, but a combination of disturbing scenes creates, in effect, a "disturbing moral tone" for
a film, as in *Cruising*. I will discuss the aesthetics of "tone" and "treatment of
a subject or theme" in chapter 4. One thing, however, is certain for these independent films of 1990: their tone/treatment violated the standards of
responsible entertainment.

Calls for an A rating would have gone unheard in 1990 if *Henry* had been
an isolated case. Between March and June 1990, however, CARA gave five X
ratings to four independently distributed films—*The Cook, the Thief, His
Wife, and Her Lover; The Killer; Dark Obsession;* and *Tie Me Up! Tie Me
Down!*—and one MPAA-member film: Triumph's *Wild Orchid*.[60] Each film
was released unrated except for *Wild Orchid*, which went out with an R since
Sony's MPAA membership precluded Triumph from releasing unrated pictures. In their columns critics proposed once again an alternative rating for
the X, complaining of the economic consequences of the category. They
chiefly cited *Cook* and *Tie Me Up!* as the work of two international directors
of renown (Peter Greenaway and Pedro Almodóvar), whose films did not
deserve to be lumped with pornography.[61] Jack Mathews, once again, was
quite vocal about a rating change and spoke for most critics:

> It is not the judgment of the raters themselves that is the flaw in the sys-
> tem; it is the adamant refusal of the MPAA to create and copyright, for
> example, an A rating—for adults only—that in an instant could right all
> the wrongs. The copyrighted A rating would be adults only; the X rating
> would be a catch-all, open classification that could be used by anyone.
> Without the A or something like it, serious filmmakers will continue to be
> limited in what they can do and adult moviegoers will get less than what
> was intended.[62]

Russell Schwartz, the vice president of Miramax, who oversaw marketing,
confirmed the current undesirability of either X-rated or unrated films in the
marketplace, pointing to the presence of unpredictable advertising hurdles
and real-estate laws prohibiting the screening of anything stronger than an R.

"Now what we're doing, [with *Cook* and *Tie Me Up!*]," he said, "is wearing the letter on our back, instead of our front."[63]

Bombastic pronouncements such as this characterized Miramax's approach to marketing its art-house product. By attacking the X rating and the industry's system of boundary maintenance, the company ignited media debates over the A rating in mid-1990. Ever since achieving enormous financial and critical success with the R-rated *sex, lies, and videotape* in 1989, Miramax chose to maximize the publicity of its films through continuous attacks on the integrity of CARA and the X rating. One can witness these tactics—what Justin Wyatt calls "marketing controversy"—being deployed in the regulation of *Scandal,* Miramax's first campaign a year earlier against what it believed were injustices of the rating system.[64]

The major spokesperson for the *Scandal* campaign and all subsequent Miramax campaigns was cochairperson Harvey Weinstein. After the British import initially received an X in mid-March 1989 for its orgy scene, he went into "marketing controversy" mode. "We were shocked to say the least," he said, about the classification. "While this is a movie about sex, we never thought it was an X-rated film."[65] Weinstein swore he never would cut the scene and appealed the rating a few weeks later, accompanied by none other than famed First Amendment attorney Martin Garbus with a phony affidavit in hand to give the impression that Miramax was going to sue.[66] Despite this nonsense, Miramax closely lost an Appeals Board vote of eight to seven in favor of retaining the X rating. With the announcement of the defeat, Weinstein marketed controversy once again. "I thought I was at the Scopes trial yesterday," he said. "I saw Garbus playing Clarence Darrow and Heffner playing William Jennings Bryan. Only in this case, Bryan won."[67] (Bryan won the *Scopes* case, too, in fact.)

Despite these pronouncements, Weinstein subsequently released *Scandal* with an R rather than unrated, editing three seconds of sexual movement from the orgy scene. Heffner recalled it was Miramax's intention all along. "By 1989, they were aware that they had fairly much of a dog there [with *Scandal*]. And if they could play it right, as they did in many other instances, they could get an audience for it. Play it right meant saying this picture should be an R. Appealing it. Getting its X. Getting certain critics . . . to insist that the X material as we saw it was really R material and they were being discriminated against."[68] "Playing it right" helped to generate almost $9 million at the box office for *Scandal* as this exploitation strategy shook the foundations of responsible entertainment. Miramax had no allegiance to the Incontestable R, to CARA, or to Valenti. If selling a film came at the expense of the rating system, so be it.

When another British film, *The Cook, the Thief, His Wife, and Her Lover*, received an X at the end of March 1990, Miramax chose this time (after losing the appeal) to release the film featuring cannibalism, frontal nudity, and child abuse uncut and unrated (with a warning that no one under eighteen should be admitted). The distributor marketed the disagreement—which in turn, inflamed calls for the A rating—by designing a poster featuring an X formed by a crossed knife and a fork, by issuing a press release deploring the idea that "a major international artist [like Greenaway] might be subjected to censorship," and by making the director and star Helen Mirren available for television and print interviews to voice long-standing criticisms of the X rating.[69] Greenaway refused to compromise his work for an R, insisting his film did not belong in the higher category because it was not "obscene": "I think in any way to cut or to reconsider these things in the context of the movie as it now stands would be certainly to go against the very reasons why I made the movie. I don't think the film is pornographic."[70] Mirren challenged CARA on moral grounds for awarding R ratings freely to slasher films: "There are no exploding heads in this movie, yet when one looks at the kinds of films that are given an R rating—*Friday the 13th* (1980) and *Halloween* (1978)—it's outrageous."[71] Comparisons to sexually violent Hollywood films by these artists reignited the debate that CARA's Rating Board and Appeals Board discriminate against independent distributors of U.S. and foreign films.

These charges put Valenti on the defensive, but he responded no differently than he had in past cases involving the X, steadfastly denying favoritism and opposing any changes to the existing category. He insisted that the rating system was merely a guide for parents, not a business plan for distributors and exhibitors to avoid the X. He defended its widespread acceptance by the majority of parents, citing (as he often did) its stable 70 to 73 percent usefulness for them in the MPAA's annual poll done by the Opinion Research Corporation.[72] He remained vigilant about the integrity of the rating system, restating that CARA was not equipped to render qualitative judgments on a film: "A ratings board can't make a distinction between artistic sadomasochism and non-artistic sadomasochism. Whether it's suitable for children is the only criteria."[73] And he also questioned once again the motives of filmmakers who cynically manipulated the rating system for economic reasons: "The publicity wizards who handle these pictures have probably all gotten a bonus. . . . They're businessmen and they're using creative expression as a bludgeon to make money."[74] Even some NATO exhibitors—who along with the MPAA distributors remained relatively silent—weighed in on the debate. Ira Korff, president of the National Amusements theater chain, stated: "I thought *[The Cook, the Thief, His Wife, and Her Lover]* had parts that were really offensive. We played it in our U.K. theaters, but I wouldn't play it here. If you end up with a couple of major distributors fighting over a semi-X, then you might see something happen."[75]

This wave of complaints by critics and creators intensified dramatically in April when the Rating Board gave an X to *Tie Me Up! Tie Me Down!* Almodóvar's film is about a former mental patient who kidnaps a soft-core porn star and tries to woo her after tying her up. The decision for CARA was inopportune, to say the least; it was the third X given to Miramax in a little over a year, and the company immediately accepted the rating. Strangely, the X may have been avoided (as would have been the film's subsequent legal battle) if Joan Graves—who had recently become the administrative director and later would be chairperson of CARA—had not accidentally told Miramax that *Tie Me Up!* had gotten an X rating and returned the film to the company before Heffner saw it. Even though Heffner saw himself as only one vote and would never overturn his colleagues on a rating decision, he required any picture initially assigned an X by the Rating Board to be shown to him so he might say, "Hey, let's talk about this again." Miramax, however, refused to set up a screening for him until they got the official X certificate. Heffner acquiesced, believing it would do more damage to the credibility of CARA if he refused. Miramax rescheduled the film later that same day, and Heffner thought it should be rated R, unlike the rest of the Rating Board examiners. "I'll believe to my dying day," he recounted, "that [Miramax was] afraid that if I saw *[Tie Me Up!]* I'd say R and then convince—not order but convince my colleagues to go to R, and they'd never have another opportunity for more wonderful publicity. And they were right."[76]

Both Heffner and Almodóvar singled out the copulation scene between Victoria Abril and Antonio Banderas as the problematic X moment, but critics pointed to the scene where Abril engages in apparent masturbatory activity with a windup toy in a bathtub.[77] The "green sheets," the forms filled out by each member of the Rating Board when rating a film, point to both moments and a scene in which Banderas watches a porno film of Abril as eliciting the X. I will discuss the specifics of their comments in chapter 4. Almodóvar, who refused to edit *Tie Me Up!* or any of his other films, including the unrated *Kika* (1993) and the NC-17 *Bad Education* (2004), appealed the R only to receive a vote of six to six to uphold the Rating Board's ruling. As with *The Cook, the Thief, His Wife, and Her Lover,* Miramax released the film uncut and unrated and advised Almodóvar, like it did Greenaway and Mirren, to market the film's controversy as much as possible.

Figure 12. Pedro Almodóvar explains to Antonio Banderas and Victoria Abril why the Rating Board gave *Tie Me Up! Tie Me Down!* (1990) an X rating.

In the U.S. and Spanish press, Almodóvar made highly candid and disparaging remarks about CARA's rating policies, questioning the standards and integrity of the X rating. He told the *Boston Globe:*

> This censorship of the industry is worse than moral censorship. When Steven Spielberg made *Temple of Doom,* which had a lot of violent scenes, he was powerful enough to cause the creation of a new rating, PG-13. So I would ask that you create other letters, other classifications. You only confuse people with this X, which just means pornography. I find *Fatal Attraction* (1987) infinitely more dangerous than *Henry: Portrait of a Serial Killer,* but they'll give *Fatal Attraction* an R and *Henry* an X. *Fatal Attraction* is a diabolical film. There couldn't be a more reactionary, conservative film than this one, which says that outside your home is where the devil is. To compare *Tie Me Up!* to *Fatal Attraction* is even more insulting. An association that gives an R to *Fatal Attraction* doesn't have the least bit of credibility. What's their ideology?[78]

"Fascist" is how he described the ideology of Hollywood films in *El País* as CARA "turn[ed] a blind eye" to the blood and violence in R-rated films like *Conan the Barbarian* (1982) and *Rambo: First Blood Part II* (1985). "We are dealing with superproducts that the industry (let's not forget the MPAA represents the industry) is interested in defending."[79]

Underlying Almodóvar's fury was a keen understanding of content regulation in the United States. He correctly observed that CARA served the economic and political interests of the MPAA signatories under a business model of responsible entertainment. Independents who don't subscribe to this ideology of entertainment often find themselves stuck with an X rating. The major distributors, though, as we have seen with many of Spielberg's films, sometimes get preferential treatment when they cross the line of responsible entertainment within a given category. Even though Heffner says that the Rating Board "is not designed (or qualified) to pass judgment on the quality of a film," to assess whether it is "good" or "bad," "moral" or "artistic," its decisions are still grounded in an ideological and self-serving notion of entertainment believed to be based on the perception of American parents.[80] This form of boundary maintenance is as subjective and unscientific as Almodóvar suggests it is, devoted to "responsible" stories and themes that many independent films deliberately challenge.

This time, though, Miramax would not simply sit back, market the film's controversy for box-office returns, and quietly accept CARA's standard for entertainment. At the behest of civil rights lawyer William Kunstler, Miramax filed a civil suit against the MPAA in the New York State Supreme Court, charging that the rating of *Tie Me Up! Tie Me Down!* was "arbitrary, capricious, and unreasonable." The complaint also contended that the MPAA was "motivated by prejudice toward foreign films and a bias in favor of those made in this country, as well as a prejudice toward independent distributors."[81] The lawsuit followed a similar one filed a week earlier in the U.S. District Court for the District of Columbia by Maljack Productions, producers of *Henry: Portrait of a Serial Killer,* who also claimed that CARA did not apply the same standards for all R-rated pictures and "breached the covenant of good faith and fair dealing." The suit charged that CARA acted in a "discriminatory fashion" by assigning the film an X although "other films containing the same or greater levels of violence" had received R ratings.[82] These two cases were the first filed against the MPAA in almost twenty years, since the filmmakers of the exploitation picture *Bang Bang, the Mafia Gang* in 1971 accused the organization of acting "arbitrarily and capriciously" as well.[83]

These lawsuits only escalated demands for revising the X rating. Of the two, *Tie Me Up!* received the most publicity since the New York State Supreme Court heard the Miramax case in June 1990, only a couple of weeks after its filing.[84] Judge Charles E. Ramos quickly dismissed the Miramax case the following month on July 19, ruling that the plaintiffs had failed to prove their case under law. He opined, "There has been no showing that the X rating afforded *Tie Me Up!* was without rational basis or arbitrary and capricious," or that the MPAA "acted in bad faith or outside of its stated function in its rating of *Tie Me Up! Tie Me Down!*"[85] Ramos questioned Miramax's good faith in launching the suit, pointing to its behavior in exploiting the X in their advertising and to its own admission that *Tie Me Up!* was not suitable for those under the age of eighteen. It "leads to the inference that this proceeding may be just publicity" for the film.

It was, however, a Pyrrhic victory for the MPAA. Ramos couched his verdict in an unprecedented criticism of the rating system, surprising everyone, including Kunstler himself: "I didn't think we would win. But never, in my most optimistic mood, did I think that even though we would lose, we would end up victorious."[86] In a fifteen-page opinion Ramos wrote that "the manner in which the MPAA rates all films, not just *Tie Me Up! Tie Me Down!* causes this Court to question the integrity of the present rating system." He took issue with the method by which CARA rated films G through X to meet the concerns of what he termed the Average American Parent (AAP). He denounced the fact that the AAP standard was determined by parents (who made up the Rating Board) rather than experts (such as psychiatrists or physicians) and that the AAP standard tolerated violence more than sexual intimacy.[87] Without a professional basis for the AAP standard, Ramos declared the rating system to be a "successful marketing strategy" for the MPAA. An "industry that profits from scenes of mass murder, dismemberment and the portrayal of war as noble and glamorous," he said, "apparently has no interest in the opinions of professionals, only the opinions of consumers." Furthermore, Ramos said the court could not "avoid the notion that the [AAP] standard is reasonable only if one agrees with it. This standard, *by definition*, restricts material not because it is harmful but because it is not average fare."

While Ramos did not find that the MPAA acted in "bad faith" in failing to copyright the X, he concurred with Miramax that "X rated is now synonymous with pornography" and that it was "a stigma that relegates the film to limited advertising, distribution, and income." He resoundingly charged that X-rated films were "produced and negotiated" to fit an R rating as determined by the AAP standard. This practice, he said, "censors serious films by the force of economic pressure" and forces American films to "deal with adult subjects in nonadult terms or face an X rating." Under the present ratings arrangement, Ramos stated, CARA has created "an illusion of concern for children, imposing censorship, yet all the while facilitating the marketing of exploitative and violent films with a seal of approval." Even though he did not find a "shred of substantiation" to suggest bias against independent distributors and foreign films by CARA, Ramos made clear that the MPAA

must assume some "responsibility to avoid stigmatizing films with an X rating" and "consider proposals for a revised rating system . . . or to cease the
practice altogether."

Like Almodóvar, Ramos demonstrated an uncanny understanding of the
regulatory forces at work within the U.S. film industry. He correctly recognized that participation in the legitimate theatrical marketplace required an
adherence to a standard of entertainment that did not include the X rating.
He also observed that the AAP is exactly the standard that CARA adheres to
in this marketplace, what this book calls "responsible entertainment." His
criticism of this policy (the stigma and abandonment of the X, negotiations
for an R) *is* precisely criticism of what I call the Incontestable R, the standard
of responsible entertainment at the R/X boundary. In his ruling Ramos correctly identified the true economic and aesthetic reality of the Incontestable
R practice: its "unprofessional" or unscientific standard, its "more lenient policy toward violence," and most intuitively, its basis as a "marketing strategy"
for the MPAA.

Valenti, still the primary public figurehead of the rating system, rebutted
these harsh, yet often accurate, assessments of the rating system by repeating
familiar rationales of CARA's mission (it only provides cautionary labels,
annual surveys attest to its usefulness for parents, etc.), while dismissing all of
Ramos's charges. "Just about everything the opinion had to say about the rating system is wrong," he said after the ruling, denying that CARA showed
greater lenience toward violence, that it primarily served the MPAA signatories, or that psychological expertise was necessary.[88] "The rating system is
not and does not pretend to be the National Institute of Health," Valenti
added. "Only parents have the authority and the responsibility to set value
standards for their children."[89] These niceties, however, were peppered by
more vitriolic criticism of Ramos's conclusions, which Valenti called "idiotic,"
rare for the MPAA president, who usually displayed grace under pressure.[90]
The growing defensiveness and weariness on the part of Valenti is explicitly
noticeable in this remark to film critic Jack Mathews: "[Ramos] made the
right decision in the case but when he got into the rating system, he was bar-
ren of any knowledge about it," Valenti said. "He presented no evidence for
his charges, no data. . . . If you make a claim, shouldn't you have some sup-
portive evidence for it? [The judge] defecates in the middle of the table and
walks away to leave somebody else to clean up the mess."[91] Valenti's fecal-
tinged retort disguised a mounting realization that the integrity of the Incontestable R was severely in jeopardy. When Ramos handed down his opinion,
Valenti publicly downplayed the significance of the ruling and remained res-
olute in his refusal to change the rating system.[92] "The only people complain-

ing about the system," he said, "are a few distributors and few critics."[93] Privately, he must have known that the twenty-two-year-old rating system was in serious danger.

While Ramos was deciding the Miramax case, a new rating service emerged from the Film Advisory Board (FAB), a nonpartisan organization founded in 1975 and dedicated to awarding quality family-friendly entertainment in all media. The FAB would provide a more informative and less costly alternative to CARA after receiving requests from several independent distributors.[94] Unlike CARA, the FAB described content (listing degrees of nudity, violence, and substance abuse) and charged only $450 to $500 to rate a film, compared to CARA, whose fees at that time could reach $8,000 for the big-budget films. The FAB's lower ratings fee did attract a small number of independent video distributors. On one hand, Turner Home Entertainment, whose family-oriented made-for-cable productions would have received no higher than a PG rating, simply bypassed CARA to save money; on the other hand, companies like Fox/Lorber Associates went with the FAB's "AO" (adults-only) rating because some of their releases would have been labeled with the stigmatized X by CARA.[95]

Even though the FAB never proved to be a formidable challenger to CARA, the company's inroads into the increasingly important video market threatened the credibility of the rating system. The stability of boundary maintenance under CARA was contingent on the absence of competition and industry-wide cooperation with the decisions of the Rating Board and the Appeals Board. Other letter ratings flooding the marketplace, particularly one to replace the X, would not only confuse the public but would damage the Incontestable R, whose integrity secured the participation of NATO, quieted government officials, and kept special interest groups at bay. Exhibitors, politicians, and reformers, however, were noticeably absent in talks for the A rating for one simple reason: no one wanted to defend a mechanism that could enable greater sex and violence—artistic or otherwise—to appear on the majority of U.S. screens. Since the MPAA won the *Tie Me Up! Tie Me Down!* lawsuit (not without criticism, though), demand for an A rating still came from those who mattered least to Valenti: the independents and the critics. With the box-office healthy and responsible entertainment intact—at least with the other categories—there was no reason for him to embrace a new category.

Many of the confrontations faced by CARA in the first seven months of 1990 had occurred, at one time or another, throughout its history. Joseph Strick sued the MPAA and Paramount in 1970 for the X rating given to *Tropic of Cancer.* Brian De Palma and Filmways marketed controversy with *Dressed to Kill* after the film earned a tentative X in 1980. Alan Parker narrowly lost his appeal for an R with *Angel Heart* in 1987. Never, though, had CARA been assaulted as continuously and relentlessly within such a short period or from so many sides. A change was inevitable, and just like the PG-13, it came from within the MPAA's own ranks.

THE CREATION OF THE NC-17

Jack Valenti, who performed a political miracle in 1968 to get the present system OK'd by the industry, has a new miracle cut out for him.
—Charles Champlin, "MPAA Ratings:
A Crisis of Confidence," 1990

By the end of July 1990, several more independent films had received X ratings from the Rating Board: *Hardware, King of New York, Frankenhooker, In the Cold of the Night,* and *Life Is Cheap . . . But Toilet Paper Is Expensive.*[96] The fact that many of these films only narrowly lost their rating appeal for an R reaffirmed to independent filmmakers and distributors their belief of CARA's bias against non-MPAA films.[97] Also heightening their outrage were reediting costs, because unlike the MPAA signatories, the independents did not have the deep pockets to cut their films down to an R, a cost, according to Miramax's Russell Schwartz, that could range from $25,000 to "well into the six figures."[98] Nico Mastorakis, president and CEO of Omega Entertainment, said that "the pressure right now on the MPAA to change the system will only continue to snowball" and that he planned to sue the MPAA if he lost his appeal for *In the Cold of the Night.*[99] He also announced his intention to create an independent ratings board paneled by major U.S. film critics, although it never came to fruition.[100]

It was a petition by the little independent distributor Silverlight Entertainment, however, that ultimately signaled a shift in rating reform. After *Life Is Cheap* lost the appeal of its X by a four-to-three vote in favor of reversing the rating, the company organized, circulated, and published a statement signed by twenty-seven prominent U.S. filmmakers urging the creation of a new adult letter rating.[101] The petition "An Open Letter to Jack Valenti"—what I will call the Silverlight manifesto—was presented to MPAA senior vice president Bethlyn Hand at a press conference on July 24, 1990, and ran in *Daily Variety* and the *Hollywood Reporter* the following day. It partially read as follows:

The "X" rating . . . has come to be universally recognized as pertaining simply to pornography. . . . We believe that it is imperative that the MPAA correct this problem by creating a new letter rating that will more fairly reflect the association's original intention in regard to adult-themed fare.

While the MPAA maintains that its Classification and Rating Administration does not censor films or force filmmakers to censor their films, the taint of an "X" rating clearly results in massive and arbitrary corporate censorship. . . .

We therefore strongly suggest that a new rating of "A" or "M" be incorporated into the system to indicate that a film contains strong adult themes or images and that minors are not to view them. This is not a compromise between art and commerce, it is an essential action designed to protect the United States Constitution. It is an issue as important as film preservation; in fact, it is film preservation.[102]

Unlike a proposal by the National Society of Film Critics in May calling for a rating to distinguish between pornographic and serious adult content, the Silverlight manifesto proposed a letter substitution only and had the weight of the artists, not critics, behind its call for action.[103] This was an unprecedented collective response by mainstream and independent U.S. filmmakers to the restrictive working conditions under the Incontestable R. Some of these high-profile signers previously admitted to cutting their films for an R in the past (Spike Lee, Adrian Lyne), while others who had made strong R films probably cut them as well (Harold Becker, Walter Hill). In most cases they remained relatively silent on the matter, behaving as willing and submissive participants within a cooperative framework of responsible entertainment that bound together the legitimate marketplace.

After this petition went out, Silverlight self-applied an adults-only A rating in its advertising for *Life Is Cheap* rather than cut the film or release it unrated. "If the [MPAA] is not ready to do that," said Silverlight president Mark Lipsky, "then we'll do it ourselves."[104] Self-interest surely motivated Silverlight's petition, but this time the now-familiar story of a failed appeal by an independent distributor confirmed Valenti's worst fear: that a "crisis of confidence" in the rating system existed both inside and outside the industry.[105]

With threats of lawsuits, self-applied A ratings, and industry discontentment, it appeared that a significant structural change to the rating system was imminent. Until June of 1990 Valenti was still very publicly opposed to a new category, since change, as Heffner always said, was a manifestation of failure for Valenti.[106] If the major distributors "came to me and said we need an A rating," stated Valenti, "I would say no."[107] The events of July changed all that. Never seriously considered by Valenti was the evaluative kind of rating suggested by Ebert, Mathews, and the National Society of Film Critics to be inserted between the R and the X that would distinguish between serious adults-only pictures and pornography. Such a rating would violate the standards of responsible entertainment that he had put in place more than twenty years earlier: "freedom of expression without toleration of license."

In various memos to Valenti, Heffner, during his chairpersonship at CARA, had always rejected an A rating in this vein because Rating Board examiners, who were only accustomed to making judgments of parental acceptability, would need to make judgments of artistic quality. How would one make subjective distinctions between "clean" and "dirty" sex, between "justified" and "exploitative" violence, he wondered? In a letter written in response to the petition by the National Society of Film Critics, Heffner said that passing judgment on the quality of a film was never the charge of CARA: "Film raters must not be empowered with two ratings that signal parents whenever films are patently out-of-bounds for youngsters under 17; one presumably for 'good' films (A) and the other for 'bad' films (X). Whatever letter or number or symbol is used for the purpose, only one rating should legitimately signal 'not for kids' . . . and it mustn't be denied to people or films we disdain."[108] Joan Graves also told the press that a dual adult rating "would invite the very censorship all of us wish to avoid."[109] On one hand, Heffner and Graves were correct. The legal ramifications of having to prove that CARA did not act (in the words of Judge Ramos) "arbitrarily, capriciously, and without rational basis" in assigning an X rating would be a nightmare for the Rating Board, especially if these distinctions were based on such subjective conditions as artistic merit. On the other hand, the economic consequences of an X rating repeatedly forced the Rating Board to apply a standard, however impartial or reasonable, that was no stiffer than an R to all MPAA-member films. It was this standard, the "Average American Parent"—one no less evaluative than a "dual adult rating"—that still lay at the center of this controversy.

When these major U.S. filmmakers finally sounded off about the X rating, they were reacting not only to the outrage by the independents but to a quiet storm of discontent surrounding two of their own: David Lynch and Martin Scorsese. *Wild at Heart* and *GoodFellas,* both with big stars and wide releases, each received tentative X ratings for violence from the Rating Board in May 1990 before they were recut to get R ratings.[110] Neither the distributors, Samuel Goldwyn and Warner Bros., nor the directors marketed controversy as Miramax did, but the press still belabored them with questions about the Rating Board and discussed them conjointly with the other controversial films. Goldwyn production chief Thomas Rothman was respectful yet equivocal in his responses after *Wild at Heart* won the Palme d'Or (best film) at the Cannes Film Festival in its uncut version. He said Lynch's popularity (he had just done the television series *Twin Peaks*) and the $10-million price tag made *Wild at Heart* "too big a movie, too important a movie, to be an X."[111] Lynch, though, was much less reserved, calling the R rating a "conspiracy" between the MPAA and NATO: "The last six films that have gone through there have gotten an X," the director said, "and they're no stronger than *The Untouchables* (1987) or any other film that's gotten an R before."[112] Leonie dePicciotto, Goldwyn's vice president of publicity, also reported Lynch's telling CARA that "if you can give *Total Recall* (1990) an R you should be able to give *Wild at Heart* an R."[113]

Scorsese, however, took a more tactful approach to questions about the X rating for *GoodFellas*, indicative of most directors working in the Hollywood film industry. Unlike De Palma, who gleefully courted controversy with the rating system, Scorsese never was one to usurp the authority of CARA. His public statements about negotiations over the R rating for *GoodFellas* were brief—"I had to trim about 10 frames of blood"—and diplomatic—"They never said, 'You'll get an X.' They never said it. But, you know, if I don't do it, will I get the X . . . ?"[114] Privately, according to Heffner, Warner Bros. cochair Bob Daly edited the film with Scorsese to get an R, particularly the moment when Joe Pesci gets his brains blown out, because the Rating Board would not budge on its violence.[115] After the R was certified at the end of June, Scorsese, dutifully once again, admitted that *GoodFellas* in fact "looked better" after cutting some violent scenes, though he did publicly wonder, like Lynch, about the amount of "bloodletting" in other mainstream R-rated pictures like *Total Recall* and *Lethal Weapon* (1987).[116] Despite Scorsese's positive spin on the rating process, *GoodFellas* and *Wild at Heart* offered further support of the view that renowned filmmakers had to cut their films to CARA's R specifications to play in the United States.[117]

The Silverlight manifesto in July, though not signed by Lynch or Scorsese, concretized their concerns, putting into play the real possibility of at least some alteration to the rating system now that the MPAA's *own* filmmakers were collectively expressing dissatisfaction with the current categories. "Nothing lasts, everything is subject to change," Valenti said in the middle of August, after the Silverlight petition initiated a meeting with representatives of the Directors Guild of America (DGA) and the Writers Guild of America West (WGA) about making improvements to CARA.[118] No independent filmmakers or distributors were invited to the private director/writer meeting, much to the dismay of Silverlight's Mark Lipsky, who questioned Valenti's good faith in the proceedings: "Cutting me and all distributors out [of the meeting] was an important way for Valenti to gain control of the situation."[119] Although Valenti was not specific about the changes to be made at the time, he remained steadfast against an adults-only category between the R and the X in his discussions with filmmakers, distributors, and critics.[120]

Valenti contemplated two other ratings as a shift away from the X designation: the NC-17 (No Children under 17 Admitted), which officially replaced the X a month later, and the RR (or A or M or another letter that signified no children under sixteen admitted) to be inserted between the R and X. The RR had, in fact, been under discussion since at least 1981, when NATO chairperson Richard Orear suggested that change to Valenti after the *Cruising* fiasco. Heffner supported either change since both restrictive ratings were "audience-related" categories rather than "quality-related" categories, something the Silverlight A rating was not.[121] Heffner even prepared a list for Valenti on the first of August in 1990, estimating which films submitted in the past year might have earned an RR instead of an X. For instance, out of the eighty-seven films given tentative X ratings in the first seven months of 1990, thirty-eight (44 percent) of them would have been rated RR. Of these eighty-seven films, only twelve (14 percent) were submitted by MPAA signatories, compared to seventy-five (86 percent) by the independents, and from the twelve MPAA submissions only five films would have been rated RR (42 percent), compared to thirty-three (44 percent) of the independents. While Heffner believed these disparities in X and RR ratings were a function of "the messages, not the messengers"—and certainly film content became stronger and more explicit in the 1980s—they still reflected a structural bias in the rating system, at least a statistical one, against the independents.[122]

These confidential discussions, however, did not stop entreaties for a nonpornographic A rating from people outside Hollywood. In August the American Film Marketing Association (AFMA)—a trade organization representing the most prominent international distributors of independent English-language movies—added its support for the implementation of such an A rating, indicating that the X hurt distribution overseas for independent films.[123] Another motion picture rating system, the Parents' Rating Service (PRS), was also announced during this time. As part of its unveiling, a PRS spokesperson directly attacked CARA's rating policies: "The notion of threatening to label a non-sexual film 'X' simply because a rating board does not like what it sees, is repugnant to all those who cherish freedom and diversity in the arts."[124] For any film dealing with "unusual subject matter," the PRS adopted one of Judge Ramos's suggestions for a revised MPAA system—the employment of psychiatrists—in determining the suitability for viewing by children under thirteen.[125]

Later that month, the situation that Valenti feared the most happened: an MPAA signatory got publicly involved in the debate over revisions to the X rating in a way not realized with *GoodFellas*. Universal received an X in June for *Henry & June* and, like Miramax, failed to remain quiet about it after further cuts still failed to earn an R from the Rating Board.[126] The film—based on novelist-poet Anaïs Nin's diary account of her troubled erotic entanglement with novelist Henry Miller and his wife, June—contained five scenes to which the Rating Board objected: a shot of a nineteenth-century Japanese woodcut of a woman being embraced by an octopus; a heterosexual love scene between Henry and Anaïs; and three lesbian scenes, including one between Anaïs and June.[127] The contract for Philip Kaufman, the award-winning director of *The Right Stuff* (1983) and *The Unbearable Lightness of Being* (1988),[128] granted him the right of final cut only if the film earned an R rating, not an X. This stipulation was standard for all directors working with MPAA signatories, but the twist here was that Tom Pollock, the president of Universal Pictures, indicated he was willing to release *Henry & June* with an adults-only rating if it carried a designation *other* than X. Complicating matters was Universal's policy of not releasing X-rated films. As a result, Pollock set a date with the Appeals Board for October 3, with the hope that the film would win its appeal and get an R.[129] *Variety*'s September 10 headline expressed the severity of Pollock's decision: "X-Rated 'June' Could Ignite Major Revolt against MPAA."[130]

Universal had confronted a similar problem with De Palma and *Scarface* in 1983, when CARA awarded the film an X. Fortunately for Valenti and CARA, the company won its appeal for an R rating. If *Scarface* had lost its appeal, CARA and Universal would have been placed in an awkward position that may well have led to a change in the X rating at that time.

Henry & June was essentially the same battle, round two, seven years later: a high-profile director, an MPAA signatory, and a sticky X rating. The difference in 1990, however, was not just the film's arrival in a more hostile and unstable rating environment but an executive willing to take on the rating system. Unlike the case of *Scarface,* in which Universal president Robert Rehme remained relatively silent as the drama unfolded around director Brian De Palma and producer Martin Bregman, Universal's Tom Pollock aligned himself up front with the director in lobbying for a new adults-only rating. Not surprisingly, Pollock's and Kaufman's arguments were distinctly similar to those expressed in the past few months by the independent distributors and film critics. Pollock differentiated *Henry & June* from pornography and exploitative films inhabiting the R category: "It is so clear that this quality film was not meant to be lumped with the hard-core stuff," he said.

"I see other films that have a combination of sexuality and violence, which I feel is far more destructive than anything in *Henry & June*. And those films are rated R."[131] Kaufman also questioned CARA's integrity—"I played by the rules and they changed them"—and impartiality: how had David Lynch's more sexually violent *Wild at Heart* earned an R while *Henry & June* received an X?[132] Once again, Heffner delivered the typical Rating Board response: "I think *Henry & June* is an absolutely beautiful splendid film. But we believe most parents would consider this out of bounds for children. All we're saying with an X rating is that this is an adult film. We are not saying it is pornographic."[133]

Whereas Heffner and the Rating Board always served the informational needs of parents when rating films, the Appeals Board often served the economic needs of the MPAA and NATO. An appeals loss for *Henry & June* could lead to a breakdown in the collusive structure of the rating system and the cooperative framework of responsible entertainment. Independents would cry hypocrisy over the film's R rating, and they would probably have a point. Universal had several options, all of them threats to the Incontestable R. First, the company could withdraw from the MPAA, taking a chance on the open market as United Artists did with *The Moon Is Blue* in 1953.[134] Second, Universal could release the film through a subsidiary, likely damaging the integrity of industry self-regulation as MGM did with *Blow-Up* in 1966. Third, Universal could edit the film to an R, undermining the credibility of the rating system even further by its failure to permit the exploration of serious adult subject matter once again. Last, Universal could keep the X for *Henry & June,* becoming the first major distributor in almost fifteen years to attempt a wide release of an adults-only film. Miramax's Russell Schwartz threatened immediate protest if the appeal proved successful. "I will cry foul from the rooftops if it's overturned. [The MPAA] will really be digging themselves into a hole with us."[135]

The appeal hearing, however, never took place, and the MPAA avoided a potentially embarrassing situation. One week earlier, on September 26, the MPAA, in conjunction with NATO, announced the replacement of the X with an NC-17 rating, making *Henry & June* the first MPAA-member film to be adorned with the outermost rating since United Artists Classics released Pasolini's *Arabian Nights* and *The Canterbury Tales* in 1979 with an X. In his public statement Valenti welcomed the change to the NC-17, but he admitted no fault to the stigmatization of its predecessor: "We have concluded that over the years some people have come to endow the X film rating with a meaning it does not have, never has had, and was not intended by founders of the rating program. It is our objective that this 'No Children Under 17

Figure 13. The film that begat the NC-17 rating: *Henry & June* (1990).
Left to right: Maria de Medeiros, Fred Ward, and Uma Thurman. Courtesy of the
Academy of Motion Picture Arts and Sciences.

Admitted' category return [the X rating] to its original intent, which simply
meant that this was a film which most parents would choose to have off limits to their youngsters under 17 years of age."[136]

Many groups and individuals critical of the X (WGA, DGA, AFMA,
National Society of Film Critics, Roger Ebert, Gene Siskel, Jack Mathews,
Tom Pollock, Philip Kaufman, and many directors of the Silverlight manifesto asking for an A rating) endorsed the NC-17. Silverlight president Mark
Lipsky, however, believed—and history would soon prove him correct—that
the NC-17 would still carry a pornographic connotation.[137] The MPAA also
added five-to-ten-word explanations to its R ratings informing parents
whether films contained violence, explicit language, and sex.[138] The new rating took effect immediately and was copyrighted so that pornographers
could not unilaterally apply it to their films.

For many years, both the MPAA and NATO were reluctant to change the
X. *Henry & June* gave them little choice but to make some kind of good-
faith modification in the rating system. Some executives still wanted the original adults-only rating, as Heffner put it, because the X provided "member

companies a convenient control mechanism in their dealings with 'runaway' creative people."[139] Director Paul Schrader put it even simpler than that: "The minute [the MPAA signatories] let Phil Kaufman make an adults-only movie, then Martin Scorsese or Brian De Palma or Stanley Kubrick will want to make one too. That's the last thing in the world they want."[140] Without an ultimate rating that stood for poison or pornography, executives feared directors would resist efforts to sign contracts agreeing to deliver an R-rated movie and then take their talent to other studios, perhaps independent ones.[141] With an ultimate rating, though, the MPAA could blame its stigmatization on the media, on the public, and on the Rating Board—anyone else but its signatories—in all matters of regulation. The NC-17, it finally was decided by the MPAA, might perform the same scapegoat function for responsible entertainment, certainly more than an RR.

NATO, however, opposed an additional adults-only category altogether—be it an RR or NC-17. The major exhibition chains feared that both ratings would shift the burden of maintaining the rating system's integrity further onto them—a complaint they have similarly had in the past, prior to the establishment of CARA through the creation of the PG-13 and beyond.[142] The introduction and sustaining of the Incontestable R had greatly assisted theater owners with policing the box office for almost a decade, but an additional age-based rating, like the RR or a cleaned-up, freshly lettered X rating like the NC-17, would cause further hardship. Greater congestion at the ticket booth, increasing theater-jumping of underage kids, and renewed community pressure—not to mention possible obscenity lawsuits—could transpire with a new rating. NATO must have finally realized like the MPAA, though, that a name change to the X was the only solution to discourage further legal action against CARA and to save the rating system itself.

After all the debates, disputes, and lawsuits over the X rating in 1990, the creation of the NC-17 did not signal a change in industry policy. CARA underwent a makeover rather than an overhaul, updating the adults-only category without fundamentally changing the business model of responsible entertainment. The NC-17 essentially ignored the criticism recently directed at CARA, that sexuality is rated more severely than violence, that the line distinguishing an R film from an X film is arbitrary, that CARA is more lenient in rating MPAA-member films than those distributed by independent companies. Instead, the MPAA and NATO displaced these concerns simply onto another adults-only letter, tabling, in effect, contestation of its rating practices for another day. The MPAA and NATO, on the one hand, could appear responsive to criticism by designing a nonpornographic adults-only category that would ostensibly permit greater artistic freedom for filmmakers. On the other hand, they could still resoundingly adhere to the same practices of responsible entertainment—"free expression does not mean toleration of license"—that had guided industry behavior throughout the existence of the rating system.

The fact that it was "business as usual" can be ascertained by two industry documents from the MPAA and NATO announcing the NC-17. The MPAA press release clearly states that the name change would restore the adults-only category to its "original design," yet it also pronounces that "the criteria for films rated NC-17 . . . will continue to be evaluated as X-rated films have been in the past."[143] More revealing, though, is a column by NATO president William Kartozian in the *NATO News*. He revealed that the NC-17 was no more or less welcome or acceptable to theater owners than the X: "In our discussions with the MPAA, it was made clear that an exhibitor may very well decide that he or she may decline to play an NC-17 film just as if that same film were rated X. Such a decision would be based on the film's content and the exhibitor's judgment on whether playing that particular film is acceptable in the communities in which that exhibitor's theaters are located. Exhibitors are permanent members of these communities, and as such, recognize the value of good community relations."[144] By treating the X and NC-17 as interchangeable, NATO could maintain the same "good community relations" as before: the prohibition of the adults-only category from their theaters. All that was needed were products of responsible entertainment from the MPAA.

The MPAA signatories made no move, however, to increase NC-17 distribution after *Henry & June*. NATO exhibitors translated their existing policies against showing X films into policies barring NC-17 films. And CARA continued overseeing tentative NC-17-rated pictures being cut into R-rated entertainment. Almost instantaneously, the NC-17 rating inherited the market functions and pornographic connotations of its predecessor.

NC-17 = X

The *Hollywood Reporter*'s October 26, 1990, headline, "NC-17 Winning Acceptance as Part of American Moviegoing," was slightly premature in its forecast of the box-office prospects for NC-17 product.[145] Other observers at the time noticed, somewhat metaphorically, that the NC-17 was little more than an X in fancy dress. The *New York Times* headline for one of Janet Maslin's columns read, "Is NC-17 an X in a Clean Raincoat?"[146] A. Alan Friedberg, chairperson of the Loews theater chain and one of the few proponents of the A rating among exhibitors, remarked that "all Jack Valenti has done is change the color of paint."[147] Film critic Hal Lipper of the *St. Petersburg Times* said, "What the MPAA has done is buy a retread to replace a flat tire."[148] Martin Grove of the *Hollywood Reporter* wrote, "After all the hoopla over revising the industry's rating system, the arrival of Universal's *Henry & June,* Hollywood's first NC-17 film, seems to bear out the notion that the more things change, the more they remain the same."[149]

The truth was that despite the new rating's initial acceptance by Universal with *Henry & June,* certain groups of reformers, exploitation filmmakers, exhibitors, and media outlets would see to it that the NC-17 would eventually acquire its predecessor's pornographic stigma. Whether the MPAA or NATO desired the adults-only rating or not, the Incontestable R would remain the standard by which Hollywood governed its products.

At first, the NC-17's inconsequentiality eluded most critics, filmmakers, and distributors. Peter Rainer (National Society of Film Critics chairperson) and Jack Mathews were both wrong in suggesting that the new rating would lead to market reform. On the day following the announcement of the NC-17 Rainer said, "By creating a category that does not have the stigma of the X, it will potentially create a situation where filmmakers are now able to explore adult themes without de facto censorship."[150] Mathews wrote that "the ban on advertising for X-rated films will not apply to the NC-17 rating at major newspaper and television stations."[151] Strauss Zelnick, 20th Century Fox president and CEO, speculated that CARA "[would] apply the NC-17 a little more freely than X" because "exhibitors will be more comfortable" with the rating.[152] Russell Schwartz of Miramax applauded the MPAA's action, saying, "This leaves the X rating with the pornographers, where it belongs. It means that the system will now function as it was originally intended to."[153] Together these observers hoped that the trademarked NC-17 would remove some of the stigma associated with X product.

The poor box-office performance of *Henry & June* did not bode well for the future of the NC-17. Lukewarm reviews, advertising complications, and an $11.3-million domestic gross for the $10-million film surely did not encourage MPAA signatories to distribute more NC-17 product. As Martin A. Grove observed after *Henry & June*'s opening weekend on approximately only three hundred screens, it "was playing the way a good art film or specialized appeal film would have played with an R rating or no rating at all. Clearly [the film] wasn't suddenly attracting mainstream moviegoers."[154] To be sure, Universal missed advertising breaks in the Sunday entertainment sections and was unable to run trailers prior to *Henry & June*'s October 5 release date because of the rating controversy.[155] More important, though, the film's lack of star power, unorthodox subject matter, and art-house qualities would certainly have made attracting a sizable audience difficult, even an audience above the age of seventeen. In fact, the box-office returns might have been much lower if Cineplex Odeon—in which Universal parent company MCA owned a majority stake—had not played the film on a quarter of its opening-day screens.[156]

Concomitant with *Henry & June*'s lack of economic success and critical support was a growing antagonism against the NC-17 from the public. When the film was announced as the first NC-17 feature, some politicians treated it no differently than they did pornography. City officials in Dedham, Massachusetts, pressured a Showcase Cinemas theater to drop *Henry & June* before its scheduled opening. The chain pulled the picture from that theater shortly after being threatened with having its license canceled.[157] In Santa Ana, California, a fight erupted between a patron and demonstrator at a theater targeted for picketing.[158] The demonstrators apparently were encouraged by overtures from a Christian talk-radio station to protest *Henry & June* and the NC-17 rating in general. In the words of one picketer: "X-rated films mean NC-17 and X-rated films do not belong in the malls."[159] In Kissimmee, Florida, efforts to establish a city ordinance—the first of its kind in the nation—making it a crime to sell NC-17 tickets to children were eventually aborted, but only after direct intervention by Valenti.[160]

Most newspapers in major metropolitan cities adopted NC-17 policies like those of the *New York Times;* they would accept ads as long as they were not "prurient or offensive" and "the main focus of the film is not the sex act."[161] A few others stigmatized the NC-17 from the very beginning. The *Birmingham (AL) News* (circulation two hundred thousand) and *Sacramento Union* (circulation seventy thousand) both refused to carry ads for *Henry & June* or any film with an NC-17.[162] "We consider the *Sacramento Union* a strong family paper," said editor Joseph Farah, "and we believe accepting X-rated movie ads—whatever they're called—would be a contradiction of our image and philosophy."[163] He also rejected the argument that the NC-17 was introduced to differentiate serious adult film from pornography: "[The] NC-17 doesn't really accomplish that at all, because if I make a pornographic movie with absolutely no redeeming social qualities at all and I submit it to be rated, it will get an NC-17. So NC-17 does not imply that there is any artistic merit to the film. . . . It doesn't accomplish that purpose at all."[164] What these reports suggest is that the R rating clearly demarcated the boundary between responsible entertainment and irresponsible entertainment for these politicians and newspapers. They believed that an NC-17 stood for pornography just as plainly as the X did. It did not matter whether the rating accompanied a serious-minded fiction film or a sexually explicit, obscene one.

Farah raised two important points. First, he correctly observed that the NC-17 was more of a stopgap measure to curb the ratings controversy than a legitimate attempt by the MPAA to produce and exhibit adults-only films. Second, he understood that nothing could prevent pornographers from appropriating the rating, as long as they had a little money. Anyone could self-apply the X, but Valenti maintained that hard-core filmmakers would never seek the now-copyrighted NC-17 rating because of the costs involved in submitting a film to CARA ($800 to $8,000, depending on the budget at the time) and because of the fact that pornography had shifted almost exclusively to the home video market. Audiences did not exist anymore for theatrical porn, stated Valenti: "When you can get a [sexually explicit] video for home, why would you want to go into town and join the raincoat crowd in some seedy movie theater?"[165] NATO president William Kartozian concurred with Valenti, suggesting that it was difficult to imagine "a skin flick being promoted with a 'triple NC-17' banner."[166]

Some hard-core distributors, however, did gravitate toward the new rating in order to capitalize on the broader marketing opportunities initially made available by the NC-17. Lou Tsipouras, president of Stardusk Productions, paid the minimum $800 fee to CARA for an NC-17 for *Radio Active,* a $200,000, sixty-five-minute sexually explicit video destined for cable and pay television. He justified the expenditure by saying it would be easier to advertise, rent, and sell the film in the home video market with an NC-17 instead of a self-rated X or no rating at all.[167] For similar reasons John Parker, president of Parliament Films, sought the NC-17 for a wider theatrical release of *Blonde Emanuelle in 3-D,* a 1978 film originally titled *Disco Dolls in Hot Skin in 3-D,* starring *Penthouse* centerfold Serena. Parker admitted that "basically, the NC-17 rating is the same as the old X, only it has a nicer title."[168] The *Blonde Emanuelle* ad that ran in the *Los Angeles Times* looked a lot like ads for pornographic films that the newspaper had refused to run for many years.[169] Other little-known exploitation flicks like *Centerspread* and *Midnight Woman* also immediately "bought" the NC-17 to gain access to the mainstream commercial market.[170]

Some religious and community groups refused to make any distinction between the X and the NC-17, condemning the new rating from the start and putting pressure on distributors and exhibitors to abandon the category. The United Church of Christ, the U.S. Catholic Conference, the National Council of Churches, and the National Conference of Catholic Bishops supported a statement urging exhibitors and media outlets to ban NC-17 films. They charged that the MPAA had "caved in to the commercial interests of those who are attempting to get sexually exploitative material into general theatrical

Figure 14. Restigmatizing the adults-only rating: the November 2, 1990, ad in the *Los Angeles Times* for *Blonde Emanuelle*.

release. . . . The change is neither in the public interest nor in the best interest of the industry. . . . We call upon the MPAA to reconsider its action. It is
an arrogant and ill-advised decision which deeply affects the public good. It
was made in isolation, without public consultation."[171]

Valenti regularly consulted with religious leaders like James Wall from the
Christian Century but not in the case of the NC-17.[172] The pronouncements
of the Catholic Church, alone, have had little, if any, effect on industry practice since the demise of the Production Code.

In their fight against the NC-17, however, the churches found allies. A
coalition of religious, family, and medical organizations—tired of having
their views repeatedly ignored by the MPAA—banded together to set up a
national association of local film rating boards similar to the last local
governmental film-rating agency in Dallas, Texas.[173] This coalition, which
included the Parents and Teachers Association and Phyllis Schlafly's Eagle
Forum, protested exhibitor laxity in barring minors from R-rated films. As
Ted Baeher, a member of the coalition, said, "We saw an instant need to keep
10-year-olds out of multiplexes that were showing NC-17 films."[174] Other
members included the American Academy of Pediatrics, Women against
Pornography, and the American Family Association (AFA), a religious fam-
ily-values organization often involved with pornographic issues and media.
They came together in mid-November 1990 at a meeting called by the
National Coalition on Television Violence (NCTV), a citizen action group
focused on television violence and efforts to curb such content. The NCTV
proposed a six-tiered rating system that also carried letters for levels of violence, sexual content, drug use, racy language, nudity, perversions, and adult
situations to be attached to theatrical films and videocassettes.[175]

These protests and attempts to construct alternative rating boards crip-
pled the prospects for all NC-17 films in the theatrical marketplace as well as
home video, now an equal and sometime larger percentage of revenue for the
MPAA signatories. The AFA's boycott of Blockbuster Video, the country's
largest video chain, influenced the retailer's decision to cease renting or selling movies with the NC-17 designation.[176] For the first three months of the
rating's existence, Blockbuster did carry once-unrated, now-turned-NC-17
films such as *The Cook, the Thief, His Wife, and Her Lover* and *Tie Me Up! Tie
Me Down!* In January 1991, however, Blockbuster reversed its corporate policy. In announcing its new no-NC-17 policy, spokesperson Ron Castell
blamed the MPAA for soiling the adults-only category: "When they revised
the X rating, we said we would wait and see how they would use the new rating. But the criteria used for NC-17 was the same as the X. So we're saying that
since the NC-17 is the same criteria as the X, we're not going to carry it."[177]

Blockbuster's about-face on the NC-17 severely threatened the very survival of the category. Jack Messer, president of the Video Software Dealers Association (VSDA, the video store equivalent of the MPAA and NATO), called Blockbuster's categorical NC-17 ban "a disservice to the retail video industry," creating "an entire class of films to be unavailable to the consumers who might desire to rent them."[178] Despite his admonition, other chains expressed concerns that stocking NC-17 films would make them vulnerable to moral crusaders like the AFA, which dropped its campaign against Blockbuster in the wake of the retailer's announcement.[179] The MPAA and NATO remained relatively absent from these negotiations, voicing their only response through an anonymous MPAA spokesperson: "It could be [that] we'll see the same thing happen with NC-17 as happened with the X. Decisions in the marketplace are not something we can do anything about."[180]

And nothing is what the MPAA and NATO did, especially given the cultural climate at the end of 1990. With 350 separate obscenity bills pending in forty-five states, the uproar over funding of the National Endowment for the Arts (NEA), and the prosecution of rap group 2 Live Crew, the major distributors and exhibitors stood back from the conservative fray, realizing full well from previous experience that participating in the adults-only market brought great risk with little economic benefit.[181] As a business committed to responsible entertainment, there was little point in defending free expression or the NC-17, now or anytime.

There was, and still remains, a considerable point in defending the integrity of the other categories of CARA. The battle over the implementation of a PG-13 rating demonstrated that policing the boundaries of responsible entertainment between the PG and R are equally as necessary—although not as vital—as the boundaries between the R and the X/NC-17. *Poltergeist* and *Gremlins* did not threaten the very existence of CARA; *Scarface* and *Tie Me Up! Tie Me Down!* did. These controversies were rarities, though. The Rating Board classified on average more than five hundred films per year from 1968 to 1999, and few of them ever became limit texts.[182] As I have shown, when industry self-regulation failed, the MPAA signatories and the Appeals Board were often accountable, not the Rating Board. Heffner and his examiners created—consciously or not—a standardized aesthetic framework that regularly guaranteed most R-rated films as responsible entertainment to Hollywood's detractors. This code of production established the formal boundaries of the Incontestable R.

CHAPTER 4

The Incontestable R
as a Code of Production

We do not censor. No one who is over 17 years of age is affected by our activities. We do not judge films on artistic merit. We are not industry spokesmen. We were set up to classify films, to provide information about the content of films, so that in our absence parents would not clamor for censorship.

—Richard Heffner, *Los Angeles Herald Examiner*, Dec. 9, 1983

As we have seen, self-regulation in the classification era required the collusion and cooperation of the MPAA signatories and NATO exhibitors to adhere to an industry-wide standard that I have referred to as responsible entertainment. This standard called for the abandonment of the product line of the X/NC-17 rating by the major Hollywood distributors, as well as entrusting the negotiation of all R-rated entertainment to the Rating Board and Appeals Board of CARA. The channeling of most products into an R rating—what I have called the Incontestable R—functioned to safeguard the industry's economic and political interests. This practice of boundary maintenance staved off calls for federal regulation of motion pictures and anticipated conflicts posed by reform groups in the distribution and exhibition of individual films.

An explanation of the social and economic pressures that motivated industry self-regulation under CARA does not account, however, for the forms its products assumed. Heffner's remarks suggest that the rating system does not pass moral or artistic judgments on a film. The rating system, he says, is designed only to signal parents just where on a rating scale—from G to NC-17—a film might be appropriate for their child.[1] This is absolutely true. Still, the Rating Board's judgments, as Judge Charles Ramos made clear in the *Tie Me Up! Tie Me Down!* case, are based on the precept of the Average American Parent (AAP), a standard with which the Rating Board abides. Ratings cast by examiners based on a film's subject or theme and its treatment of sex, language, violence, and drug use might be decided by majority vote, but these votes are grounded in an ideology of entertainment shaped around American parents, particularly white middle-class parents. "We were rating for the people who were going to the ballot box and vote to have the industry censored if the ratings weren't right," Heffner said.[2]

How, then, might these concerns and pressures lead to a CARA certification, especially one over which the Rating Board and a film distributor disagree? As I mentioned in chapter 1, Lea Jacobs provides a model for analyzing the complex ways in which social conflicts and disputes surfaced in representation in fallen women films of the Production Code era. In *The Wages of Sin* Jacobs viewed the self-regulatory process as a series of narrative and formal compromises between the Studio Relations Committee/PCA and studio producers that internalized these social concerns. These negotiations, occurring before films went into production and primarily at the script stage, involved systematic, localized elements of narrative structure, character motivation, endings, and patterns of narration. Because each instance of self-regulation was a unique, individualized response, Jacobs's model allowed for variation and inconsistency from film to film and accounted for broader changes in society and the operations of external agencies.[3]

Jacobs's model of industry self-regulation as a constructive force that shapes film form and narrative still applies to CARA, but its mechanisms and strategies of boundary maintenance are completely dissimilar. Under classification the localized sense in which the regulatory operations of the SRC and PCA produced specific structures of narratives is nonexistent. There are no established rules regarding religious doctrine, morality, or "Dos and Don'ts"; CARA only examines films after their completion, placing the burden on executives, screenwriters, and directors to make films with a particular rating in mind before their submission to the Rating Board. In most cases the distributor and the Rating Board agree to the assigned rating; nothing in the film is changed. Other times, the Rating Board plays a more active role in the classification process. In order to achieve a desired rating, the distributor needs to recut (and perhaps recut again) the film to the Rating Board's satisfaction. When a compromise cannot be reached on a rating for a finished or recut film, the distributor can appeal the rating to the Appeals Board. These disputes are unavoidable, especially since Rating Board examiners never tell a filmmaker *how* specifically to cut a film, only describing in the most general terms the offending moment or scene. Without a written code of production or a hands-on approach to editing, or uniformity between the Rating Board and the Appeals Board, ratings determinations will always show inconsistencies and gaps, just as Production Code seals did when Joseph Breen and his predecessors and successors issued them.

The industry's commitment to responsible entertainment is itself an invocation of broader social forces, but the mechanisms by which these forces surface in specific rating categories cannot easily be gathered or understood. CARA is the final stop in a long line of self-regulatory strategies by producers and distributors concerning the handling of various representations and issues. Files and ballots concerning CARA's operations were unavailable to researchers until Heffner made available his oral history and correspondence for study. What these papers reveal, particularly in the case of limit texts involving the boundary between R and X (or NC-17), are the specific scenes, if not shots, that crossed over into NC-17 territory only to come back to the terrain of the Incontestable R after a negotiation process with the Rating Board. Sometimes these scenes or shots remained intact, if a distributor won an appeal through the Appeals Board.

These acts of boundary maintenance, though different in procedure and philosophy from the PCA, clearly show the constructive role that CARA plays in shaping film form and narrative in the R rating. Rating Board examiners may not "arrange" an NC-17 film into an Incontestable R, but its majority consensus to a distributor's edited cut of a film involves the same strategic forethought of public offense used by the second PCA in assessing threats to the MPAA's economic and political interests. For a film to ultimately receive an R by the Rating Board is not simply a matter of a distributor's eliminating the offending content—although this does happen, and sometimes it entails only a few seconds. The restructuring of a film by a distributor also involves "speculating" what might be considered an aesthetic of responsible entertainment by the Rating Board at certain historical moments. Supplementing and rearranging footage, changing camera angle and distance, and replacing dialogue—in addition to deleting material—are some of the particular textual practices and configurations that guide an instance of regulation by a distributor in the classification era. These acts of accommodation allow us to consider boundary maintenance under CARA as a prohibitive and productive process like the PCA, as something that is not only done to texts but something that also creates and shapes texts, ideologies, and meanings.

The availability of R, NC-17, and/or unrated versions of the same films enables us to reconstruct this process of self-regulation. Different versions represent the original cuts submitted to the Rating Board and the final cuts released into U.S. theaters. This chapter analyzes these versions alongside press accounts, personal interviews, and Heffner's papers to provide an entryway into a conceptualization of responsible entertainment shared by the Rating Board and distributors at certain historical junctures. Where the treatment of sex and nudity are concerned—two of the criteria on the Rating Board's evaluation sheet—a set of remarkably consistent stylistic constraints and conventions emerges, which govern the threshold of the Incontestable R between 1992 and 1997.

To suggest that the Rating Board abides by a kind of "production code" during this time frame, I will first examine the general operations of CARA, discussed in part throughout this book but here presented in a comprehensive manner. The day-to-day activities of the Rating Board have generally remained the same for almost forty years, but nuances of policy, representation, and membership shift with administrations, making it difficult to verify that my account is completely and currently accurate. I have tried to provide the most up-to-date information, which has become increasingly scarce since Heffner left office in 1994. Next I will perform a case study of *Basic Instinct*, one of the most notorious limit texts in the history of the rating system. This account will permit us to reconstruct an instance of film regulation under CARA as a complex network of explicit and implicit norms of the Rating Board combined with stylistic choices made on the basis of pure guesswork by the filmmaker or distributor. Finally, I will analyze the various versions of several films released after *Basic Instinct* to argue for the institutionalization of certain representational codes governing sex and nudity that remained impermissible for an R rating. I will show that the line between an R and NC-17 is much more obvious and consistent than commonly believed, for either MPAA-member or independently distributed films.

How CARA Works

The Classification and Rating Administration, known as the Code and Rating Administration until 1977, operates under the jurisdiction of the Motion Picture Association of America, a Hollywood trade organization that engages in collecting royalties, detecting and eliminating film piracy, and negotiating international film treaties for its members.[4] The MPAA is funded almost entirely by fees paid by six members, the major distribution companies in 2007: Paramount Pictures Corporation; Sony Pictures Entertainment, Inc.; 20th Century Fox Film Corporation; Universal City Studios LLLP; Buena Vista Pictures Distribution (Walt Disney); and Warner Bros. Entertainment, Inc.[5] Located in Sherman Oaks, California, CARA consists of two separate arms: the Rating Board and the Appeals Board. CARA's funding comes from fees charged to producers and distributors for the rating of their films. As of 1999 these fees ranged from $2,000 to $10,000, depending on the acquisition cost of the film, the gross revenue of the submitter for the previous fiscal year, and whether the submitter was involved in the film's financing.[6] The Advertising Administration, which oversees all advertisements and press materials for rated motion pictures, is officially part of the MPAA, not of CARA.

MPAA chief executive officer Dan Glickman (2004–present) oversees CARA, as did previous MPAA president Jack Valenti (1966–2004), and selects the chairperson of the Rating Board.[7] In the CARA era these chairpersons have been Eugene Dougherty (1968–1970), Aaron Stern (1970–1974), Richard Heffner (1974–1994), Richard Mosk (1994–2000), and Joan Graves (cochair 1997–2000, chair 2000–present). The Rating Board is composed of eight to thirteen full-time and part-time salaried people hired to serve three-to-five-year terms and headed and selected by the chairperson. The Rating Board members are mainly parents (raising children currently or having raised them in the past). In only a few instances have their identities been disclosed to the public, the most recent instance occurring in Kirby Dick's documentary *This Film Is Not Yet Rated* (2006).[8]

Rating Board executives watch three, sometimes four, films each day. Although there is no official quorum, under Heffner's administration no ruling on a film had been carried by less than five or six people.[9] After each film viewing the members complete "green" ballots, spelling out their reasons for the rating according to the following criteria: subject or theme and the treatment of language, violence, sex and/or nudity, and other (for example, drug use).[10] The examiners ask themselves the same question for each criterion: "Is the rating I am about to apply one that most parents in America would find accurate?"[11] The Rating Board then gives the film an overall rating based on these assessments. Each rating is decided by a majority vote. The producer or distributor has the right to inquire about the reasons for the rating and can choose to try for a less severe rating by editing the film. The reedited film goes back to the Rating Board and the process begins again. The MPAA president officially takes no part in rating decisions. Except in very special circumstances like the *Tie Me Up! Tie Me Down!* affair, Heffner always stuck to protocol with the Rating Board.

If producers or distributors are displeased with the rating given by the Rating Board, they can appeal the decision to the Appeals Board, which moved from New York to Los Angeles in 1993. The Appeals Board is composed of eighteen to twenty-four individuals, including the president of the MPAA plus one representative from each MPAA member; exhibitor representatives designated by NATO, equal to the number of MPAA-member representatives; and no more than four independent distributors, periodically determined by the Policy Review Committee (made up of MPAA and NATO members of CARA), who agree in writing to submit all their films to CARA.[12] After screening the film, the appellant explains why he or she believes the rating was wrongly assigned and suggests a less-restrictive one; this person may offer the oral testimony of two witnesses. CARA's chairperson then states the reasons for the film's rating, and the producer has an opportunity to rebut. After excusing the two opposing representatives from the room, the Appeals Board discusses the hearing and, in a secret ballot, votes to uphold or overturn the rating; a two-thirds vote of those present is required to overturn the rating. The Appeals Board's decision is final, although it has the authority to grant a rehearing at the producer's request. If the producer is still not satisfied, he or she can release the picture unrated. As I demonstrated in chapters 2 and 3, these rules are not steadfast, especially when the rating of one of the MPAA-member companies is at stake. Roughly 920 movies were reviewed by the Rating Board in 2005; eight of these were appealed, and two were overturned.[13]

In addition to submitting a film for a rating, all written and visual materials for rated motion pictures must be submitted to the Advertising Administration. This includes theatrical and home video trailers, print ads, radio and TV spots, press books, and videocassette packaging. In order to assure parents that children will not be seeing a trailer with R or NC-17 material in it, most trailers are approved for "all audiences," meaning that no scenes in it would be rated higher than a G. These "all audiences" trailers carry a leader with a green background for the projectionist, describing the rating of the film advertised, and a green band encircling the trailer reel. Other trailers are approved for "restricted audiences" because of their content. Their use is limited to films rated R or NC-17. The leader for "restricted" trailers has a red background, and the reel has a red band to alert projectionists so that they do not show the wrong trailer with the wrong picture. Trailers, says Bethlyn Hand, former head of the Advertising Administration, are disapproved by her staff of four mothers "nine out of ten times" the first time around. "I don't want anyone to be offended by what we approve here," remarked Hand at her retirement in 2003 after twenty-seven years of MPAA service. "Parents are very protective of what they did not select for their kids to see. And with a trailer, you're a captive audience."[14]

As of this writing the public faces of CARA are Glickman and Graves, who unlike Heffner, are quite closemouthed about the inner workings of the rating system. Their remarks mirror those of Valenti, litanies of half-truths and pretenses that conceal the economic and political motivations behind CARA's operations. For example, Valenti often noted that CARA has one sole mission: to give advanced cautionary warnings to parents so they can make responsible decisions about the moviegoing of their children. "We serve parents of America. We do not serve producers, distributors, or film critics." He also commonly said that the Rating Board, unlike its predecessor, the Production Code Administration, does not rate the quality of a film: "There are no dos and don'ts. It doesn't place values, good *or* bad, on the picture." When we compare these statements to those of Glickman and Graves, they may well have been spoken by Valenti himself. Glickman said, "The underlying purpose is not to censor [films]. It's to give a rating that parents will understand and [use to] properly guide their children." And Graves, when asked about the NC-17 awarded to Atom Egoyan's *Where the Truth Lies* (2005), remarked, "What we're supposed to do is rate the film the way we think most American parents would rate it. We're supposed to reflect standards, not set them. Our board believes that most parents would think it's in the adult category."[15]

By releasing few details regarding individual rating decisions and denying access to its internal documents and memos, CARA continues to operate in a shroud of secrecy over the standards of its categories. Heffner's oral history and papers at Columbia University stop at 1994. Otherwise, not much is publicly known about CARA's rating guidelines and practices since that time. What is commonly presumed is that the Rating Board follows a language rule and a drug-use rule. With language a single occurrence of any of the "harsher, sexually derived words" guarantees at least a PG-13 rating, even if the word is used as an expletive. If this word is used more than once as an expletive or once in a sexual manner, the picture gets an R. Heffner explained the difference as " 'Oh f[uck]!' " versus " 'I want to f[uck] you.' " Director Albert Brooks puts it more crudely: "If you say, 'I'm going to fuck you over,' that's a PG-13. If you say, 'I'm going to fuck you over the desk,' that's an R."[16] A two-thirds-majority vote by the Rating Board can, however, give a lesser rating to a film containing the word *fuck*, if the examiners believe it to be more appropriate. Any drug-use reference also guarantees a film at least a PG-13, with a three-quarter majority of the Rating Board needed to overturn it. Short as this list of rules might be, they still provide some insight into the negotiation of responsible entertainment at the level of dialogue.

In these instances films generally earn an automatic rating. The majority of ratings deliberations, however—especially those involving sex, nudity, violence, and mature themes—are made on a combination of quantitative and qualitative grounds, what Heffner has called the "treatment" of subject matter. Rating Board examiners may not intentionally judge how "good" or "bad" a movie is, but they do apply a standard for rating categories that is dependent on interpretation. Questions such as "Is this film too mature for kids under 13?" or "Might parents find this kind of violence too upsetting for a child without adult supervision?" or "Do certain sexual images warrant an NC-17?" all involve subjective assessments that emerge from the formal and narrative treatment of these issues. "We're not dealing with Euclidean geometry here" was Valenti's oft-repeated rejoinder to accusations of bias toward certain kinds of entertainment by CARA. "It is a group of parents making a judgment."[17]

Nevertheless, rating criteria predicated on subjective levels of suitability for children are still grounded in industry assumptions over a set of cultural values shared by its audience. These assumed values or "national mores," as William Paul suggests, always involve issues of morality, ethicality, and ideology, leaving them inadvertently open to criticism. "Whose mores determine the national mores?" he queries. "The point is that no code to govern the content of art can ever be value neutral. The values of a specific class at a specific time inform every aspect of the Production Code that began to be stringently enforced in 1934. From a contemporary viewpoint, this is most forcefully clear in the Code's ban on miscegenation as subject matter for a movie."[18] Discreet treatment of miscegenation was eventually allowed in the Code's 1956 revision, and then all mention of the term was expunged from the 1966 Code of Self-Regulation. CARA, of course, never followed the rest of the PCA's regulatory conceptions for harmless entertainment, but the Rating Board's still functioned according to an unidentified and nebulous cluster of national mores thresholds soon to be institutionalized as responsible entertainment under the Heffner administration. Boundary maintenance of the Incontestable R filtered out those images, words, and themes found objectionable or inappropriate for Hollywood entertainment by the Average American Parent (as Ramos suggested) or the white middle-class audiences who might vote at the "ballot box" to have the industry "censored" (as Heffner suggested). These assumptions were certainly not "value neutral" as they helped to distinguish an R rating from an X/NC-17 for Rating Board examiners.

How CARA articulated the social values associated with responsible entertainment in its rating policies and practices for the R/X boundary can best be seen by the accusations perennially made by critics and filmmakers about the Rating Board's lenient approach to violence in comparison to sexual matters. As early as 1969, Arthur Knight noticed that "incest, regicide, and self-mutilation," in the G-rated, ancient Greek tragedy *Oedipus the King*, "are apparently 'acceptable for all audiences, without consideration of age'—so long as they take place off screen and there are no nude scenes." Two decades later, the same cry was heard from critics. Sam Frank states, "The [Rating B]oard's double standards are blatant. Explicit acts of nonstop murder are acceptable in an R movie but explicit sex acts are not." Richard Corliss believes that the system "punishes eroticism with an X rating, yet rewards violence—from rape to dismemberment—with an R." Many movie directors concur with this assessment. Phillip Noyce believes that the Rating Board is "far more lenient about acts that end life than those that engender it." Philip Kaufman says, "You can cut off a breast, but you can't caress it." Jean-Jacques Annaud claims, "There is too much violence—heads are chopped off and it's still an R. But to take the girl you love to bed is wrong. Why the hypocrisy?"[19]

Valenti, whose public declarations about the rating system were often specious and inaccurate, responded to such claims in a candid and logical manner that bore out some of the mores of responsible entertainment. He said that CARA treated violence less severely than sex partly because violence is more difficult to classify and qualify than sex and partly because Americans are more offended by sex than violence.[20] "What is too much violence? Is John Wayne at Iwo Jima killing a thousand Japanese more violent than the Boston Strangler?" Valenti mused. "But with sex—there's nudity and you know what it is. There is also a deeply ingrained Puritan ethic in this country, and people who are uptight about these things tend to be more uptight about sex than violence, although violence is very much monitored by the rating system." In this oft-repeated adage Valenti described the system of boundary maintenance under classification, one of an ongoing determination of the dividing line between "too much" and "all right" for each category so that "people who are uptight" cannot find fault with Hollywood's products. To stave off those "uptight" politicians and moral reformers, Valenti sometimes offered a few insights about the way in which CARA arrives at its decisions for violence: "The intensity, graphic depiction, and accumulation of the problem play a role in how severely the film will be rated," he said. One hit in the face might qualify for a PG, "but if that man is hit 10 times in the face and blood is shown all over, then that film is probably at least a sure PG-13."[21]

Without production guidelines for specific categories, especially when an R rating is at stake, filmmakers are oftentimes shocked and angry by what they believe is an undeserved NC-17 being assigned to their film. When the Rating Board informs a filmmaker that his or her film is "too much" for an R, examiners never describe how to cut its violence or sex down to the lower rating. Editing a film thus becomes a guessing game, claims one producer, who was given an NC-17 because "the film just feels too sexy." "I'm forced to cut my movie, but I have no parameters," he said. "The guidelines for each rating are one paragraph long, no specifics. If they'd just say, 'four fucks,

Figure 15. Prelude to the "explicit sexual content" in the NC-17-rated *The Dreamers* (2004).

two goddamns and one motherfucker is an R,' at least I'd know what to cut."[22] In certain instances CARA identifies the precise scene that elicited an NC-17 but still refrains from providing specific editing advice. "We never tell a director what he or she can or cannot put into a film," says Richard Heffner. "We refuse to be editors. . . . If a director doesn't like the rating we give, he is welcome to bring us another version. We will look at it and change the rating or not, according to what we see. Or he can go to the appeal board."[23]

CARA's brief explanations for its R and NC-17 ratings provide us no more clarification to the Rating Board's distinctions between an R and an NC-17. For example, the Rating Board rated two versions of *The Dreamers* (2004), an NC-17 version for theatrical and video release and an R version strictly for video release. Its explanation for the ratings—an NC-17 for "explicit sexual content" and an R for "strong sexual content and graphic nudity, language and some drug use"—alone reveal little.[24] The differentiation, however, between "explicit" and "strong" sexual content in the two explanations clearly suggests a norm does exist between the R and the NC-17, one the Rating Board must make aesthetic valuations on.

The secrecy of the industry's self-regulatory operations made it quite difficult for journalists and researchers to determine CARA's methodologies, thought patterns, and biases behind the Incontestable R for some time. A filmmaker's presumptions of CARA's inconsistent and arbitrary decisions that occasionally emerged in the trade and popular press offered the only insights into the formal norms and conventions of the Incontestable R. Fortunately, the growth and profitability of the home video market has led to the availability of various rated and unrated versions of films on video, laser disc, and DVD to help us analyze the differences between the R and NC-17 ratings. Accompanying the original versions in the video marketplace are (1) unrated director's cuts of theatrical R-rated films, (2) R-rated versions of NC-17 and unrated films, and (3) uncut foreign releases of R-rated films. Often supplementing the films are interviews, trailers, and separate audio tracks with filmmaker commentary that contain discussion of the rating process and the negotiations that took place between the filmmaker and the Rating Board to earn the picture an R rating.

Now, with the availability of Richard Heffner's oral history, papers, and memoranda, primary evidence from the Rating Board's perspective sheds great light on the distinctions between the R and the NC-17. For instance, the seven "green ballots" for *Tie Me Up! Tie Me Down!* reveal each examiner's reasons behind the rating they applied to five different criteria in the film, as well as to the reason each gives for the film's general rating. A breakdown of the ratings is as follows for this pre-NC-17 classification film: four PGs and three PG-13s for subject or theme; seven Xs for sex and/or nudity; six Rs and one X for language; one PG, two PG-13s, and four Rs for violence; and six Rs and one X for other (which is almost always drug use). All the examiners awarded the film on the whole an X. Specifically, this is one examiner's account of the sex and/or nudity in the film:

> Very graphic sexual scene between Marina and Ricky, reel 4-1000; view from her head down as nude on bed, he on top and she says "I'll put it in"; see her hand go down by his crotch as she directs him inside her; graphic thrusting begins followed by graphic side view full length[,] her legs in air[,] he thrusting, loud sexual sounds—1042—followed by graphic aerial views that are seen in side by side mirrors on ceiling[,] of full length his bare rear thrusting between her legs, just like real life—1097—continues with closer views as she asks him not to "take it out" in shoulders and faces only view as they sit facing each other engaged.[25]

Even though no R-rated cut of *Tie Me Up! Tie Me Down!* exists outside of Almodóvar's original version, these green ballots—the only ones in the Heffner files besides *Star Wars* (1977)—illustrate some of the red flags in representations of sex and nudity that are problematic to the Rating Board. "Full

Figure 16. A tentative NC-17 for language: Big Gay Al and friends in *South Park: Bigger, Longer & Uncut* (1999). Copyright 1999 Warner Bros.

length" (full shots, or the entire body, in the film frame), "bare rear thrusting" (onscreen pelvic movement during sex), and verbal references to "putting it in" and "taking it out" (insertion and withdrawal of the penis) are all formal elements that differentiate between the R and NC-17 versions of the same film, giving credence to Valenti's claim that "nudity itself is not automatic grounds for an R rating. It depends how sensuous the scene is."[26]

The rest of this chapter focuses on the sex and/or nudity criterion of CARA's rating system in cases involving the R and NC-17 boundary. Most films reported in the press and made available in alternative versions on video dealt almost exclusively with these two issues. A few notable cases since 1990 did involve language (*You So Crazy* [1994]; *Clerks* [1994]; *South Park: Bigger, Longer, & Uncut* [1999]), theme (*Kids* [1995]; *Happiness* [1998]; *A Dirty Shame* [2004]), and violence (*Natural Born Killers* [1994], *Kill Bill Vol. 1* [2003]). My focus, however, on controversial films concerning sex and nudity does not mean to suggest that other Rating Board criteria are applied inconsistently at the classification stage. Heffner recollects that most appeals actually dealt with violence rather than sex because distributors "sort of expected sex to get an X." A breakdown by rating criteria of the number of tentative X ratings awarded by the Rating Board and the number of appeals heard by the Appeals

Board is unavailable, but I would suspect that distributors were less reluctant to market controversy over X-rated violence and language than sex because of the potential for greater public outcry.[27] Hollywood's audiences—and subsequently Hollywood's products—have historically been more tolerant of violence than sex; the Production Code, as Stephen Prince has demonstrated, permitted greater stylization of violence than the erotic.[28] Additionally, obscenity laws in the United States—undoubtedly related to the country's Puritan streak and justification for violence—exclusively involve instances of sexual conduct. Exhibitors cannot be prosecuted for graphic violence, so there is less necessity to regulate its representation than sex and nudity.

By analyzing press accounts, different film versions, and Heffner's papers one can provide strong evidence for the uppermost formal boundaries of the Incontestable R at particular historical moments. These resources make it possible to confirm and debunk, to separate truth from hype, many published reports of CARA that circulated false or misleading information about the rating system as a result of Valenti's stranglehold on media communication. These resources also help to reveal the constructive nature of film regulation under CARA, a process less like the collaboration between the studios and the PCA in the *arrangement* of content for a seal, and more like the *speculative* delivery of content for a specific rating by filmmakers in an ongoing process of *negotiation* with the Rating Board. *Basic Instinct* provides the most detailed and comprehensive account of this system of industry self-regulation at work.

Basic Instinct and the Incontestable R

The stigmatization and abandonment of the X/NC-17 by the mid-1970s compelled the Rating Board to devise formal strategies for the uppermost echelons of the Incontestable R—commonly referred to as a "hard R"—in order to effectively police the boundaries of responsible entertainment for the MPAA and NATO. Critics incessantly berated CARA for this practice—of imposing artistic constraints on filmmakers—but the Rating Board was just simply following orders: all the MPAA signatories and many of the independent distributors wanted to avoid the X/NC-17. Valenti's standard response to accusations of "censorship" from critics and filmmakers is certainly valid: "I can't ask or force an exhibitor to do anything, and I can't ask or force a director to cut one bit of film. Whatever he does on an economic basis is up to him." On the other hand, *New York Times* film critic Vincent Canby is equally justified in remarking that the system is not truly "voluntary": "A producer can 'volunteer' to have his film remain undistributed, unadvertised and unplayed, if he refuses to make the 'required cuts' to get an R rating."[29]

Both men's comments belie the real truth of "volunteerism" and the rating system. The MPAA signatories control venturesome talent by forcing them to sign R contracts as much as artists knowingly sign R contracts in exchange for their films' distribution by MPAA signatories. Responsible entertainment comes with a price tag as well as an aesthetic. CARA, in a way, just helps filmmakers fulfill their contractual obligations. Some directors, like Paul Schrader, find these compromises, grounded in the political and economic motives of the MPAA and NATO, appalling. "This means that usually you make the movie you want, and show it to the ratings board. And they say that and this is a problem, and you change it, to get an R. So they're saying that they're not censoring anyone, but what's happening is that you have to censor yourself, and then you come back to the board, and they may imply, 'You haven't censored yourself enough.'"[30] Others, like Paul Verhoeven, believe that cutting a film down to an R rating is a condition of working in Hollywood, where one always has to balance artistic aspiration with industrial economics: "If you want to be in this business, you have to realize that people, companies[,] are investing money and are dependent on the success of the movie in order to survive." Consider *Basic Instinct,* he says. "The movie cost $45 million, so you cannot say 'fuck you all.'"[31]

Verhoeven was contractually obligated to deliver an R on *Basic Instinct* to TriStar (a division of Columbia and owned by MPAA member Sony), a stipulation that he was quite accustomed to at the time. Each one of the Dutch director's previous U.S. pictures—*Flesh + Blood* (1985), *RoboCop* (1987), and *Total Recall* (1990)—earned a tentative X from the Rating Board before being cut down to an R. *Basic Instinct* went through the same editing process, just with more notoriety. Together with *Cruising, Scarface,* and later *Natural Born Killers,* it was one of the most controversial films that the Rating Board faced under Heffner.[32]

Like any limit text, *Basic Instinct* stirred intense discussion and gossip, especially over its graphic sex scenes, almost eighteen months before the film's March 1992 opening. In August 1990 the *Los Angeles Times* reported that writer Joe Eszterhas and producer Irwin Winkler left the film because Verhoeven wanted to have explicit heterosexual and homosexual sex scenes with frontal nudity.[33] Reports such as these generated tremendous publicity and buildup for *Basic Instinct,* much of it already discussed elsewhere. In *The New Censors* Charles Lyons provides a lengthy account of the social protests during the film's production and release. Outrage from the political Left (National Organization of Women and Queer Nation), protesting the film's misogyny and homophobia, and the Right (Cardinal Roger M. Mahony), publicly calling for an updated Production Code, put CARA in the center of debate over various lifestyle issues. Stephen Vaughn presents a history of the film's publicity manipulated by the press, TriStar, Carolco (the financier), Eszterhas, Michael Douglas, Sharon Stone, and Verhoeven.[34] Even though he knew he had to cut *Basic Instinct* for an R, Verhoeven still intended to push the limits of the rating system. The challenge for him with *Basic Instinct*, he said, was to see how far he could go in the United States with a major star like Michael Douglas. Stone even coyly attested to its probable rating showdown. "Michael Douglas and I went as far as *anyone* could go. So far in fact, that I don't know how they'll *ever* get a rating."[35]

From its unanimous NC-17 by Rating Board examiners (including Heffner) in mid-November 1991 until its R certification in February 2002, *Basic Instinct* went through the most arduous, if not the longest, negotiation process for an R rating ever at CARA. Ultimately, the Rating Board had no choice but to give the picture an R; Verhoeven was contractually obligated to deliver one, and TriStar would not release the film with an NC-17. The distributor would submit the film to CARA if it had to, even without Verhoeven's permission, until it got the lower rating. As Richard Heffner recalled about the negotiation process, *Basic Instinct* was "never going to [get] anything other than a hard R. But we would, as we did with all films, try to help these bastards enable us *responsibly* to give it an R rather than NC-17."[36]

The ensuing rating struggle dealt with five specific scenes involving explicit sex and graphic violence: the ice-pick murder that opens the film, the anal sex scene between Douglas and Jeanne Tripplehorn,[37] the so-called "fuck of the century" scene between Douglas and Stone, the elevator murder of George Dzundza, and the closing sex scene between Douglas and Stone.[38] After the first screening of *Basic Instinct*, the Rating Board made Carolco and Verhoeven aware of these problematic scenes. Verhoeven confirms this, stating that he knew *what* to edit for an R, just not *how* to edit:

> They said we have problems with the violence in the first act and in the scene of the stabbing. Then we have a problem in the fifth reel, and we have a problem in reel seven, etc. I think they had problems in four or five reels altogether. With the big love scene between Sharon and Michael, they simply said it was too long and too strong. They didn't say that shot or this shot. In fact, we tried to get them to be more specific, but they said, "We won't tell you; we're not going to cut your movie. You cut your movie; you give us something we can accept. All we can tell you is that it's too long and too strong."[39]

Of no NC-17 concern was the infamous interrogation scene of Stone in the police station where she crosses her legs and presumably reveals her vaginal area. Yet the press reported it, erroneously, as one of the major stumbling blocks of the NC-17.[40]

Over the course of eight edited submissions to earn an R, Verhoeven said the Rating Board objected to the film's overabundance of nudity, sexual grinding (rotation of the pelvises in the act of sexual intercourse), and explicit sex and violence.[41] The director replaced shots with alternative ones, omitted others, or reduced in length images of oral sex, violent lovemaking, multiple stabbings, and sexual grinding he believed to be NC-17 in nature. His speculation was dutifully and mutually noted in a weekly ratings-pending report prepared by then-examiner Joan Graves that summarized the history of *Basic Instinct*'s negotiation with the Rating Board up to its penultimate edit.[42] This report, analyzed alongside the unrated (NC-17 first cut) and R-rated (final cut) versions of the film, unveils a revealing portrait of the regulatory process, one in which Heffner and Graves uncharacteristically gave editing details to Carolco and Verhoeven and in which the Rating Board reviewed individual scenes.[43] First, the ratings-pending report undeniably demonstrates the Rating Board's awareness and approval of a director's aesthetic choices as he or she progresses toward an Incontestable R. Second, it unmasks the formal norms and conventions of the Incontestable R that the Rating Board would implement and systematize for the treatment of sex and nudity for the next several years. To prove these claims, I will discuss the alterations in the formal and narrative design of the three most problematic scenes in *Basic Instinct*—the initial ice-pick murder, anal sex, and "fuck of the century" scenes—before applying these findings to subsequent films.[44]

In the NC-17 ice-pick murder scene, in which a nude blonde (a concealed Stone) stabs her lover to death, the Rating Board objected to "full body shots" of Stone stabbing the man and full body shots of Stone astride him and "grinding away" on him from both rear and side views. The R version eliminates graphic long shots of stabbing, of torn flesh, and splattering blood, as well as reduces the number of stabs visibly entering the body from six to one (two stabs were still too much for the Rating Board). The reduction of sexual grinding has also been reduced to "two revolving motions" to the satisfaction of the examiners.

In the NC-17 anal sex scene, the Rating Board objected to the "violent lovemaking and rear entry portion" after Douglas throws Tripplehorn against a couch in an act of rage. The R version suggests rough sex instead of rape, as the entire section of the scene from the "point at which he rips off her panties" to Douglas collapsing on top of her has been eliminated. The result

Figure 17. Responsible entertainment and the medium shot of missionary sex: Michael Douglas and Sharon Stone in *Basic Instinct* (1992). Courtesy of the Academy of Motion Picture Arts and Sciences.

is an extremely awkward jump cut. The shots removed are Douglas dropping his pants (revealing his bare behind) and entering Tripplehorn from behind (removing the inference of anal sex) as she protests, "No, please, no, ow!"; three-quarter shots of grinding, close-ups of Tripplehorn's pain/pleasure; and Douglas's orgasm.[45]

The NC-17 "fuck of the century" scene between Douglas and Stone after their sexual foreplay at a nightclub was the most troublesome to the Rating Board. Graves told Carolco that "the only areas that could be eliminated as a problem were those of head and shoulders only." Several shots were of great concern to the Rating Board: a "side view of [Douglas's] penis as he mounts her," full body shots of Douglas "thrusting" into Stone, full body shots of Stone sitting "astride" Douglas and grinding (where one can see her rear), and "one view from the headboard in which you could see down her body including the pubic hair." The R version dramatically shortens the sex scenes, removing the close-up of cunnilingus, a long shot of fellatio, a shot of Stone's erect nipples, and any evidence of pubic hair during the sex act. Full body shots of sexual thrusting and grinding have been reduced in number, sometimes replaced with a close-up of a face. Douglas's penis was covered by an "optical." The obscured ceiling-mirror long shot of Stone giving oral sex to Douglas has been shortened from approximately three and a half seconds to two seconds.

The lengthy negotiation over the many NC-17 submissions of *Basic Instinct* reveal that murder, homosexuality, nudity, and sexual behavior were not taboo in and of themselves: their methods of treatment were. In other words, the means by which Verhoeven narratively presented and stylized these subjects originally did not meet the standards of the Incontestable R. Yet the process of recutting the film and negotiations with the Rating Board lays bare what these treatments may entail. They include full body shots of fornication; prolonged sexual thrusting or grinding; onscreen imagery of anal sex or oral sex, and the visibility of pubic hair or the penis during a sexual act; and knives physically penetrating the body.

In total this speculation and negotiation, according to Verhoeven, amounted to a final cut of *Basic Instinct* that was forty-two seconds shorter than its uncut European counterpart: twenty-two seconds were cuts, and twenty seconds were replaced with closer or wider shots of the same take.[46] During the production process Verhoeven assured himself that he would have sufficient material on the editing table to work with in cutting the film from an NC-17. He knew from prior experience, especially in regard to sex and nudity, what qualified for an R rating:

> All the sex scenes in *Basic Instinct* were shot from a lot of different angles. We realized during the shooting that some of the angles, especially the one when Michael is between Sharon's legs and licking her vagina, would not be acceptable. Even when we looked at it in the replay because we were shooting simultaneously with video, we were all really laughing. . . . We knew we would never get away with that. But we went as far as we could, although each time I felt there could be a problem with the MPAA, I shot further away, from another angle, with a different light or whatever, so I had a lot of different possibilities. And so the MPAA could not force me to cut things out. I always offered them another solution that was less explicit without changing the scene. So if you compare the NC-17 to the R-rated version in terms of running time, they're not very different but their intensity is different.[47]

"For every close-up," added Verhoeven biographer Rob van Scheers, "[Verhoeven] also took a medium one just in case, and for every medium shot he also recorded a wide shot."[48] Verhoeven's awareness of the formal strategies to earn an R rating not only points to his familiarity with the boundaries of sex and nudity between the R and the NC-17. It also suggests that definite stylistic standards operate on a consistent basis with the Rating Board and that its "production code" can be cracked by a savvy director.

Basic Instinct, I will demonstrate, adhered to the same sex and nudity norms for an R by the Rating Board as other films of its time. The Rating Board may have allowed *Basic Instinct* to touch the outermost boundaries of the Incontestable R, but it certainly did not allow the film to cross them. Despite the film's R rating, though, many critics still believed *Basic Instinct* exemplified CARA's arbitrary practices and favoritism toward the MPAA. David Ansen wrote in *Newsweek:* "Why does the ratings board consider [*Basic Instinct*] an R movie and deem *Henry & June* NC-17? Only one answer suggests itself: explicit eroticism is OK if accompanied by hostility and muti- lated flesh, but God save our children from the sight of two undressed people up on screen giving each other simple pleasure." John Hartl of the *Seattle Times* wrote that the R rating for *Basic Instinct* "suggests that the rat- ings board can be worn down, especially by a studio with a $50 million investment."[49] These remarks surely exhibit the kinds of misunderstanding and confusion over the policies of the Rating Board discussed throughout this book, no doubt caused by Valenti's veil of secrecy on the rating system. Even so, these critics and many other viewers found *Basic Instinct*'s R rating "contestable." Why?

One reason for this accusation clearly lies in Carolco's game-playing and dishonesty with the Rating Board. The financier screened the unexpurgated version of *Basic Instinct,* not the R-rated one, for critics with the MPAA seal and certificate number attached to it.[50] Even if Janet Maslin's scathing review in the *New York Times* comes from an NC-17 screening of the film, her remark—"the altering of several explicit images does not significantly change the film's overall *tenor*"—points to a stronger explanation for *Basic Instinct*'s notoriety.[51] The film's overall tenor or *tone*—as the term is frequently em- ployed in this book and elsewhere—still felt NC-17-ish to many viewers.

Of the many definitions of *tone* offered by the *Oxford English Dictionary,* those most pertinent to the concerns of regulators are (1) a state or temper of mind; mood, disposition; (2) a special or characteristic style or tendency of thought, feeling, behaviour, etc.; spirit, character, tenor; esp. the general or prevailing state of morals or manners in a society or community.[52] When applied to cinema, tone reflects the attitude or atmosphere of a film and the feeling or sensation experienced by a viewer. How exactly a film communi- cates this frame of mind for different users—through style, performance, narrative—is difficult to determine. We have seen Rating Board examiners, film critics, and other consumers of motion pictures use words like *graphic, explicit, strong,* and *intense* to describe films whose tone either adheres to or transgresses an assigned CARA rating. For the Rating Board, however, an *interpretation* of a film's tone always carries with it a qualitative *evaluation* of the film's tone as well. This interpretation or evaluation is predicated on the MPAA's commitment to responsible entertainment and a film's projection as responsible entertainment to audiences, especially when an NC-17 is at stake.

In fact, "tone" provides a common denominator between the PCA and CARA, between harmless entertainment and responsible entertainment. Lea Jacobs discussed tone as an important concern of Joseph Breen's in managing potentially offensive material after 1934. Tone involved signifiers beyond the level of dialogue and action—nonverbal elements such as set design, camera movement, music, lighting, performance, and costuming—that could render an individual scene or entire film objectionable and in violation of the Production Code. As discussed in chapter 1, *Baby Face* (1933) emphasized these visual elements to undercut the narrative logic of sin, guilt, and redemption of the fallen woman genre, whereas *Anna Karenina* (1935) employed these elements in support of these generic norms. Since tone required more interpretative work than plot analysis or characterization in analyzing a scene's potential "harmfulness," Breen increased his office staff in 1934 to more thoroughly negotiate revisions with producers over these nonverbal aspects. We can comprehend these more "extensive elaborations" of the Production Code's moral principles as tonal "checkpoints," ensuring unity of harmless entertainment every step of the way.[53]

The systematic activity of monitoring shifts in tone—as well as arranging other formal and narrative elements at the production level—did not migrate from the PCA to CARA. Filmmakers and distributors prepared their films for classification outside the regulatory apparatus of CARA. When the film finally arrived at CARA after postproduction, the Rating Board could only evaluate its status as responsible entertainment for a particular rating category at the level of spoken dialogue and onscreen behavior. Other elements that contribute to a film's tone—camerawork, performance, set design, etc.— were beyond the purview and operations of the Rating Board. Filmmakers and distributors themselves had to interpret earlier in production whether these aesthetics might also push their films into a rating category they did not desire. With little editing feedback from the Rating Board, revisions could be hit or miss, dependent on degrees of available footage, financial resources, and a willingness to shape one's film to suit the norms of a preestablished yet uncharted rating category.

The NC-17 reception of the R-rated *Basic Instinct* is a result, I believe, of the Rating Board's inability to regulate into responsible entertainment many of the film's tonal irregularities. Heffner alludes to these irregularities in his daily log during *Basic Instinct*'s negotiations as the cause of an NC-17: It "seems as though [the] whole film is just a backdrop to sex and violence moments . . . which are not frequent, but are overwhelming in intensity when they occur, which may be good filmmaking technique but remains out of the mainstream."[54] While the Rating Board could adhere to its own circumscribed conventions for the Incontestable R, it had little control over the treatment of the film's subject matter through nonverbal means. Subjects such as lesbianism, nontraditional sex, sadomasochism, and murders by ice pick may receive NC-17 consideration by the Rating Board, but they are not necessarily excluded from an R, perhaps not even from a PG or PG-13. Formal elements such as Jerry Goldsmith's haunting score, Sharon Stone's sultry performance, and Jan De Bont's claustrophobic cinematography most likely contributed to the perception that *Basic Instinct* was not an Incontestable R, because these elements are nearly impossible for CARA to regulate.

In fact, the Rating Board did help arrange *Basic Instinct*'s nonverbal elements in the direction of responsible entertainment, mostly because of its status as a big-budget MPAA-member film partly financed by Douglas. Graves got Verhoeven to darken the sex scenes so they "played more mainstream" and assisted editor Frank Urioste with the grinding and stabbing scenes.[55] Despite this rare though still discriminatory intervention by the Rating Board (that is usually the province of the Appeals Board), the examiners could not forestall criticism of *Basic Instinct*'s R rating. The fiction of *Basic Instinct* created an unsettling sense of perversity, pornography, and potency that some viewers thought crossed the line of the Incontestable R. Whether this uncomfortable or disturbing tone emerged from a single scene or an aggregation of scenes, the same or similar pronouncements have historically been made for other R-rated texts discussed throughout this book: *The Exorcist, Cruising, Dressed to Kill, Scarface, Angel Heart*. Surprisingly, as we will see in chapter 5, Verhoeven's next film, *Showgirls* (1995), the first, and still the only, big-budget NC-17 release, would not have any of these problems.

Basic Instinct demonstrates that the Rating Board cannot always guarantee an Incontestable R. Oftentimes, when a film still "felt" NC-17 despite its R rating, the Rating Board was not able to regulate the nonverbal aspects of potentially offensive material in the direction of responsible entertainment. With the onscreen treatment of sex and nudity, however, the Rating Board showed remarkable consistency and standardization for the Incontestable R between 1992 and 1997. Any anomalies, as often is the case, could be traced to the Appeals Board.

1992: The Sex and Nudity Norms of the Incontestable R

We are not a censoring agency. We've checked over the script and we feel that since Madonna's got all of her clothes on in the courtroom scenes, the use of the facility is totally appropriate for us.

—Christine Yorozu[56]

Following *Basic Instinct*, five films in 1992 flirted with or accepted NC-17 ratings, some with controversies, others without. All of them, though, involved the treatment of sex and nudity: two films released by MGM, an MPAA signatory—*The Lover* (1992) and *Body of Evidence* (1993)—and three films from independent distributors—New Line's *Damage* (1992), Aries's *Bad Lieutenant* (1992), and Fine Line's (the art film division of New Line) *Wide Sargasso Sea* (1993). This new wave of films with adult appeal led critics to challenge once again the criteria for an NC-17.[57] Filmmakers again leveled claims of favoritism against the Rating Board, referring to their uncut versions as being no more sexual than the R-rated final cut of *Basic Instinct*. They were wrong.

So far in this book, I have invalidated charges of unfairness, hypocrisy, and arbitrariness of the Heffner Rating Board by pointing out Valenti's suppression or misinformation to the press, the marketing of controversy by distributors, and the underhandedness of some appeals hearings. A closer analysis of the sex and nudity in these films reveals that clear narrative and formal demarcations do, in fact, exist between the R and the NC-17 in the months after *Basic Instinct* and several years afterward, at least for these Rating Board criteria. By comparing the same narrative elements (vaginal sex, oral sex, anal sex) and formal elements (shot framing, shot duration, shot replacement) in the uncut NC-17 or unrated version with the R-rated version (as I did with *Basic Instinct*), I will show that the Rating Board's regulations are overwhelmingly consistent, clear-cut, and unbiased in dealing with MPAA-signatory and independent product.[58]

Despite not having access to a weekly ratings-pending report like the one Graves kept on *Basic Instinct*, I can easily observe and define the sex and nudity conventions of the Incontestable R. At the time, though, these norms were still unknown to most filmmakers, so most distributors marketed their controversy to the fullest. In terms of nudity no double standard exists for men and women. Full frontal exposure of the male and female body is permissible, but medium shots and close-ups of an actor's face in the same frame as another actor's genital area are not permitted. The representation of sex is more complicated. Masturbation and oral sex movements are allowable off-camera and in certain cases involving long shots, darkened scenes, or obscure camera angles, but the actors must always be clothed. In addition, three-quarter or full shots of sexual grinding and thrusting can last only a few seconds, and pubic hair can never be shown in this shot. Exceptions include darkened long shots and scenes with clothed actors. Shots of naked lovers in a missionary or female-dominant position are permitted as long as there is no sexual movement. Also, onscreen simulated shots of the penis being inserted into the vagina and anal sex are not permitted. For both sex and nudity, though, a single shot can warrant an NC-17.

Body of Evidence

Body of Evidence tells the story of a lawyer (Willem Dafoe) brought under the spell of his client (Madonna), who is on trial for "fornicating to death" her lover in order to inherit his multimillion-dollar estate.[59] When MGM received word in August 1992 that Body of Evidence got a tentative NC-17 for its "explicit sexual scenes," the distributor, and the film's director, Uli Edel, had no quarrel with the Rating Board's decision. Speaking for both MGM and Edel, executive producer Steven Deutsch remarked, "We understand why they gave [Body of Evidence] the rating. The question we are now asking ourselves is 'Do we want to change it?'" If MGM had released the film with the adults-only rating, Body of Evidence would have become the first major studio film to test the NC-17 waters since Henry & June. However, said Deutsch, "the big difference between us and [other producers who faced the NC-17 dilemma] is that we have the most famous woman in the world. What we want to research over the next several weeks is what that means to this film to go out with the NC." In contemplating the economic risks associated with the adults-only rating, MGM considered the fact that the "woman" Deutsch referred to—Madonna—may be perhaps the best box-office insurance an NC-17 picture could ever have. This especially would be the case if Body of Evidence turned out to contain, in the words of Deutsch, "the most explosive erotic scenes performed in any mainstream film, making Basic Instinct [look like] a cartoon" in comparison.[60] Deutsch's remarks are a bit misleading here since, at this time, he was comparing the uncut version of Body of Evidence to the R-rated cut of Basic Instinct. Even when compared to the uncut version of Verhoeven's film, however, Edel's uncut movie goes much further in its sexual explicitness.

Two scenes of sexual grinding and one scene of cunnilingus are longer and more explicit than comparable ones between Stone and Douglas in Basic Instinct: a shot of Madonna straddling Dafoe in their first sexual encounter, a scene between Dafoe and Julianne Moore making love missionary style, and a scene in which Dafoe gives oral sex to Madonna on the hood of a car. In addition to these shots of greater explicitness, Madonna's pubic hair is clearly visible in one long shot where she kneels astride a man (but facing away from him) and makes love; Madonna masturbates under her skirt on-camera in another scene; and anal sex between Madonna and Dafoe is implied by another scene, although the narrative does not make reference to it. In fact, the mise-en-scène of each sexual act above warrants an NC-17 on its own, and certainly the movie could not be passed for an R in that state.

By the end of October, two months after receiving the NC-17, MGM chose to cut *Body of Evidence* for an R rating. "Madonna could have overcome a lot of the stigma of the NC-17," said Deutsch about the decision, "but what we became aware of was that in the audience's mind, there is still no difference between the NC-17 and the old X."[61] Although this observation is indeed true, MGM, more than likely, had never planned to adopt the NC-17 anyway. The distributor had always planned a wide release for *Body of Evidence* because a successful opening weekend would reassure exhibitors that it could still open films after the box office underperformance of *Rush* (1991), *Of Mice and Men* (1992), and *Diggstown* (1992).[62] Equivocating over an R or NC-17 also served to market the film's notoriety following bad word of mouth coming from the test screenings.

As a result of this decision the R version of *Body of Evidence* (only two minutes shorter than the NC-17 version), is decidedly more tame. Contrary to Deutsch's generous assessment that none of the sex scenes were "totally removed" and only "minor portions" of three sex scenes were cut, MGM manipulated, trimmed, or eliminated from nine scenes every shot of sexual grinding, masturbation, anal sex, and oral sex from the NC-17 version.[63] The same rating demarcations that guided the editing of *Basic Instinct* applied in the case of *Body of Evidence,* suggesting that the Rating Board is not arbitrary in its judgments for the Incontestable R.

Sexual grinding. All full shots from the NC-17 version have been cut or reduced in length to a few seconds in the R version: (1) the second scene of the film (Joe Mantegna's first appearance) eliminates a video monitor shot of Madonna astride a man by using alternative footage containing different angles; (2) a later video monitor shot of Madonna astride a man with her pubic hair visible is cut and replaced with alternative footage; (3) the first sex scene between Dafoe and Madonna has been shortened from ninety seconds to its initial thirty-nine seconds (Madonna is naked on top of Dafoe in a full shot in both versions; however, at the point where she begins to move her torso in the NC-17, the R version cuts to the following morning's scene); and (4) all onscreen shots of Dafoe and Moore's grinding torsos in the NC-17 are

Figure 18. Defanged for an R rating: Willem Dafoe and Madonna in *Body of Evidence* (1993).

removed in the R (except for a one-second glimpse of Dafoe's behind). In the R version a postcoital missionary full shot of Dafoe and Moore remains from the NC-17 since the lovers are stationary.

Masturbation. Madonna's masturbation scene, in which she fondles herself onscreen underneath her skirt, has been cut in its entirety for the R. All that remains is Madonna wetting her finger and sticking it down her skirt, the camera cutting away before she begins to move her hand.

Anal sex. The "rape" of Madonna by Dafoe in the R version eliminates a two-second camera pan that reveals sexual grinding higher up on Madonna's behind than is customary for vaginal penetration. The audio track accompanying Madonna's close-up—the sound of her screaming in pain as Dafoe anally penetrates her off camera—has been cut from the NC-17.

Oral sex. The oral sex scene on the car is essentially cut for the R except for one brief, dark long shot of Dafoe performing cunnilingus on Madonna. Shots of Madonna's pubic hair during sexual activity have also been removed; however, the end of this scene in the R version contains a nine-second grinding shot not in the NC-17. The grinding is longer than generally accepted by CARA for a full shot, but the scene is dark, and Madonna and Dafoe are almost fully clothed (Madonna is naked from the waist down with her genital area unexposed).

These formal alterations to the NC-17 version of *Body of Evidence* significantly defanged the sex scenes from this B-level *Basic Instinct*. Perhaps MGM should have accepted the more restrictive rating for *Body of Evidence,* given that it debuted on 2,052 screens on January 15, 1993, to terrible reviews. The $20-million film opened to only a $7.5-million box office, believed to be at the time among the ten lowest opening weekends for pictures playing on nineteen hundred or more screens. Its box office then dropped by 59 percent the following week.[64] MGM considered pulling all prints so that the NC-17 version could be reissued in two months (per MPAA rules) but decided against it as a new run might hurt video sales.[65] *Body of Evidence* was released in its R-rated theatrical version and unrated video version almost six months later.

Damage

The same day MGM announced *Body of Evidence* would be trimmed for an R to avoid what MGM cochairperson and co-CEO Alan Ladd Jr. called "the stigma of the NC-17 label," the Rating Board handed out the adults-only rating to another film. When *Damage*—a story about a married politician (Jeremy Irons) having an affair with his son's fiancée (Juliette Binoche)—received an NC-17 in October 1992, its internationally acclaimed director, Louis Malle, publicly criticized the Rating Board for the label. He accused CARA of "aesthetic myopia" for failing to distinguish between art and pornography and for giving R ratings to gratuitously violent movies like *Basic Instinct*. "I am stunned, just shocked," he said. "If *Basic Instinct* got an R, I think I deserve a PG-13. This is a very passionate movie. But there is no ice pick. There is no murder. There is no rape."[66]

Martin A. Grove's editorial in the *Hollywood Reporter* on the unrated press-screened version of *Damage* exposed how manifest Malle's stupefaction of the Rating Board's standards for an R rating really was in the industry:

> After watching Louis Malle's *Damage* last week I couldn't for the life of me understand how the MPAA could have rated that version of the film NC-17. I spent the entire evening waiting to see something on the screen that was so sexually hot it would justify the controversial rating, but found absolutely nothing of the sort. In fact, there was significantly less sex and nudity in *Damage* than there was in the R rated *Basic Instinct*. . . .
>
> In discussing *Damage* . . . with others who have seen it, I couldn't find anyone who believed it really merited an NC-17. "Next to *Basic Instinct*, there's no comparison," observed one veteran film marketer I spoke to, who asked to be anonymous so as not to prejudice the MPAA against him or his future product. . . .
>
> *Damage* . . . is simply not an erotic movie that could satisfy anyone who bought a ticket expecting the sexual titillation that NC-17 or its predecessor X rating connote. There's very little nudity in the film and the one scene that shows Miranda Richardson bare-breasted is a totally unerotic scene of grief and anger triggered by a key plot point.[67]

Grove clearly is unaware that the treatment of sex and nudity—not its accumulation—can earn an NC-17, that the Rating Board (but not the Appeals Board) is undiscriminating in awarding NC-17s, and that the adults-only rating is not only reserved for "sexually titillating" films. This latter misperception was also expressed, perhaps exaggeratingly so, by New Line president and CEO Michael Lynne: "Louis Malle does not make films that are pornography, or that pander to baser instincts."[68]

Grove's and Lynne's renouncement of *Damage*'s NC-17 was surely provoked by the controversial, one-minute scene in question—where Irons and Binoche, seated on the floor naked, engage in some rough but unrevealing sex. In fact, the scene is "backlit," said Malle, "so there is no frontal nudity," and as a result, the scene does not contain any genitalia or pubic hair either.[69] The Rating Board assigned an NC-17 because the nude actors are having sex in a medium long shot that lasts twenty-five seconds, far too long for CARA policies regarding sex in an R rating.

Even though Malle was contractually obligated to produce an R picture, New Line Distribution president Mitchell Goldman said the company had "every intention of maintaining the artistic integrity of *Damage* as Louis Malle originally intended it."[70] New Line appealed the NC-17, and the rating was upheld by a majority vote of six to five.[71] Apparently the stigma of the NC-17 won out, as *Damage* was reedited to an R for a wide release with Malle's cooperation.[72] Malle shortened the scene in question by three seconds, breaking up the problematic shot into three above-the-waist close-ups edited together by dissolves.[73] In these close-ups, Malle performed an optical zoom on one shot taken from the NC-17 version and substituted another shot with previously unused footage. The R still contains a brief long shot of the actors in a nude embrace, but it is postcoital (as in *Body of Evidence*), with no sexual movement.

Malle's unfamiliarity with the rating system and Lynne's public statements that its procedures were "arbitrary" and "unfair" overshadowed the fact that the Rating Board was actually consistent in its polices.[74] Examiners applied the same standards to the R version of *Damage* that they did to *Basic Instinct* and *Body of Evidence,* even though it only involved one disputed scene of fewer than thirty seconds of screen time. New Line, together with Malle's agent, Sam Cohn, complained that they were only altering "seven seconds" to change the rating from NC-17 to R, but seven seconds, says Heffner, "can change a picture from G to NC-17" if the particular moment onscreen is very "explicit."[75] Malle's treatment of the sex scene in the R version—replacing long shots with close-ups—certainly made it less explicit and delivered a responsible tone more in line at the time with other representations of the sex act in the Incontestable R.

The unsubstantiated and misinformed claims about the Rating Board's practices by the filmmakers of *Damage* ultimately earned the film free publicity at CARA's expense, like many other marketed controversies. This time, shortly after the film's release, Malle himself admitted that New Line's wailings, in part, were designed to buy *Damage* a month of press coverage: "My friends at New Line told me, 'we don't mind if we have an NC-17 for a while, because we'd like to get a little publicity.'" In fact, *Damage* was actually rated "18" in England, meaning no one under eighteen could see the film, and Malle did not complain one bit to the British press about the rating. Reflecting back a year later from its U.S. release, however, Malle still believed that industry politics were behind the NC-17 rating of *Damage*. "I think it was a bad situation," he said, "that simply came from the fact that it was the end of the year and the MPAA had been accused of letting a number of films like *Basic Instinct,* for instance, get away with an R rating. They wanted to maybe . . . just make an example. I think we'd been taken on this controversy almost by accident. That's what I strongly believe." Malle's conspiracy theories join those of *Body of Evidence*'s Stephen Deutsch, who said that CARA "is reeling from *Batman Returns* (1992) criticism that it applied toughness to sexuality more than violence. I believe if they had *Basic Instinct* to rate over again it would be NC-17."[76] These assumptions, I will continue to show, are unfounded.

Wide Sargasso Sea

Unlike the case of *Damage,* Fine Line dutifully accepted—without any complaints or regrets—the NC-17 given to *Wide Sargasso Sea* in August 1992.[77] Ira Deutchman, president of Fine Line, was willing to take a chance on the NC-17 and, like few others before or after him, commended the Rating Board's practices. "Given the difficulty of trying to be everything to a population as diverse as America's," he said, "it's a lot to ask of the [MPAA] to be much better than they are. They are making an honest attempt to be representative of society, and I don't see why we can't accept that there is certain material that is suitable for adults and not for children."[78] His approbation, however refreshing it may have appeared to the Rating Board, was probably no more than a marketing ploy. *Wide Sargasso Sea* was a low-budget period piece from Australia without any stars, but Deutchman could certainly bank on NC-17 notoriety to attract art-house audiences. Whatever the case may be, director John Duigan's adaptation of Jean Rhys's novel (a "prequel" to Charlotte Brontë's *Jane Eyre*) about sexual obsession and madness in the mid-eighteenth century West Indies featured a lot less sex than *Basic Instinct, Body of Evidence,* or even *Damage.* Even so, *Wide Sargasso Sea* violated the parameters of the Incontestable R.

As usual, many critics failed to see the rationale behind the film's NC-17. John Hartl of the *Seattle Times* said *Wide Sargasso Sea* is no more salacious than the R-rated *Basic Instinct.* Others erroneously attributed the rating to a nonsexual shot of male genitalia. Kenneth Turan of the *Los Angeles Times* wrote that the "NC-17 rating is apparently due in part to a brief shot of male frontal nudity." The *Atlanta Journal and Constitution*'s Steve Murray remarked that "a frontal shot" is still "taboo" in Hollywood and "the main reason for the NC-17." And Mick LaSalle of the *San Francisco Chronicle* declared that the NC-17 should therefore be known as the "weenie rating." This belief that a rating double standard exists among the sexes for frontal nudity is positively and perennially false, contradicted most recently in the early 1990s by the appearance of Jeremy Irons's penis in *Damage* and the R rating given a few months later to Harvey Keitel's genitals in *The Piano* (1993). Jack Valenti has been forthright in stating that there are no rules against male frontal nudity in an R film and has even clarified the point at which the representation of the penis may cross over into the NC-17 category. "If you saw a guy sidling across a room, and he turns, it's one thing. But if he's in bed and engaged in coupling, well, that's different."[79]

Certain critics correctly observed, however, if in somewhat broad terms, the grounds on which the Rating Board awarded the NC-17 to *Wide Sargasso Sea.* Vincent Canby of the *New York Times* wrote the film had "complete nudity," and *Variety*'s Lawrence Cohn described the "frequent nude and sex scenes" as "tastefully handled, though a couple briefly have the explicit content that earned 'Sargasso' an NC-17 rating."[80] The "completeness" and "explicitness" of *Wide Sargasso Sea*'s love scenes that Canby and Cohn remark on, but cannot fully explicate, point to the sexual images regularly edited from NC-17 films to earn an R rating: a lengthy full shot of sexual grinding between a nude man and woman, a ten-second three-quarter shot (slightly below-the-waist) of sex in the standing position, and a close-up of a man fondling a woman underneath her dress onscreen. These shots may be less exploitative in tone than, say, *Body of Evidence,* but their explicitness and duration still transgressed the boundaries of the Incontestable R.

Indeed, with a few cuts *Wide Sargasso Sea* could have avoided the NC-17 rating. This was made clear in its video release when Fine Line offered the film in its original NC-17 theatrical version and an R-rated video-only version with all three shots noted above completely edited out. One other shot eliminated from the NC-17 version was a close-up of Karina Lombard's dress being torn apart (revealing her breasts) in a fit of marital rape by her husband. Remaining in the R version was male frontal nudity presented in a nonsexual manner. While no written accounts of the rating negotiation exist for the video release of *Wide Sargasso Sea,* Fine Line must have decided simply to cut the problematic scenes in their entirety rather than waste money on "crafting" an R version for stores, like Blockbuster Video, that would only purchase a single copy. These clearly prohibitive acts in shaping film form and narrative differ quite dramatically from the more productive strategies (optical zooms, lighting adjustments, footage replacement) as shown for *Basic Instinct, Body of Evidence,* and *Damage.* While still constructing the boundaries of the Incontestable R, these prohibitive methods would almost always be employed in editing theatrically released unrated or NC-17 films for the ancillary market.

Bad Lieutenant

Like Fine Line, Aries Film Releasing embraced the NC-17 rating when it acquired U.S. distribution rights for *Bad Lieutenant* in August 1992. Abel Ferrara's follow-up to *King of New York,* one of the ten films that received an X in the first seven months of 1990, was quite unlike the more demure *Wide Sargasso Sea,* with its fleeting moments of sex. *Bad Lieutenant* wore its NC-17 on its sleeve, raw. Rating Board examiners probably gave it an X for every one of its criteria. Among many unpleasant things, Harvey Keitel plays the boozing, gambling, cursing, trigger-happy, scuzzball father of four, who also happens to be a cop and the film's protagonist; he masturbates outside a car after forcing a teenage girl to pantomime how she "sucks a guy's cock"; he graphically shoots up drugs stolen from police busts with fellow addicts; and he investigates a crime of a nun brutally raped on an altar—her vagina lacerated with a crucifix by two Latino boys. Clearly, Ferrara's uncompromising and frank treatment of corruption, decay, and redemption was nowhere near what the Rating Board would regard as an Incontestable R, what reform groups would perceive as responsible entertainment, or what most people would consider good taste.

Aries could not market controversy out of the NC-17 for *Bad Lieutenant* even if it wanted to. Ferrara did not give them any choice either. "I demanded the right to make an unrated picture contractually," he said. "I told [producer Edward R. Pressman] up front it would be a triple-X picture. . . . There's one version of *Bad Lieutenant* and that's it. It's an adult film but not necessarily for a limited audience."[81] Ferrara capitulated, however, to an NC-17 and R release on home video through Artisan.

Four scenes in *Bad Lieutenant* were drastically reedited to obtain this R for video, severely mangling the original film without any regard for narrative coherence. They were Keitel's sex and alcohol binge with two women, the rape of the nun, Keitel's masturbation, and the heroin injection scene. It suffices to say, without going into the specific alterations of each scene, that their running time was greatly reduced (for example, the rape scene was cut from forty-nine seconds to fourteen seconds), and sexual grinding, the showing of pubic hair during a rape, and simulated fellatio were eliminated from the NC-17 version. While the R-rated video release managed to meet the standards applied to other theatrically released, R-rated films in the early 1990s, the editing process, said Aries president Paul Cohen, was preposterous because "the [Rating] Board gave the rating for the tone and you can't cut a tone."[82]

The R-rated *Bad Lieutenant* demonstrates that the Rating Board is not equipped to deal with a film whose tone—what Ferrara calls the "mood" of a film—so incessantly defiles the sensibility of responsible entertainment.[83] Like fellow adults-only rated *Henry: Portrait of a Serial Killer* and to some extent Ken Russell's *Whore* (1991), *Bad Lieutenant* approaches sex and violence in a naturalistic, ambivalent fashion; its low-budget, shaky camerawork, improvisation, and wandering plotlines conjure up feelings of dread, amorality, and rage that cannot simply be regulated with dialogue replacement or editing tricks. Unlike *Wide Sargasso Sea,* these films do not have a sense of "quality" Heffner speaks of, "films that looked good enough, that were written smartly enough, that were directed or produced well enough for parents not to have to say 'Oh, my God, we can't let our children within two miles of this film.'"[84] Production value, therefore, does play a role in the rating process.

Accompanied by good reviews, especially for Keitel's performance, *Bad Lieutenant* managed to expand its release into a few mainstream venues with its NC-17. It also demonstrates that some NATO exhibitors were willing to show NC-17 films, a fact made exceedingly clear with *Showgirls* in 1995 but one surprisingly averted by *The Lover* three years earlier.

The Lover

The Lover was based on Marguerite Duras's largely autobiographical novel about a fifteen-year-old French girl's (Jane March) affair with a twenty-seven-year-old Chinese aristocrat (Tony Leung) in 1920s Indochina. A major international success before it opened in the United States, the film received an NC-17 from the Rating Board in April 1992. In a move described by *Variety* as the "quintessentially unconventional director's cut,"[85] director Jean-Jacques Annaud edited the film at his own behest, despite protests from distributor MGM, who bought the U.S. rights to the 115-minute European version.

The circumstances surrounding the rating negotiation of *The Lover* were more mundane than controversial.[86] Amid a series of conflicting trade reports, it appears that Annaud had first unofficially submitted the unrated European version to the Rating Board for its opinion. After being told the film probably would be rated NC-17, Annaud cut three and a half minutes from graphic sex scenes in the film and sent it back to the Rating Board to be officially rated. About this version MGM's cochairperson and co-CEO Alan Ladd Jr. showed great ignorance or, better yet, greater marketing savvy when he said, "There is no graphic sex in *[The Lover]* and certainly nothing in this picture that you haven't seen before." Every examiner believed otherwise, giving the film an NC-17 rating, said Heffner, because it was "sexually so strong that it couldn't be anything other than NC-17."[87] In an attempt to resubmit the film for an R, Annaud cut another eight and a half minutes, mostly dealing with pace. At MGM's request Annaud reconsidered this approach and subsequently appealed the rating, reinserting the eight and a half minutes of footage into the film before the hearing.

In what Heffner would call a "terrible mistake," the Appeals Board overturned the NC-17 by a seven-to-three majority decision. Heffner cites two reasons for the Rating Board's defeat. First, he did not have a prepared statement like he usually did to argue against the appellant's case because there was such certainty that the film would lose its appeal. Second, MGM's vice president Kathie Berlin successfully played the *Basic Instinct* card soon after that film's release, arguing convincingly during the appeal that the explicit sex

Figure 19. The most explicit R-rated film of its time: Jane March and Tony Leung in
The Lover (1993). Copyright 1992 Renn Productions.

scenes in *The Lover* showed romantic heterosexual love rather than promoting gratuitous sex and violence. In two separate interviews Berlin confirms
this strategy. "I talked about *Fatal Attraction* and *Basic Instinct*," Berlin told
the *New York Times*, "which showed violent lovemaking and lesbianism, and
most of the lovemaking is Michael Douglas throwing someone over the back
of the chair." "In *Basic Instinct*, it wasn't lovemaking," she told the *Los Angeles
Times*; "it was rough violent . . . f—ing was the word I used. I said, 'If you're
worried about what kids are seeing, worry about that!'"[88] To also attest to the
film's "no sex without love" morality, Berlin brought in Annaud, sexuality
educator Lennie Roseman, and letters of support from psychiatrist Sandra
Leon and *Seventeen* editor Midge Richardson.[89] Despite the Rating Board's
defeat, Heffner found her arguments "cleverly made" in the wake of *Basic
Instinct*, a momentum perhaps lost four months later when *Damage* narrowly
lost its appeal.[90]

Even though the appeal for an R was successful, Annaud removed the eight
and a half minutes of cuts he had made prior to the appeals hearing for a 103-
minute U.S. theatrical release in October 1992, thus rendering the film twelve
minutes shorter than its European counterpart. In addition, Annaud edited
out a voice-over stating the girl's age—fifteen—because of current cultural
fears of child abuse.[91] Even in its shorter version, *The Lover* contained the
most explicit depictions of sexual intercourse to appear in an R-rated film

throughout the 1990s. It may not have included shots of oral, anal, or other forms of nontraditional sex found in *Basic Instinct,* but its images of intercourse were more sexually graphic and longer than similar scenes in the R-rated *or* unrated versions of Verhoeven's film.[92]

There are five major sex scenes in the R version of *The Lover.* Each one involves the missionary position, with March appearing full-frontal and Leung naked from behind. The first three scenes are the most sexually explicit. Both actors are fully nude, simulating sexual intercourse in a completely realistic manner. Long and full shots of the two of them "grinding" repeatedly occupy the frame. For instance, in the third sex scene when the two nude actors make love on the floor, the camera does a one-minute slow dolly in from a long to a full shot. With *Basic Instinct* and other films, the shot framing and time duration of sexual intercourse was usually replaced with alternative angles or cut after a few seconds of grinding. None of these formal conventions of the Incontestable R are present in *The Lover.*

Even though *The Lover* earned its R rating from the Appeals Board, the Rating Board still receives the brunt of criticism from members of the public who disagree with a film's final, assigned rating. This setup, as we have seen, breeds inconsistency, confusion, and hostility in the rating system. Filmmakers would argue—and rightly so—that "you passed so and so movie with this and that, so you must pass mine," even though the film received an R only on appeal. Critics would complain—and rightly so—that the system is arbitrary and doesn't work. Filmmakers over the next few years continued to refer to *Basic Instinct* as the outer limit of sexual imagery for the R rating. *The Lover,* for some reason, never served as their cited precedent, even though it was much more graphic in its R version than the Verhoeven film. Attempts, however, to imitate *Basic Instinct*'s success by one-upping the film's notorious sex scenes failed at the box office. While the quality of these films can be debated, the Rating Board's norms cannot; each film closely abided by its standards of sex and nudity for the Incontestable R.

THE INCONTESTABLE R AFTER HEFFNER

Because I appeared naked in [Color of Night]*, because you see me frontal nude, you're going to assign an X rating to it. I mean, why is it okay for Sharon Stone to go, "Hello, everyone, I'm Sharon Stone," and that's okay?*
—Bruce Willis, *CNN Showbiz Today,* 1994

Following *Basic Instinct,* the MPAA signatories and independent distributors released a succession of R-rated sexual thrillers in 1993 that flirted with the

NC-17. *Sliver* (cut to an R), *Boxing Helena* (won its appeal for an R), and *Dangerous Game* (lost its appeal for an R), like *Body of Evidence,* though, failed at the box office. Nevertheless, the Rating Board's formal boundaries of sex and nudity for the Incontestable R were consistent with films from the previous year. Their rating battles testified to the rampant confusion and misinformation still surrounding the Rating Board's practices and procedures, a process undoubtedly fostered by a distributor's exploiting of the NC-17 and CARA's secrecy with filmmakers and the press.

Richard Mosk replaced Heffner as chairperson of CARA on July 1, 1994. Even though no primary documentation of the Rating Board's activities exists from this point onward, the same standards of sex and nudity applied until the end of the decade. The first manufactured controversy under the Mosk administration involved Jane March once again, in Disney's *Color of Night* under its Hollywood Pictures banner. The MPAA signatory and Cinergi, the film's production company, inflamed the polemic often suggested about the Rating Board's double standards for male and female nudity in order to market the beleaguered picture. Director Richard Rush had already been fired off the film—an erotic thriller about an emotionally vulnerable psychologist (Bruce Willis) and a woman from his therapy group (Jane March)—during postproduction because of budget overruns, negative test screenings, and disagreements over a releasable cut of the film. The latter issue arose in part from the Rating Board's objection to certain images of sex and violence in Rush's first cut. Since Cinergi was contractually obligated to deliver an R-rated cut to Disney—who would not release an NC-17 picture—*Color of Night*'s release was subsequently pushed back from April 29 to August 19, 1994.[93]

Early in the editing process *Variety* reported that the controversy involved two scenes featuring full frontal nudity of March and Willis that had to be cut to avoid an NC-17. This account would prove to be correct but not due to the hypocrisy of the Rating Board. Willis erroneously told CNN that the sex scenes were recut because "the female nude form gets an R rating and the male nude form gets an X rating," a story that the news media were more than happy to run with. *Newsday* linked *Color of Night*'s rating difficulties and its penis problems to CARA's supposed "slip-up" with *Basic Instinct* two years earlier. *Boston Herald* critic Stephen Schaefer called the rating battle the "Will we-or-won't we see all of Willis?" campaign.[94] Other publications suggested that the only way to see his penis would be in Rush's original and unrated version of the film on video.[95] As part of the settled creative dispute that saw him removed from the film, Rush won the right to have his version—and only his version—released on home video.[96]

Director's cuts are traditionally released on video in addition to, not in place of, the theatrical film version. Like *Basic Instinct, Body of Evidence, Damage,* and *Dangerous Game* in the pre-DVD 1990s, they almost always involved the original cut of the film submitted to the Rating Board. The "director's cut" of *Color of Night,* however, included seventeen more minutes of footage, a different ending, additional subplots, and more sexually explicit material.[97] When looking at the U.S. video version of the film, though, one sees nothing more explicit than what was permissible in R-rated films of the time.[98] Both Willis and March singly kiss each other's pelvic regions, but there is no suggestive oral sex or visible pubic hair in the frame during these acts that may raise the red flag for Rating Board examiners. Many potential NC-17 shots have been trimmed through a series of dissolves to avoid lengthy, sexual grinding.[99] Perhaps three individual shots were objected to, yet these can also be explained by the Rating Board's norms for the Incontestable R. A five-second crane shot of March astride Willis in the pool contains little sexual movement and it is questionable whether they are making love at all. A two-second close-up of grinding torsos reveals no pubic hair. And a brief full shot of Willis, his penis visible, in the pool—but not engaged in a sexual act—does not violate any standards for the Incontestable R. These three shots, in my opinion, could not have been responsible for the film's potential NC-17 rating.

What was responsible were ten seconds of sexual conduct removed from the European theatrical cut for U.S. and Canadian video sales and rentals, and one shot involved Willis's penis.[100] The European video release of *Color of Night* actually contained different nude footage from what appeared in the North American video release. The aforementioned two *scenes* of full frontal nudity of Willis and March that *Variety* suggested were supposedly the causes for the NC-17 may actually have been *shots*—and these two shots are featured in the European video release. Both occur underwater, and they involve separate shots of pubic hair and a lover's face in the same frame. Willis kisses the inside of March's thigh and her pubic hair is revealed; March kisses the inside of Willis's thigh and his penis is revealed. These two shots are always given automatic NC-17s by CARA, and, by no surprise, they last exactly ten seconds.[101]

It stands to reason that these ten seconds were NC-17 in nature, or else they would have been included on the R-rated North American video release. It also stands to reason that since Disney refused (and still refuses) to release unrated or NC-17 films, these mercurial ten seconds would have been the contentious shots arresting the film's theatrical release as well. As I have argued before, the onscreen treatment and sexual context of the penis (visible in sexual grinding, proximity to another actor's face), and not just the

Figure 20. Manufacturing controversy over the Rating Board's supposed double standards for male and female frontal nudity: Jane March and Bruce Willis in *Color of Night* (1994). Courtesy of the Academy of Motion Picture Arts and Sciences.

presence of a penis, could warrant an NC-17. Jack Valenti alluded to this detail for *Color of Night:* "If Bruce Willis had stepped out of a shower and was toweling himself, or was reaching for a telephone and there was a fleeting glimpse of nudity, [the rating] would probably be an R. But if you're shown totally nude and screwing somebody on a bed, that's something else."[102]

Like so many other rating battles before it, *Color of Night* is another misrepresentation, overstatement, and fabrication of the Rating Board's practices. Since a shot of Willis's penis did not singularly warrant an NC-17 for *Color of Night,* after all, one of two things happened: the Rating Board did not advise Disney of the exact shots necessary to avoid an NC-17, leading to insinuations of sexism; or Disney knew about the cuts but manufactured a controversy instead. Despite Richard Rush's not knowing the exact truth, he confirmed the fact that Disney management stirred up a ratings dispute: "From the beginning this was a kinky picture. It was Disney's plan all along to use the erotic elements to attract an audience. There was a tacit conspiracy between the press and the PR department to exploit the NC-17. Most of the papers suggested I was fighting for an NC-17, which was wrong. I had signed a contract to deliver an R-rated film."[103] Secrecy and subterfuge, once again, lead back to the R/NC-17 boundary.

After the box-office failure of *Color of Night* the MPAA signatories abandoned the sexual thriller genre and left the soft-core theatrical field to their newly developed art-house subsidiaries and the independents. Unlike their more mainstream brethren, these mid-1990s films were unrated or carried an NC-17 for sexual explicitness. The MPAA and non-MPAA-member distributors prepared video-only R versions alongside their original theatrical versions in order to accommodate outlets like Blockbuster Video, Wal-Mart, and Kmart, who have policies against carrying NC-17 movies. These films included October's *When Night Is Falling* (1995), Trimark's *Kama Sutra: A Tale of Love* (1996), and Sony Pictures Classics' *Broken English* (1996, released in the U.S. in 1997). Despite their art-house pedigree, they still adhered to the standards of the Incontestable R in their edited versions for video.

Like the filmmakers of *Color of Night,* the filmmakers of *When Night Is Falling* charged the Rating Board with having a double standard for its rating process—this time with homosexuality. The Canadian drama about a female university professor (Pascale Bussières) who's engaged to a fellow academic (Henry Czerny) but falls for a bisexual circus performer (Rachael Crawford), received an NC-17 in October 1995 for what October partner and comanaging executive Amir Malin called two scenes of lesbian lovemaking in the film. "It is our strong belief that had the two scenes involved heterosexual lovemaking, we would have received the less restrictive R rating," he said. Malin subsequently procured the assistance of the Gay and Lesbian Alliance against Defamation (GLAAD), who put out a press release stating, "By giving the film an NC-17 rating, it sends a very strong message that same sex couples engaging in intimacy are not fit for the general public." CARA's response to these charges managed to inflame the controversy even further. As usual, the Rating Board refused to comment on the specifics of the *When Night Is Falling* case, stating only that the two "explicit sex scenes" would be considered "out of bounds" for children under seventeen by "most American parents."[104] The *New York Times*' rejection of the film's print ad (an embraced Bussières and Crawford partially concealed by a bed sheet) seemed to confirm Malin's and GLAAD's allegations of a double standard.[105] An overwhelming thirteen-to-one vote at the appeals hearing to uphold the NC-17 sealed it for them.[106]

These exchanges were an all-too-familiar scenario, the usual tête-à-tête of hype, mistruths, and vagaries among CARA, filmmakers, and the press about the rating system. After the appeal it was revealed that the two contentious scenes were, in fact, one heterosexual (Bussières and Czerny) and one homosexual (Bussières and Crawford) love scene. Director Patricia Rozema said, "Either there was a misunderstanding on the part of October, or the MPAA backpedaled like crazy when they saw how [Amir's claims] looked in print."

Figure 21. The *When Night Is Falling* (1995) ad rejected by the *New York Times*. *Los Angeles Times,* Nov. 12, 1995, Calendar section.

Despite this revelation, Rozema still suspected homophobia and racism on the part of CARA: "I wish you knew how cautious I am to brandish the word *homophobia,*" she said, "but with the MPAA, I have to. The irony is that people looking for that really horny scene, or that new sexual position they've never seen, well they won't find it. Nothing here is designed to titillate, which is what pornography does." Joan Graves, who recently became the MPAA vice chairperson, dismissed the idea of differing sexual standards, stating that it was "the degree of graphic sex" in *When Night Is Falling* that earned it an NC-17, not the type of nudity or sexuality. Even so, Rozema refused to cut or alter any of the film's love scenes, and October released it unrated. She remarked, "The decision of the ratings board shows an extremely limited vision, and I don't want to honor their classification criteria by accepting this rating."[107]

Strangely, October released only an R-rated version of *When Night Is Falling* on video in the United States. A comparison of the R version with the uncut British video release of the film (the same one as the U.S. theatrical release), however, makes clear that the Rating Board and Appeals Board awarded the NC-17 in an arbitrary manner. The uncut/NC-17 heterosexual love scene contains torso close-ups and long shots of sexual thrusting and grinding with the characters' buttocks in the frame; the homosexual love scene contains torso close-ups of sexual grinding and shots of masturbation with Crawford's hand right outside the frame. For the R-rated video release October (with or without the assistance of Rozema) edited the first scene by replacing the close-up with a dissolve involving two "incontestable" shots and deleting the long shot altogether; in the second scene all the masturbation shots are removed, and only above-the-waist medium shots and close-ups remain. These sex and nudity revisions for the R rating of the film correspond to other R-rated films throughout most of the 1990s.

Despite Rozema's and Malin's claims to the contrary, homophobia did not play a role in the NC-17 rating for *When Night Is Falling.* The Rating Board does, however, treat sexual behavior differently and admittedly so for an R rating. Speaking for his tenure at CARA, Heffner does not disagree that anal sex may have warranted an X/NC-17 over an R since he believed most American parents would agree it deserved a harsher rating.[108] Certainly, CARA's ratings-pending report for *Basic Instinct* illustrates great concern for rear entry positions and the inference of anal sex. *Body of Evidence* eliminated all inferences of anal sex for its R-rated theatrical release. *Pulp Fiction* (1994), regulated under Mosk, may have adjusted the standards of Heffner's administration with its offscreen depiction of sodomy. Surely, by the time of the R-rated *Brokeback Mountain* (2005), standards governing anal sex and the Incontestable R had changed. Graves, speaking shortly after that film's release, echoed her comments of eleven years earlier: "The criticism that gay sex scenes draw more restrictive ratings than straight ones is wrong. If something is graphic enough to be R, it's graphic whether it's homosexual or heterosexual." Yet in the same statement Graves admits that a gay kiss might earn a PG-13 instead of a PG because parents might feel younger children are unfamiliar with homosexuality.[109] These comments certainly suggest that for CARA responsible entertainment still retains some of the same puritanical and moralist elements pertaining to sexuality that harmless entertainment had under the PCA.

When *Kama Sutra: A Tale of Love*—a romantic tragedy about a queen (Sarita Choudhury), a lusty king (Naveen Andrews), a love-smitten sculptor (Ramon Tikaram), and a servant girl (Indira Varma) who sleeps with the king on his wedding night—was given a tentative NC-17 in February 1997, director Mira Nair was completely befuddled for the reasons behind the rating. Her confusion was evident in the following statement: the Rating Board "wanted us to cut out the full frontal nudity, and to eliminate a scene where the two women make love to each other."[110] The latter cut she described was not from a traditional love scene but from a scene of one woman demonstrating on another woman how to "mark" a lover's body. While the subject of "marking" itself is not off-limits to the R, it is the treatment of these and other subjects, not the acts themselves, that were responsible for *Kama Sutra*'s NC-17 rating.

Instead of adopting the NC-17, Trimark released the film unrated in theaters, then distributed it unrated and R-rated for home video. Approximately forty seconds from three scenes have been removed for the R version. The first scene of foreplay between Varma and Andrews had two shots removed: a full shot of Andrews pulling a red garment off of Varma and exposing her frontally nude in a full shot (this was replaced in the R version with a close-up of her face) and a close-up of Andrews kissing Varma's thigh with her pubic hair visible in the frame. The second scene that was cut featured Tikaram astride Varma. Two close-ups where his buttocks (facing the camera) gyrate as she clenches her feet have been removed. The largest cut in *Kama Sutra* (thirty seconds) occurred in the "marking" scene discussed above. As Choudhury stands up in profile, Varma kneels down to kiss Choudhury's torso and legs. Medium close-ups of Choudhury's pubic hair are exposed in the same frame as Varma kisses her. This shot was completely removed in the R version.

The pubic hair shots in the above scenes of *Kama Sutra* have always been NC-17 material because of the proximity of an actor's face to another's genital area. The cuts in the second scene are standard Rating Board rejections because lengthy sexual grinding, especially close-ups of fornication, are forbidden in the R rating. Why Nair replaced the full frontal shot of Varma with a close-up is unknown but explainable. I do not believe the Rating Board found Varma's pose too frank, soft-core, or risqué for the R rating. Instead, I think that Nair *misinterpreted* the Rating Board's objections to the scene—which may have come through in a memo or a phone conversation broadly as "explicit sexual content in this scene was NC-17"—to include *all* full-frontal shots. Without any clear guidance on editing the scene from the Rating Board, Nair most likely cut more footage than necessary to get an R rating. Overdetermining the standards of the Rating Board in cases like *Kama Sutra* probably occurs more often than realized in the classification era. As *Basic Instinct* and other limit texts from MPAA signatories have demonstrated, the Rating Board sometimes does give specific editing information for big-budget Hollywood films. Trimark, like many other independent distributors, may not have been as well accommodated by CARA as the major distributors sometimes are.

Despite the existence of "regulatory courtesies," the standards of the Rating Board remain the same for the MPAA signatories and the independents. The New Zealand film *Broken English*, about a doomed love affair between a Maori man and a Croatian woman, offers a case in point, being one of the few films to be distributed with an NC-17 by an MPAA signatory. Released by Sony's art-house division, Sony Pictures Classics, in July 1997, *Broken English* received an NC-17 almost a year earlier for a single shot taking place during a robust, bed-breaking, heterosexual love scene. The camera dollies in from a full shot of the two nude lovers making love in a variation of the missionary position into a three-quarter shot that contains sexual grinding. The shot is undoubtedly NC-17, a fact confirmed by director Gregor Nicholas after the film's appeals defeat. He was told by an Appeals Board member that he "could have shot it another way, like from the waist up," that "[the Appeals Board has] to draw the line somewhere," and that "we can't expose the youth of America to buttock-thrusting of this type."[111]

Critics actually recognized this "buttock thrusting" aesthetic in *Broken English* as NC-17 in nature, its intensity and duration truly hard to mistake for an R rating. Leslie Rubinkowski of the *Pittsburgh Post-Gazette* noticed the self-evidence of its NC-17 as well: "You'll be able to pick it out, no matter how good your English is."[112] Janet Maslin of the *New York Times* concurred, isolating the shot from the rest of the film. "*Broken English* is rated NC-17," she said. "The reason: a sex scene that without explicitly depicting genitals is simply too acrobatic and lifelike to be fake. That forbidden rating does not reflect the larger spirit of the film."[113] These statements reconfirm Heffner's claim that a single shot can determine a film's rating. Rather than reconstruct the film with different formal elements, as the directors of *Damage, Body of Evidence,* or *Kama Sutra* had, Sony Pictures simply cut the forty-three-second shot for its R-rated video version.

These analyses of *When Night Is Falling, Kama Sutra,* and *Broken English* demonstrate that the Rating Board employs the same standards of sex and nudity for video releases as it does for theatrical releases. The editing done for an R on video releases corresponded with rating practices regarding sexual grinding, masturbation, and pubic hair for theatrical releases. The Rating Board does occasionally modify its policies for the treatment of these acts, not through amendments like the Production Code Administration, however, but through more subtle and unpublicized means in response to social and cultural shifts in the definition of responsible entertainment.

The Rating Board's approach to the representation of masturbation and oral sex changed in the mid-to-late 1990s as a result of a greater liberalization of sexual matters in music, television, and other cultural media. From Pee Wee Herman's arrest and the *Seinfeld* "The Contest" episode in the early 1990s to the Monica Lewinsky scandal and daytime talk shows of this period, stories about fellatio, cunnilingus, and masturbation permeated the media, turning once private speech into public discourse. How exactly these elements were acknowledged by the Rating Board and negotiated with filmmakers cannot be determined without internal documentation of CARA's practices. Even so, the treatment of these sexual acts in the films themselves—most notably *Jade* (1995) *Boogie Nights* (1997), and *Two Girls and a Guy* (1998)—are more explicit than films in the first half of the 1990s, suggesting these broader social forces shifted the boundary thresholds of the Incontestable R.

Two old nemeses of the rating system were behind *Jade:* director William Friedkin and screenwriter Joe Eszterhas. The film about a clinical psychiatrist (Linda Fiorentino) by day, hooker by night, who is suspected of murder, received crushing reviews and performed disastrously at the box office in October 1995. Though ill-fatedly, Paramount used sex as the film's main selling point in its marketing campaign. The trailer hinted at "secret fantasies" and "secret lives" that "go too far," and the poster art underscored the film's primary subject matter with the tagline "Some fantasies go too far." Accompanying these words was a picture of Fiorentino, her back to the spectator, with the suggestion that she is receiving oral sex; a hand appears on her waist in the lower left corner of the poster.[114] Highly suggestive for Advertising Administration approved poster art, the one-sheet for *Jade* and the film itself appears to have set a new regulatory standard for CARA.

What was so peculiar about *Jade* was the absence of any rating controversy. Neither the *Hollywood Reporter* nor *Variety* carried articles on any dispute

Figure 22. Shattering the taboos of onscreen oral sex: Linda Fiorentino and Chazz Palminteri in *Jade* (1995). Copyright 1995 by Paramount Pictures.

between the filmmakers and the Rating Board. There was no report of an appeal, nor did Paramount or Friedkin use a potential NC-17 as a marketing ploy to stir up interest for the film. When an extended unrated version of the film was released a few years later on video with twelve minutes of footage (mostly exposition) not shown in theaters, Paramount's video marketing department did not promote its added sexual elements.

Still, the R version contains many "taboo" shots previously impermissible in other R-rated films. One scene—the third of three scenes featuring police-men watching Fiorentino performing various sexual acts with a client on videotape—contains a one-second onscreen shot of simulated cunnilingus.[115] Similar violations occur in the final sex scene: a two-second medium shot of cunnilingus is clearly visible onscreen, and two one-second full shots of a man (the one outside the frame of *Jade*'s poster) performing oral sex on Fiorentino. No pubic hair is visible during these oral sex scenes in *Jade*; Fiorentino is always partially clothed by a nightie.[116] Yet the Rating Board passed these sexual aesthetics for an R when previously, the degree of explic-itness of the acts—even a one-second full shot of a man's face between a woman's legs or vice versa—had been taboo for the rating. Studio favoritism probably played a role in the isolated nature of *Jade*'s transgression of the norms of responsible entertainment. Without primary documentation from CARA, however, this explanation remains only a guess.

Two years later, though, it would be hard to imagine not having shots of masturbation, fellatio, and cunnilingus in a film about the 1970s porn industry. Indeed, the NC-17 was not easy to shake for distributor New Line and director Paul Thomas Anderson, who submitted fourteen different versions of *Boogie Nights* to the Rating Board in the summer of 1997 before getting an R.[117] The film's principal postproduction executive, Joe Fineman, described the rating dilemma in a memo to Anderson: "The [Rating Board] found that *Boogie Nights* contained much more sexually graphic material than in *Showgirls* or *Henry and June*. Remember, you have two lengthy jerking off scenes, four graphic sex scenes showing tits, humping and bare asses plus the Roller Girl's full frontal. That's a real sweatload of sex compared with the NC-17 pictures I mentioned above." Contractually obligated to deliver an R, Anderson says ninety seconds of the film were cut to satisfy the Rating Board, not whole scenes, just trims to shots, mainly from what the director called "Mark Wahlberg's ass, humping." The Rating Board specifically had a problem during the rating negotiations with "how long humping goes on" and "humping and talking at the same time," Anderson remarked. "So we just went and shot a shot of Nina Hartley, and I said: 'Nina, hump one, stop, say your lines, and we'll move on.' And we did that and put it in and got an R."[118]

For a film about an industry built on the concept of gratuitous sex, however, *Boogie Nights* was quite restrained in what it reveals to the audience. Much of the sexual action is implicit rather than explicit in the released R version.[119] The only remaining thrusting shots from the bootleg uncut version occur in the limousine scene with Roller Girl (Heather Graham) and a young guy off the street, about two seconds of obscured grinding. All the intercourse scenes of Wahlberg's "humping" have been eliminated. The porno shoot between him and Julianne Moore contained close-ups, cutaways, reaction shots, above-the-waist medium shots, and a long shot of the two actors nude in a stationary fornication position but never any sexual grinding full shots. These shots along with Graham's and Wahlberg's nonsexual full-frontal shots, conformed to Rating Board standards of sex and nudity.

Boogie Nights' scenes of masturbation and fellatio violate existing norms of the Incontestable R, however, suggesting that the Rating Board changed its policies regarding these sexual acts. A seven-second, split-screen, three-quarter shot of Graham giving fellatio to Wahlberg and a one-second, three-quarter shot of Melora Walters doing the same to Wahlberg appear in the R cut. And Wahlberg's masturbation scene in front of a mirror shows his hand moving up and down in a three-quarter shot, although his penis is out-

Figure 23. Paul Thomas Anderson directing Heather Graham in *Boogie Nights* (1997). Courtesy of the Academy of Motion Picture Arts and Sciences.

side the frame.[120] Previously, all hand movement had to occur outside the frame, even in the R-rated video version of the sexually graphic, NC-17-rated *Crash* (1996).

The reports of the editing of *Boogie Nights* never focused on the Rating Board's liberalization of its masturbation and oral sex policies; instead, the media reinforced the same untruths and distortions perpetuated about the rating system. Peter Bart, the usually astute editor of *Variety,* conjured up old industry myths to account for Wahlberg's penis shot in the final image of *Boogie Nights*. "Since the rating board has always in effect barred male frontal nudity, the unveiling of the penis posed a similar problem," he wrote. "The upshot: it's there, but briefly. Does the fact that viewers get a peep rather than a full-fledged glimpse of Mark Wahlberg's 13-inch member justify an R rather than an NC-17? Perhaps, since we've been assured that the organ is a prosthetic rather than the real thing—hence the scene can be rationalized as a fantasy sequence."[121] While this "peep" actually is a twelve seconds long, three-quarter shot, this shot of full frontal male nudity certainly was unparalleled. As I have shown, however, the Rating Board has no double standards on frontal nudity as long as it occurs outside of sexual activity—Julianne Moore in *Short Cuts* (1993) and Amy Irving, Amy Locane, and Dennis Hopper in *Carried Away* (1996) have plenty of nonsexual full-frontal screen time in these R-rated films. The Rating Board cares nothing about ideological distinctions like fantasy and reality, just "Mark Wahlberg's ass, humping."

Whereas the R negotiation for *Boogie Nights* took place over a number of explicit scenes, the contretemps over Fox Searchlight's *Two Girls and a Guy* dealt with just one: a six-minute, silhouetted, oral sex number between Robert Downey Jr. and Heather Graham. *Variety*'s Todd McCarthy described the film—about a two-timing actor (Downey) whose two girlfriends (Graham and Natasha Gregson Wagner) find out about each other's existence—as "a bout of quite hot and, at least for an American movie, unusual sex."[122] This sex scene was solely responsible for the film's official NC-17 rating ("for a scene of explicit sexuality") in November 1997.[123] Its "unusualness" was not lost on some members of the Appeals Board that same month, which upheld the NC-17 in a close seven-to-seven vote, telling the film's director, James Toback, that the scene was "groundbreaking" in its sexual depiction.[124] Toback, who was contractually obligated to deliver an R on *Two Girls and a Guy,* set out to trim the scene himself. After a rare second appeal saw the film fall one vote shy (seven to five) of the two-thirds majority needed for an R, Toback recut *Two Girls and a Guy* and was finally awarded an R in April 1998 by the Rating Board after the film's fourteenth submission.[125]

Toback despised the Rating Board but, like few other directors, astutely understood the logic behind its policies of responsible entertainment. "They're not rating movies for the Average American," he said. "They're rating movies for a fringe group of potential adversaries who might protest and write letters. That's the fundamental hypocrisy of the [Rating Board]." He stated that the oral sex scene "didn't just disturb them, it freaked them out totally . . . [yet] . . . [they] can be as intellectually shabby and blockheaded and inconsistent and capricious as they want to be, and they're unanswerable. You can bang your head against a wall, and it's still their wall." These rare moments of rationality from a filmmaker about the rating system, though, gave way to the hype and misunderstandings by *Two Girls'* distributor and the press. David Dinerstein of Fox Searchlight believed the oral sex scene was raw and intense but "doesn't go beyond what any other film that's currently out is doing, especially *Boogie Nights.*" He was wrong. Amy Wallace of the *Los Angeles Times* shared the same opinion in writing that "anyone who's seen *Boogie Nights* . . . will probably judge *Two Girls* to be the tamer film by far."[126] She was wrong as well.

In fact, *Two Girls and a Guy,* just in this one scene, is more graphically explicit, in my mind, than *Boogie Nights,* even though neither film shows genitalia or pubic hair in its depictions of masturbation and oral sex. In the fellatio segment of *Two Girls and a Guy* two separate three-quarter shots (with Graham's back to the camera) reveal her giving oral sex to Downey Jr. for three seconds and masturbating him for two seconds. A one-second close-up of the masturbation is also present. In the cunnilingus segment, two one-second close-ups of Downey (with his back to camera) kissing Graham's buttocks are followed by a fifteen-second full shot (though darkly lit) of him licking and fondling her genitals. All of these shots, though, had been trimmed down from the NC-17 version, edited according to the temporal norms of sexual grinding and thrusting adhered to across a broad spectrum of films from the time of *Basic Instinct* to *Boogie Nights.* "Instead of Heather Graham's elbow going up and down six times," Toback said, "it's three times; instead of Robert Downey being on his knees in a successful effort to give pleasure orally for seven seconds, he's doing it for 3½ seconds."[127]

Boogie Nights and *Two Girls and a Guy* clearly set new standards for the representation of masturbation and oral sex in R-rated films by 1998. Except for the anomaly of *Jade* in 1995, the more graphic stylistic treatment of these sexual acts had been negotiated out of R-rated films since 1992 and perhaps as far back as the early 1980s. A liberalization of Rating Board standards can best explain this shift, along with greater public tolerance for the treatment of such acts in the realm of responsible entertainment. Before long, masturbation (outside the frame and represented by onscreen hand movements) became a major plot point in R-rated films like *Psycho* (1998), *There's Something about Mary* (1999), and *Me, Myself & Irene* (2000). Oral sex played a central role in R-rated films like *American Pie* (1998) and *Scary Movie* (2000).

At the same time that the Rating Board was quietly reshaping the contours of sex for the Incontestable R in the 1990s, however, the MPAA reified responsible entertainment on its end through the continual abandonment of mainstream NC-17 films—except in one instance—MGM/UA's *Showgirls* in 1995. The film met with little controversy and even smaller box office. Through its failure, though, *Showgirls* proved one thing: an NC-17 film could in fact be marketed, advertised, and exhibited like any R-rated film.

CHAPTER 5

Showgirls

THE FEASIBILITY AND FATE
OF THE NC-17 RATING

*I just do not believe that there will be all that many NC-17 films
coming down the pike. . . . I seriously doubt that many investors will be
rushing to put their money into projects which have a built-in
structural limitation to their financial success.*
 —NATO President William Kartozian, *NATO News,* March 1991

After *Henry & June* the Motion Picture Association of America, the National
Association of Theatre Owners, and the Video Software Dealers Association
overlooked the cosmetic change in the X rating and went back to business as
usual: the business of the Incontestable R and responsible entertainment. The
MPAA signatories shunned the distribution of mainstream NC-17 films. Few
mainstream movie houses would play NC-17 films. Most major video-store
chains refused to carry NC-17 films. The year after the rating change, film
critic Peter Rainer lamented, "It's one thing to sanction more adult-oriented
movies; it's another thing to make them."[1] A number of mostly forgettable
NC-17 films were released in the following years, and none removed the economic liability and moral stigma of the category. *Whore* (1991), *Dice Rules*
(1991), *Bad Lieutenant* (1992), *Wide Sargasso Sea* (1992), *Bank Robber* (1993),
Man Bites Dog (1993), and *You So Crazy* (1994) were not distributed by MPAA
signatories, played in few mainstream theaters, and contained noncommer-
cial elements that made them untenable in the mass market. In 1995, however,
Showgirls renewed the possibility that the NC-17 rating could be a viable
commodity.

MGM/UA, the MPAA-member distributor of *Showgirls,* tried to keep in
mind what Richard Maltby describes as the necessary conditions for the
consumption of a Hollywood film: "A 'good' movie is one that gives us our

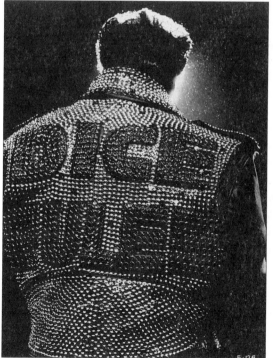

Figure 24. *Whore* (1991).
Figure 25. *Dice Rules* (1991).
Two independent, early
adopters of the NC-17
rating.

'money's worth.'"[2] MGM/UA believed that the combination of NC-17 sexual rawness, a lot of bare-breasted nudity, a big Hollywood budget, and *Basic Instinct* director Paul Verhoeven would provide viewers with a worthwhile experience in exchange for their time and ticket price.[3] That did not happen, and *Showgirls* bombed at the box office.

Ever since then, the MPAA signatories have not released a single NC-17 film targeted at multiplexes for mainstream audiences. All MPAA NC-17 product, along with NC-17 and unrated product from the independents, has been destined for art houses and niche audiences, expanding only in a few instances to mainstream theaters. This chapter argues that *Showgirls*—had it been successful at the box office—may have removed some of the stigma still attached to the NC-17 category today. I will first examine the marketing of *Showgirls* in order to debunk many long-standing industry myths of the marketplace that fueled the stigmatization and practical abandonment of the X/NC-17 rating. Contrary to popular thinking, MGM/UA actually faced few barriers in securing prime advertising, promotional spots, and exhibition outlets for *Showgirls*. Next I will discuss how the film's scathing reviews and box-office disaster nullified any progress made for the legitimization of the NC-17 rating. *Showgirls* alternatively validated the commercial unfeasibility of the NC-17 rating and the commercial feasibility of the Incontestable R to the MPAA signatories. I will then analyze the inconsequential sixty-second difference between the NC-17-rated theatrical and R-rated video releases of *Showgirls*. After all the hype, *Showgirls* turned out to be nothing more than a glorified R-rated movie. Finally, I will talk about the fate of the NC-17 after *Showgirls*, a rating subsequently applied only to U.S. independent and foreign films. Case studies of the unrated *Kids* (1995) and *Happiness* (1998) demonstrate how the industry's systematic bias toward the Incontestable R drives out of the marketplace independent films that fail to correspond with the norms of responsible entertainment, even those films originally intended for distribution by MPAA-member companies. The purchase of independent distributors like Miramax and October and the creation of in-house art-house subsidiaries by MPAA signatories since the mid-1990s have further marginalized and stigmatized the NC-17 and its "sister," the unrated film. Consequently, fewer and fewer films carrying these tags play in mainstream theaters or art houses.

THE MARKETING SUCCESS OF *SHOWGIRLS*

It was commonly believed that the inability to secure exhibition venues, the loss of ancillary markets, the high probability of backlash, and the difficulties of advertising adults-only material made an NC-17 film an extremely risky investment for the MPAA signatories. Nevertheless, these obstacles failed to dissuade MGM/UA from purchasing the North American distribution rights to *Showgirls* from Chargeurs, the film's foreign backer.[4]

Showgirls tells the tale of Nomi Malone (Elizabeth Berkley), who hitches her way into Las Vegas to become a dancer. She is intrigued by a show at the Stardust, a nightly music-and-dance extravaganza full of gymnastic G-string dancers. Nomi, knowing she has to start small, becomes a stripper at the second-rate Cheetahs, where she gets extra tips for lap dancing in a private booth. Eventually, she sleeps her way into the Stardust show and replaces its star, Cristal Connors (Gina Gershon), after pushing her down a stairway. Success, however, comes at a cost. After seeing her best friend get gang-raped at a celebration party, Nomi decides to hitchhike back home and leave sin city.

When initially shopping the project to production studios, Verhoeven made final cut a mandatory condition of any contract for *Showgirls;* he was no longer willing to commit his film to an R rating in order to ensure a wider audience, as he had done with *RoboCop* (1987), *Total Recall* (1990), and *Basic Instinct* (1992).[5] According to the director, "When I first read the script, I told Joe [Eszterhas, the screenwriter] I wouldn't consider it unless we found a film company that gave the O.K. I didn't want to go through the *Basic Instinct* experience, going back to the [MPAA] 300 times."[6] After three straight box-office hits Verhoeven felt he had earned the right—or gained the clout—to demand final cut for his next project, a privilege given to very few directors working in Hollywood. If it happened to be rated NC-17, then so be it.

So why did MGM/UA purchase a property with the NC-17 condition attached? First, MGM/UA was the only MPAA signatory not publicly owned—the company answered to the European bank Credit Lyonnais—so the distributor had a degree of freedom to distribute controversial films that its competitors lacked.[7] Second, *Stargate* (1994) had been its only hit since *Thelma and Louise* (1991). MGM/UA believed that an NC-17 film would definitely generate publicity, controversy, and profit. Third, *Showgirls* would reunite Verhoeven with Eszterhas—whom critic Christopher Goodwin called "the Barnum and Bailey of cinematic psychosex."[8] Since *Basic Instinct* earned $352 million worldwide, their partnership guaranteed MGM/UA some box-office insurance in domestic, foreign, and video markets.

In seizing the chance to make an NC-17 movie, MGM/UA violated industry policy governing responsible entertainment. By giving Verhoeven final cut of *Showgirls,* the distributor also disrupted Hollywood's traditional practice of arranging products into an Incontestable R. MGM/UA placed total control of *Showgirls* in the hands of the artist, hoping to profit from a controversial rating. It was this sort of opportunism that Valenti often said would pose the greatest threats to CARA, because such short-term profitability for one MPAA signatory would threaten the long-term stability of the entire industry.

MGM/UA obviously did not care. *Showgirls,* like all Hollywood films, was intended to be a "moneymaker" but, in the words of one critic, a "starmaker" and "groundbreaker" as well.[9] With a relatively modest $40-million budget, MGM/UA heavily promoted the film's production values and sensationalistic elements to an adult audience, intending to open the film as widely as possible. First, Frank Mancuso, chair of MGM/UA, believed that *Showgirls* was "a commercial project, and with the size and pattern of the release that there's an opportunity for the film to gross a substantial amount of money."[10] The film also featured the potential star-making motion picture debut of Elizabeth Berkley, a teenage actress from the television show *Saved by the Bell.* The role of Nomi Malone was a make-or-break role for Berkley, whose unclothed appearance during half of the film could incite cheers or jeers. Last, with its abundance of sex and nudity, *Showgirls* clearly was a test of the acceptability of provocative, erotic, NC-17 films in mainstream markets. Verhoeven recognized this potential: "It's not soft porn. I don't know if it's titillation or not. But it does take nudity for granted. . . . Women are topless and that's how it is. . . . It also pushes the envelope portraying sexuality in a more precise way than you normally do in American movies."[11] In good faith or rather through gentlemanly hubris, Verhoeven even agreed to defer 70 percent of his $6-million director's salary until the movie turned a profit.[12]

Since the NC-17 automatically excludes most teenagers, *Showgirls* needed to promote itself in a dramatic fashion to an adults-only audience to recoup its costs. Without any previous NC-17 marketing strategy of this magnitude to borrow from, MGM/UA maximized the potential audience for *Showgirls* by making it as ubiquitous as possible, unabashedly promoting its forbidden nature and raw sexuality in a way unseen in any advertising campaign to come out of Hollywood in a long time. The marketing plan was indeed shrewd, innovative, and effective and managed to solve a number of problems previously thought to be intractable when selling an NC-17 film.

First: *Where can you advertise a trailer of an NC-17 film, and can it contain any representative images?* It was commonly believed that most television stations would not advertise X or NC-17 films. This, however, was untrue. The four major broadcast networks had a policy of airing advertising spots for NC-17 films on a case-by-case basis. In the case of *Showgirls* only NBC refused to carry the trailer, though the network gave permission to its owned-and-operated stations and affiliates to carry it at their discretion. The trailer ran on the other three networks after 10 p.m., just an hour later than the standard

cutoff time for R-rated films. For movie houses the MPAA's Advertising
Administration approved both a "green band" and a "red band" trailer of
Showgirls, enabling the film to be promoted to adults attending movies with
any rating, not just those rated R or NC-17.

Showgirls' first theatrical summer teaser, approved for general audiences
in a "green band" trailer, promised "a movie event so erotic . . . so dangerous
. . . so controversial . . . that we can't show you a thing"; this onscreen text was
followed by a shot of Berkley running her tongue along a shiny pole. The
second "red band" trailer was shown only with R-rated films and outlined the
film's story through images of breasts, lesbianism, and catfights.[13] Capitaliz-
ing on the notoriety of the Verhoeven/Eszterhas team of *Basic Instinct,* this
trailer promised that "last time they took you to the edge; this time, they're
taking you all the way." The most provocative footage of *Showgirls* was saved
for the 250,000 copies of an eight-minute home video trailer MGM/UA
released to video stores on September 11, 1995, eleven days before the film's
premiere. It included bare breasts, sexually explicit scenes, and graphic violence. Free of charge to consumers eighteen or over, the video could be picked
up at all major retail outlets, except Blockbuster Video.[14] Many stores had to
order additional copies because the demand was so great.[15] An executive from
a rival distributor called this "a brilliant move. Whether the consumer picks
up the tape or not, it had the veneer of something special . . . that just might
be a little nasty."[16] This multitiered strategy of marketing the trailer for *Showgirls* demonstrated that an NC-17 film could reach adult audiences through a
variety of traditional and nontraditional means.

Second: *Where can you advertise the film in print?* Contrary to industry
belief, many newspapers, not just the *Los Angeles Times, Chicago Sun-Times,*
and *New York Times,* were willing to accept ads for NC-17 films, provided that
the artwork was not offensive.[17] In addition, although the Advertising Administration had little tolerance for sexuality and nudity in newspaper advertising—as shown in the cases of *Jason's Lyric* (1994) and *Ready to Wear* (a k a
Prêt-à-Porter [1994])—it approved the *Showgirls* advertisement for mass distribution.[18] By designing an appealing, but not revealing, promotional ad that
met the standards of the Advertising Administration and the policies of mass
media outlets, MGM/UA was able to purchase a flood of print spots. The
advertisements and poster art featured a revealing shot of Berkley with what
appeared to be a never-ending leg and the words "Leave your inhibitions at
the door."[19] Only the *Daily Oklahoman* and the *Fort Worth Star-Telegram*
refused to carry the ad. Outdoor advertising included banners on airplanes,
taxi panels, kiosks, bus shelters, and billboards over Times Square and Venice
Beach. MGM/UA especially targeted the eighteen-to-thirty-four male

audience by placing advertisements next to the box scores of Labor Day sports sections.[20]

Third: *How do you convince theater owners to show the film?* Never before had there been an NC-17 film with such commercial potential. Niche films like *Bad Lieutenant* or foreign films like *Wide Sargasso Sea* were always destined for a limited release on the art-house circuit; national multiplex chains would rarely consider these NC-17 films for their theaters. In contrast, the Hollywood-produced *Showgirls* confronted exhibitors with a difficult decision: whether or not to assume the risk of showing an adults-only film that could be a moneymaker at the multiplex. Exhibiting the film meant that theater personnel would have to check teenagers' IDs at the box office—potentially creating box-office gridlock—and monitor those trying to sneak into *Showgirls* from another movie. MGM/UA, aware of exhibitor uncertainty toward an NC-17 product, showed theater owners an eight-minute teaser trailer (likely the same one released to video stores) seven months prior to the film's release to assure them of *Showgirls'* legitimacy and non-pornographic quality—in other words, to demonstrate its "responsible" nature.[21] The distributor even provided theater owners with the finished film before its release to further reassure them.[22] And, as an extra incentive for exhibitors, MGM/UA offered to pay for an extra usher to stand outside the *Showgirls* screenings to catch theater jumpers.

MGM/UA's strategic wooing of exhibitors transformed any appearance of exploiting the NC-17 rating into the appearance that it was concerned for child welfare. Although some pressure groups, such as the American Family Association, still found *Showgirls* a "hard-core porn movie," many exhibitors considered the film appropriate for their screens and not synonymous with pornography. Only two theater chains, Cinemark in Texas and Carmike in Georgia, refused to change their policy against showing NC-17 films. James Edwards Sr. of Edwards Theatres, who booked the film, admitted that he might have refused the film a few years before, "but times change . . . and if we want to stay in business, we have to change." Nevertheless, Bruce Corwin, president of Metropolitan Theatres, would have preferred a less restricted rating: "Obviously, we'd all love to see it come in with an R. It makes it easier for everyone."[23] There were also two other significant reasons for *Showgirls'* inroads into mainstream exhibition: (1) multiplexes recently built as stand-alone buildings by large chains were not subject to the once-common lease restrictions from malls barring NC-17 films; and (2) operators in the older buildings violated their lease agreements to show the film.[24]

Fourth: *How profitable can NC-17 films be in the ancillary markets?* With expected revenues from box-office sales then accounting for one-fourth of a film's total revenues, the profitability of the television, video, and overseas markets was (and remains) an important factor in deciding to produce any film, NC-17 rated or not. Of all video stores at the time, 30 percent would not rent NC-17 product, 50 percent of the sell-through market (notably Block-buster, Wal-Mart, and Kmart) would not carry NC-17 films, and pay cable outlets HBO, Showtime, and Viewer's Choice (pay-per-view) would not run films with the NC-17 rating.[25] Overseas, an NC-17 film featuring nudity and sex could be banned throughout much of the Middle East and the Far East and might face harsh age and advertising restrictions in certain countries in Europe and Latin America. It would appear, then, that MGM/UA was taking a big financial risk with *Showgirls*.

The MPAA signatory, however, paid only $10 million for the film's North American distribution rights, an amount it was almost certain to earn back in the ancillary markets even if *Showgirls* failed at the box office. Chargeurs, the producer, must also have thought that it had a can't-lose situation on its hands, as the company insured itself against a catastrophic drop in the film's ancillary value by preselling all its overseas distribution rights, reportedly getting top dollar in Japan.[26] *Showgirls'* reasonable $40-million production price tag made such deals possible for Chargeurs, and it was also undoubt-edly the case that Verhoeven's name attached to a big-budget "sex" film from the United States lured distributors to purchase the film even prior to its completion.

As expected, on July 19, 1995, CARA gave the NC-17 to *Showgirls* for "nudity, erotic sexuality throughout, graphic language, and sexual vio-lence."[27] Verhoeven wasn't worried about the film's chances for the adults-only rating, however: "I knew we had nudity enough for an NC-17."[28] Perhaps to Verhoeven's chagrin, few people expressed moral outrage about the film's nudity, violence, or tone. One of the few reform groups that spoke out against *Showgirls* was the Christian Film and Television Commission, which urged "moral Americans" to boycott the film.[29] Morality in Media also criticized the film, condemning its subject matter and MGM/UA's efforts to market the film in neighborhood theaters and video stores.[30] The organization decided to forgo demonstrations so as not to attract con-sumers to the film. A spokesperson for U.S. Senator Bob Dole said that these organizations were doing precisely what the presidential candidate sug-gested in his "nightmare of depravity" speech, and he applauded them for their efforts.[31] Ironically, actress Gina Gershon claimed that *Showgirls* was "the perfect Bob Dole movie. . . . It's all about morals and values. . . . It just happens to be done topless."[32] The lack of cultural and political debate sur-rounding the film certainly made it appear that most of the public cared

Figure 26. Shattering NC-17 myths without shattering the box office: Elizabeth
Berkley in *Showgirls* (1995). Courtesy of the Academy of Motion Picture Arts and
Sciences.

little that an NC-17 film (or at least that *Showgirls*) was playing in their
neighborhood theaters.

With the film's U.S. premiere approaching, there was a media blitz for
Showgirls. Berkley demonstrated the art of lap dancing *on* David Letterman
during his late-night show. Joe Eszterhas took out a full-page ad in *Daily
Variety* and, in an open letter to the public, blasted the studio's male-targeted
marketing campaign by encouraging women to see *Showgirls* for its story and
not for its sexual content. In an interview Eszterhas also attacked the ratings
system itself, encouraging underage teens to "use [their] fake IDs" to get into
Showgirls.[33] MGM/UA published a book about the making of *Showgirls* that
contained explicit photographic outtakes and stills from the film. The distributor also launched an extremely well-trafficked Web site that received more
than one million hits daily (fifty thousand to seventy-five thousand was considered a success at that time), which translated to about 175,000 people.[34]
The site, which children could access despite a warning that its contents were
off-limits to anyone under seventeen, featured nude photos, a dialogue sim-
ulator with the performers, and a link to the *Playboy* Web site.

Showgirls' successful marketing inroads, theatrical guarantees, and relative
dearth of controversy proved that an MPAA signatory could successfully distribute an NC-17 film with little economic or political risk. The warnings that

the rating would fail to secure advertising and theatrical venues were certainly unfounded. Most important, *Showgirls* revealed, to some extent, that an NC-17 film could be validated as responsible entertainment. Gerry Rich, MGM's vice president of worldwide marketing, pointed out that "the whole myth that you couldn't release an NC-17 film widely was just that—a myth."[35] The question still remained, though: would *Showgirls* attract a paying audience, with its large amount of nudity, sex, and strong subject matter? If so, and if the film had "reasonable success," said Verhoeven on the day of its release, "the people at the studios may think, 'OK, we can make NC-17 films.' The freedom that will be obtained will be beneficial to the directors and ultimately to the public."[36]

The Box Office Failure of *Showgirls*

This is a gamble worth taking. If there are consequences, we'll all have to live with that. [Showgirls] is an adult movie, but so what? It's entertainment. It's honorable. American audiences are strong enough to accept this movie. You're not going to be ashamed to see your neighbor in the movie theater when you see Showgirls.
                    —Paul Verhoeven, *New York Times,* July 21, 1995

Despite opening on September 22, 1995, in 1,388 theaters, a record for an NC-17 film (about the same as *Clockers* and *Dangerous Minds* that year and more than half the standard number for big-budget Hollywood releases at the time), *Showgirls* was a box-office disaster in the United States. The hype surrounding the film proved to be an unfulfilled tease for critics and audiences alike as *Showgirls* earned only $8.1 million in its first week (a per-screen average of $5,845). Worse, *Showgirls* fell precipitously (60 percent) in its second week, to a box-office total of $3.7 million (a per-screen average of $2,531)—eventually grossing slightly more than $20 million domestically. Its failure can be attributed to its poor word of mouth and to the fact that critics almost unanimously gave it some of the most abominable reviews in recent memory; Dana Kennedy of *Entertainment Weekly* called it the "worst movie in history."[37]

Even though Verhoeven and Eszterhas had repeatedly stressed the film's nonsexual elements of female empowerment and morality, reviewers condemned nearly everything about the picture, citing the incompetent performances (particularly that of Berkley), the dullness of the narrative, the disturbing gang rape of Molly, the laughable dialogue, the inclusion of only one "real" sex scene, and the unerotic sexual imagery. Janet Maslin of the *New York Times* found the film a "bare-butted bore." Kenneth Turan of the *Los*

Angeles Times called Berkley's Nomi "an irritating self-absorbed twerp." William Cash of London's *Daily Telegraph* wrote that *Showgirls* "reduces eroticism to the banal level of the Playboy Channel" and "is simply a hardcore version of *Baywatch*." Anthony Lane of the *New Yorker* said that the film's depiction of lust and sexuality "should not be shown to people *over* seventeen." And Richard Corliss of *Time* believed that the film wasn't sexy, "only X-ie."[38] Most damaging, critics tended to find the characters in *Showgirls* unsympathetic, a characteristic inconsistent with the affirmative cultural function of entertainment that Hollywood has always constructed.[39]

Mockingly coined "Fleshdance" and "*All About Eve* in pasties," *Showgirls* certainly did not live up to the expectations it had created. One exhibitor said, "If it wasn't NC-17, it would never get any interest out of you, me, or anyone else." Since *Showgirls* contained only one scene of simulated sexual intercourse, perhaps men in the audience, wrote John Leland in *Newsweek*, were disappointed with the sex and eroticism. Tom Shone of the *Times* believed that the only people who would get excited by *Showgirls* were "those too young to see it." Verhoeven eventually admitted that there was a "perception problem" with *Showgirls* because the advertising promised a sexy, pornographic movie. "That was wrong," he said. "The trouble was, audiences went looking for thrills and emerged unaroused and that made them hate the film."[40] Or perhaps the three million people estimated to have seen the eight-minute video trailer had already concluded that the film was unsatisfying as erotic entertainment and never considered paying $7 to see it at the theater.[41]

Consumers seemed happy, however, to pay $3 to rent *Showgirls* on video—in both NC-17 and R versions—as demand for the film racked up more than 250,000 preorders in North America, significantly more than the average for a film with similar box-office take.[42] MGM/UA released both versions itself without the assistance of the sales force or back office operation of Warner Home Video, which exercised an option in its distribution agreement with MGM/UA not to handle titles greater than an R.[43] Before the theatrical release of *Showgirls* Verhoeven neither wanted or expected to cut the film, since MGM/UA contractually could not force him to do an R-rated version.[44] Apparently, he changed his mind. After consuming more than $50 million in production costs and marketing while only earning $20 million at the box office, Verhoeven felt responsible for *Showgirls*' failure and made two versions available to video outlets to help Chargeurs and MGM/UA recoup their investment. Blockbuster Video, Hollywood Video, and other video outlets with policies against carrying adults-only product unequivocally accepted *Showgirls* for rental once MGM/UA cut the film down to an R, proving that

NC-17 films could be exploited fully in the ancillary markets if cuts were made to the theatrical versions.[45]

The film's ability to secure advertising, to open wide on almost fourteen hundred screens, to reap more than $8 million in its opening weekend, and to secure distribution at the major video outlets had many industry watchers, like John Burnham of the William Morris Agency, soon predicting an increase in NC-17 production by the MPAA signatories: "I think that big studios are going to be much more open to it. Studios will be interested in anything that has that kind of ability to open so successfully.... The NC-17 rating is no longer tainted, now that it's confirmed that it can succeed in the intended market of release."[46] Marc Platt, president of TriStar Pictures, believed an audience still existed for an NC-17 film despite *Showgirls'* poor showing at the domestic box office. "If an NC-17 film were a great movie," he said, "there would certainly be an audience. There are still substantial hurdles with NC-17 films that one must overcome in bringing the film to the marketplace. I don't believe those hurdles will necessarily disappear, but I do believe that if an audience finds a film satisfying, then they will go to that film, regardless of its rating."[47] The *Hollywood Reporter* remained uncertain about *Showgirls'* impact, remarking that the film was "hardly a test" of how well an NC-17 rating would succeed with a mass audience.[48]

Why, then, has no MPAA signatory "tested" the waters with a moderately budgeted NC-17 film since *Showgirls* in 1995? Why did Verhoeven turn out to be correct when he remarked after *Showgirls'* box office failure that "Studios will be hesitant to make NC-17 movies" and "My advice to myself or anybody else is . . . don't make [an NC-17] for more than $20 million"?[49]

The fact remains that it does not serve the political and economic interests of the MPAA distributors and NATO exhibitors to market an NC-17 film. A few isolated incidents occurred in the Midwest and South as city officials, religious groups, and concerned citizens protested screenings, organized boycotts, and shut down some theaters showing *Showgirls* in Bismarck, Memphis, and Tupelo.[50] By this time, though, bad reviews and poor box office had completely neutralized any controversy over the film. Had *Showgirls* been a hit—which it certainly could have been—these events might have galvanized more opposition from reformers. This never happened, but MCA vice chairperson Tom Pollock, the executive behind Universal's *Henry & June* five years earlier, summed up the rating's viability for the MPAA signatories: "There's no law that says NC-17 films can't work . . . but the primary business of Universal Pictures and all the studios is mass entertainment, not pushing the boundaries of sex and violence. It doesn't have to do with moral reasons. It has to do with monetary reasons."[51]

A *Hollywood Reporter*/Robinson Lerer Sawyer Miller Poll taken almost two months after the release of *Showgirls* supports Pollock's argument, suggesting that the NC-17 still carries the X-rating's stigma of pornography and turns away a substantial segment of the mass audience.[52] In a telephone survey of 1,009 adults ages eighteen and up, the poll found that 34 percent of its respondents would be less likely to attend a film if it was rated NC-17 and 24 percent would refuse to attend an NC-17 film even it received critical acclaim. Of the respondents, 69 percent said they would see a critically acclaimed NC-17 film. Nevertheless, the rejection by one-quarter of the population, when factored with high ticket prices and viewer preferences, made mainstream success for an NC-17 film extremely difficult. The pollsters concluded that low-budget NC-17 films had better commercial prospects than big-budget ones, especially those aimed at youths eighteen to twenty-four years old and minorities; more than twice the number of nonwhites than whites said the rating would make it more likely for them to see a film. These results reinforce the fact that *Showgirls*' proven viability in the marketplace had not greatly affected the NC-17's desirability among a majority of Hollywood audiences. Why intentionally have "an uphill fight," by restricting the paying audience to grownups, observed 20th Century Fox distribution executive Tom Sherak shortly after the *Showgirls* collapse.[53] "If you have an excellent story, don't you want as many people as possible to see it?"[54]

A different explanation for the failure of *Showgirls* and the abandonment of adults-only films by the MPAA signatories was presented by director Amy Heckerling, who expressed skepticism that "there's an audience that necessarily wants its porn from Hollywood."[55] As discussed in chapter 4, ever since *Basic Instinct,* theatrically released erotic thrillers had fizzled at the box office in the 1990s. *Body of Evidence* (1992), *Sliver* (1993), and *Color of Night* (1994) were followed by *Jade* (1995), *Striptease* (1996), *Lolita* (1998), *The Player's Club* (1998), and *Wild Things* (1998), which were all unsuccessful. "Sex just doesn't play at the movies anymore," argued Alyssa Katz in the *Nation* in 1998. "Voyeurism went private with the arrival of the VCRs, at exactly the time AIDS hit, and it has stayed at home, and on television, ever since."[56]

Heckerling and Katz may be right in some respects, but two industrial factors had also worked against *Showgirls*. First, the flood of sex thrillers that followed *Basic Instinct* all but drowned the genre's commercial value at the theaters.[57] Second, soft-core eroticism, of the kind that *Showgirls* used as a publicity stunt, could be seen on pay cable and rented at any video store—privately and at a much cheaper price.[58] Mainstream audiences already had access to original pay-television programming such as Showtime's *Red Shoe*

Diaries and straight-to-video erotic thrillers like *Indecent Behavior* (1993). Playboy Entertainment also had successfully produced a number of low-budget, erotic features directly for video and cable, as well as produced video calendars of its magazine's playmates. Since Blockbuster Video and other conservative chains carried many of these videos, as well as the R-rated *Showgirls* spin-offs *Lap Dancing* (1995), *Midnight Tease 2* (1995), and *Stripteaser* (1995), home viewing sales skyrocketed at the expense of soft-core theatrical fare. "After all," says Katz, "who wants to sit next to some pervert while watching smut?"[59]

Although *Showgirls* neither took off at the box office nor spawned an NC-17 revolution, it ironically (yet maybe not surprisingly) emerged as a midnight cult movie in New York and Los Angeles, much like *The Rocky Horror Picture Show* (1975). After Betty Buckley, the star of *Sunset Boulevard* on Broadway, hosted a *Showgirls* party at Planet Hollywood in February 1996, MGM/UA relaunched the film in theaters as high camp, imitating the audience participation that had accompanied Buckley's fete.[60] At the first midnight shows in March, the distributor hired drag performers to pass out scripts that cued viewers to shout along with the characters' lines and to sexually gyrate and lap dance beneath the screen during *Showgirls'* most memorable moments.[61] "Maybe this kind of ritualistic cult popularity isn't what I intended," said Verhoeven, who wasn't consulted on the rerelease, "but it's like the resurrection after the crucifixion."[62] Nevertheless, *Showgirls* managed to break the record of Pia Zadora's *The Lonely Lady* (1983) for the most Golden Raspberry Awards, the Oscar's doppelganger given out annually before the Academy Awards.[63] The film received seven awards, including worst picture, actress (Berkley), and screenplay. Even Verhoeven was on hand to pick up his worst director award, remarking that "at least this appreciation is better than nothing."[64]

When *Showgirls* was released on video in both an NC-17 and R version, Verhoeven only had to cut sixty-one seconds after going through four submissions to the Rating Board.[65] The limited amount of cutting and the relative tameness of the theatrical version surprised even Verhoeven: "On *Basic Instinct,* we went back to them nine times to get an R," he said. "We cut about 45 seconds. I thought it would be much worse with *Showgirls.* We'd probably lose three or four minutes. . . . Knowing the script, everybody agreed that it would not be possible to make this movie as an R without too much cutting. In fact, we were all wrong."[66] An additional twenty seconds were replaced with different camera angles or optical zooms, and some sex scenes were sped up to shorten their duration.[67] Yet almost all the stage and sexual nudity was kept in the R version, which means that it would have been relatively easy for

Verhoeven to cut the film down from an NC-17 for a wider R-rated theatrical release.

Three major scenes in the NC-17 version of *Showgirls*—the lap dance, swimming pool, and rape—were modified in the R-rated video release. For Berkley's lap dance on Kyle MacLachlan, full shots of her touching her genitals through her G-string and touching MacLachlan's genitals through his pants were replaced with close-ups of their faces. Much of Berkley's lap dance had its NC-17 full shots replaced with above-the-waist medium shots. And MacLachlan's six-spasm orgasm was reduced to one spasm. For the pool lovemaking scene between Berkley and MacLachlan the same editing techniques were employed: medium above-the-waist shots replaced long shots of sexual grinding, and the overall reduction of the length of the sex scene was reduced. An additional shot of Berkley reaching into the water to insert MacLachlan's penis inside her vagina off-camera was cut for the R version. For the rape of Gina Ravera, penetration and sexual grinding full shots were entirely cut as well. A medium reaction shot of the rapists is also shortened.

Additionally, other scenes were trimmed for the R. During Berkley's first stripping number, a long shot of the actress sexually placing her fingers inside her G-string have been replaced with a close-up of her face. In the same scene a shot of fellow stripper Rena Riffel's vulva as she crawls on the floor was cut. In a later strip scene a mock grinding performance onstage between a nude Berkley and Riffel and a shot of Berkley running her genitals down alongside a pole have been shortened and replaced with above-the-waist shots and close-ups of their faces. Oddly, the "period-checking" shot during Berkley's dance-turned-lovemaking session with Glenn Plummer in his apartment was left intact in the R version. In this scene Plummer places his hand in Berkley's tights because he refuses to take her word that she cannot make love because of her period. Perhaps the Rating Board felt the nonsexual nature of the shot was permissible for an R. Chances were they had never been faced with such an editing decision before—and probably never will be again.

The trivial nature of these alterations suggests that the overall tone of the NC-17 *Showgirls* did not radically challenge the concept of responsible entertainment. The film's success in overcoming many of the impediments thought to be associated with the NC-17—exhibitor apprehension, reform group disapproval, and media boycott—might also be attributed to its "feeling" and "looking like" a typical R-rated film to Hollywood's audiences and detractors. As scholar Linda Ruth Williams remarked, "Verhoeven goes no further than he did in *Basic Instinct,* and not as far as the average straight-to-video erotic thriller."[68]

This historical account of *Showgirls* demonstrates that Verhoeven always intended *Showgirls* to play for mass audiences and that MGM/UA did everything to make sure the film would play to those audiences in a majority of NATO theaters. Most independent films embracing the NC-17—before *and* after *Showgirls*—however, invariably challenged the boundaries of the Incontestable R in ways unimaginable for Hollywood films and almost exclusively for the art-house circuit. While the *Rating Board* did not award NC-17 ratings to independent distributors in a discriminating manner, the *rating system* did actively reward R ratings to films that subscribed to the notion of responsible entertainment, be they released by the MPAA signatories or the independents. One either plays by the rules of the MPAA and NATO or gets shut out of the mainstream marketplace. It is often as simple as that.

THE INDEPENDENTS AND THE NC-17

If you really want to make something badly enough and you can work it into a budget of $7 million or $8 million or $9 million, there's a good chance of getting it made. Maybe not by a major. Independently, I'm talking about.
—Martin Scorsese, quoted in Roger Ebert and
Gene Siskel, *The Future of the Movies,* 4.

Showgirls is the exception to the rule. The MPAA and NATO never rallied behind the X/NC-17 rating because of its obvious economic and political liabilities: cutting one's audience in half while doubling public grievances generally meant less money at the box office. By "closing down production" of X/NC-17 films and "locking them out" of many first-run exhibition sites, these trade organizations distanced themselves from the adults-only rating now wholly embraced by exploiteers and pornographers. CARA was the glue that cemented this arrangement; the Rating Board ensured almost all MPAA and NATO products carried an R rating in order to reinforce the image of Hollywood as a site of responsible entertainment. With the Incontestable R in place by the mid-1970s, the MPAA managed to regain the two most important components of vertical integration of the classical period: distribution and exhibition. "Cooperation and collusion," noted Jon Lewis, "protect[ed] the studios against the vagaries of the marketplace, the American zeitgeist, and all those so-called independent producers and distributors."[69]

A built-in dissociation and segregation of R-rated Hollywood products from NC-17 or unrated independent fare already had its roots in the Production Code era. As Eric Schaefer demonstrates in *"Bold! Daring! Shocking! True!": A History of Exploitation Films,* the success of the MPAA's self-regulatory policies in the sound era lay in its ability to preclude non-industry-certified films from being shown in mainstream picture houses. Schaefer argues that from 1927 until World War II the independent films of the period (exploitation films, particularly sex-hygiene films), by being excluded, helped to define and shape the nature of mainstream Hollywood entertainment. "Just as surely as 'the Breen Office' was another strategy to consolidate power in the hands of the majors," he says, "it also functioned to marginalize the exploiteers by denying seals to their pictures. Without Code seals, exploitation films were, for all intents and purposes, barred from the lucrative first-run houses in large cities that were run by the majors. The Code and its enforcement also served to shape the dominant image of what movies should be vis-à-vis exploitation."[70] Classical Hollywood's desire to separate itself from exploitative fare served, therefore, to reinforce the perception of Hollywood filmmaking as a dependable business enterprise and to present the MPAA as an organization committed to harmless entertainment.

Efforts to separate the mainstream from the "mutant" were vital to Hollywood because of the public's inability to distinguish between films made by the MPAA and those produced by the independents. Calls for movie reform in the Production Code era, states Schaefer, "were invariably directed at Hollywood, but not necessarily Hollywood *films*," because in the public's mind, all motion pictures were regulated by the PCA under the watchful eye of the MPAA.[71] Schaefer's observation applies equally to the classification era. Motion pictures playing in mainstream exhibition houses are still assumed to be "Hollywood films," whether or not they are distributed by an MPAA signatory or certified by CARA. The very design of the Incontestable R was intended to forestall criticism of motion pictures by reformers and legislators, but CARA could never fully regulate the content of MPAA (*Basic Instinct*) or independent films (*Henry: Portrait of a Serial Killer*) or control the behavior of NATO exhibitors (*Cruising*). To many reformers, for example, a Brian De Palma film—be it distributed by Filmways (*Dressed to Kill*), Universal (*Scarface*), or Columbia (*Body Double*)—still was misogynistic or violent rubbish and not responsible "Hollywood" entertainment.

Since exhibitors can choose to show any film they want, the MPAA could at least—with the help of the majority of NATO members—maintain the illusion of responsibility with independent products by containing their representations within the norms of the R rating. As I showed in chapter 4, the majority of independents released their films NC-17 or unrated, but almost all MPAA signatories cut their films for an R. This way, the less "responsible" X, NC-17, or unrated independent films would migrate to the art houses, whereas the more "responsible" R-rated MPAA and independent films would play in mainstream theaters. Still, some NATO exhibitors did book NC-17 or unrated independent films alongside MPAA product in their theaters, hoping, just like the distributors themselves, that the explicit and unedited elements of sex, violence, and language would reap greater box-office fortune than an edited R-rated version of the film.

Marketing controversy became the primary mechanism for independent distributors to circumvent the Incontestable R and wrestle control of the marketplace away from the MPAA, at least on a case-by-case basis. Miramax, in particular, built its reputation and success on this strategy, sometimes releasing its pictures with an R *(Scandal)*, sometimes releasing them unrated *(The Cook, the Thief, His Wife, and Her Lover)*, but whenever possible releasing them in an atmosphere of heated dispute with CARA. *Kids*, released two months before *Showgirls* in 1995, appeared to be another opportunity for Miramax and its cochairpersons—Bob and Harvey Weinstein—to exploit and deride the rating system. It was not to be, as the Weinstein brothers— who had sold Miramax to the Walt Disney Company two years earlier but had remained at its helm—found out. Miramax, a once-proud marketer of controversy, became a token subsidiary of responsible entertainment, a harbinger of things to come for NC-17 and unrated films.

Kids was hardly Incontestable R material. Photographed in an unflinching documentary style with a tone of chronic despair, the unnerving and uncompromising film chronicles twenty-four hours in the lives of a band of thrill-seeking New York teens, with one girl, who has picked up the AIDS virus, looking to find one of her earlier lovers to tell him the bad news. Miramax paid $3.5 million for *Kids*' worldwide distribution rights after its screening at the Sundance Film Festival. Its notoriety spread by word of mouth after its screenings at the Cannes Film Festival and reports from *Film Comment* (*Kids*' "disturbingly erotic vision . . . may make the film unreleasable") and *Variety* (*Kids* "is poised to become one of the most controversial films ever made").[72] The film's violation of many of the most obvious tenets of responsible entertainment, however—frank depictions of teenage sex and drug abuse, racial violence, gay-baiting, and rape—practically guaranteed that it would be rated NC-17 by the Rating Board.

Historically, Miramax's motto—"any publicity is good publicity"—had manufactured interest in its films, regardless of whether the distributor cut a film for an R rating or released it unrated. On most occasions of appeal, Miramax lost (*Scandal; The Cook, the Thief, His Wife, and Her Lover; Tie Me Up! Tie Me Down!* and *The Advocate* [1994]); occasionally, it won (*Clerks*). All this changed in 1993 when Disney purchased the company for approximately $75 million, and it became what Justin Wyatt termed a "major independent."[73]

Once unfettered and autonomous, Miramax now faced obstacles previously unknown to it in distributing a film and securing exhibition sites: (1) as a subsidiary of Disney, the company had to follow Disney's family-friendly corporate policy; (2) as a subsidiary of an MPAA signatory, it could no longer release unrated films and had to consider the concerns of NATO exhibitors in its acquisition of films; and (3) as a subsidiary of a publicly traded corporation, it had become vulnerable to popular opinion expressed by stockholders, politicians, religious leaders, and the press.

The intent of the merger, as Wyatt pointed out, was to keep Miramax's and Disney's business operations separate. The deal would give Disney an arthouse division, enabling the company to produce movies for a portion of the adult market not reached by its Touchstone division. As for Miramax, the deal would make the Weinsteins personally wealthy, while giving their company greater access to capital, funding to shift into production, wider distribution overseas, and better ancillary deals in home video and pay television after years of financial strain. Soon after the merger, however, the constraints of corporate ownership were made manifest; Miramax could no longer market films through media controversy under the ownership of Disney. Or could it?

In 1994 Miramax was forced to return Martin Lawrence's verbally explicit *You So Crazy* to HBO (who in turn sold it to Samuel Goldwyn) after the film lost its appeal to reverse the Rating Board's NC-17. At the time, Bob Weinstein downplayed the role of the NC-17 and Miramax's new status as a subsidiary of Disney for the relinquishment of the film:

> We can and we [will release NC-17-rated films]. But we felt this film had crossover appeal and that unrated was the best way to go. And now that we are a part of a major company, which is a signatory to the MPAA, that option is not available to us. We are an autonomous division [of Disney] and we have the ability to release a film as NC-17. We can run our division as we see fit. But it was not in our best interests—or Martin Lawrence's— to go out with an NC-17.[74]

What Weinstein fails to mention here is that Miramax had no choice but to abandon the project because, in addition to Disney's commitment as an MPAA signatory not to release unrated films, Disney's corporate policy is not to release NC-17 films. Therefore, Miramax—whose fortunes and laurels as a genuine independent derived from distribution of difficult, unconventional, and nonresponsible product—now had its hands tied as a major independent.

This "unfortunate situation," as Bob Weinstein called it, reemerged shortly thereafter with *Priest* (1994), a film about a gay clergyman.[75] Even though *Priest* carried only an R rating, Disney was under pressure by Roman Catholic groups and company shareholders to prevent Miramax from releasing the film.[76] This time, however, Disney was powerless to stop the film's release; the company's charter with Miramax, as Walt Disney Motion Picture Group chairperson Joe Roth put it, allowed its subsidiary to release *any* film within certain budgetary limits as long as it carried no rating higher than an R.[77] How long this "marital strife" could last between the major independent and its corporate parent is evidenced by two opposing quotes in *Newsweek* about the boycott of *Priest:* "We were terrified that we *wouldn't* get a controversy," said a Miramax source; "They're shameless, and they're embarrassing us," said a Disney source.[78]

It became apparent in the case of *Kids* that the Miramax/Disney relationship could not function as long as Miramax continued with its usual acquisition and marketing strategies. Spooked by reports from Cannes that Jack Valenti—even before seeing *Kids*—did not believe it could be edited for an R, and director Larry Clark's retort that "I'm not going to edit out a single f[uck]ing frame," Disney sold the rights to the film to the Weinsteins in June 1995 even before it was submitted for a rating.[79] The Weinsteins, in turn, set up a new company, Shining Excalibur Pictures, created solely to distribute *Kids*. Reminiscent of *The Man with the Golden Arm*, *Blow-Up*, and other Production Code–era films released through an MPAA subsidiary, this maneuver, said Harvey Weinstein, was not the result of Disney's worries about the film's content:

> We expect [Shining] Excalibur to be a one-shot deal. . . . [W]e're not in the NC-17 business. But—with Disney's consent—we'll keep it going should another one arise. The company can help us defend ourselves against the conservative right. It's protection for movies that have edge. . . . Creating this company was the perfect solution—unprecedented as far as I know. It's the opposite of going head-on. Though we're at a tremendous risk—losing Buena Vista's clout in the home video market and pay TV markets—if I were Disney, I'd have made the same decision. Especially in this political climate, they have a grand name and reputation to protect.[80]

Kids received an NC-17, and, not surprisingly, the Weinsteins marketed its rating controversy just as they had with films under the Miramax banner.

This time, their campaign rallied behind the cultural urgency of the film and the obligation they had as distributors to make sure that children were not restricted from seeing *Kids*. Shining Excalibur CEO Eamonn Bowles led the charge: "It's our opinion that R is the correct rating. By giving it an NC-17 rating, they are taking away the parental right to take their possibly vulnerable children to see this—which might help them open a discourse about

Figure 27. The antithesis of responsible entertainment: *Kids* (1995).

what kids have to face today." And the Weinsteins, as before, solicited noted public figures for their support at the appeals hearing. Attorney Alan Dershowitz, who was earlier hired to fight the *Clerks* appeal, complained that "the rating system fails when it comes to a film many American parents want their children to see. They believe, rightfully so, this film could save lives." Former *Sassy* magazine editor and author Jane Pratt remarked that "*Kids* creates a forum for discussion between parents and their teen-agers." Valenti inadvertently helped to sensationalize the film's release. He stated "that parents in America would be grateful for the decision," and that "if ever a movie should be barred from viewing by children, *Kids* may be that film. . . . I believe, and I would hope that most exhibitors would agree, that *Kids* is a movie that children should not see."[81]

More than likely, Valenti's outspoken antipathy for *Kids* and influence over the Appeals Board ensured an NC-17 would be given to the film. In the past his intervention in appeals hearings protected the economic interests of the MPAA signatories by helping to overturn harsher ratings for *Poltergeist, Scarface,* and other big-budget films. With *Kids* the MPAA's political interests this time were at stake; the film was already an object of censure from parents, pressure groups, and government officials. Dershowitz was probably correct in his charge that Bob Dole's recent attacks on Hollywood entertainment, particularly *Natural Born Killers* (1994), had impacted the Appeals Board vote of sustaining the NC-17.[82] Probably fears of theater boycotts and the inability to police theaters for minors determined the appeals votes by the MPAA and NATO majority. Whatever the reasons for the NC-17, Valenti was not going to allow Miramax to destroy the integrity of the rating system with a political hot potato like *Kids*. He certainly was not going to sanction a major independent's end run around its MPAA corporate parent.

Kids could have effectively subverted the industry's regime of self-regulation had only one of the following four possibilities happened: Disney made an exception for its no-NC-17 policy; the Rating Board gave it an R with a disclaimer, a tactic used for Spielberg's PG-rated *Jaws* ("some material may be too intense for younger viewers") and the R-rated *Saving Private Ryan* (1998: "includes intense, prolonged realistically graphic sequences of war, violence, and language"); the Appeals Board was swayed by platitudes of social responsibility and overturned the Rating Board's rating (as in *The Lover*); or more than just a handful of NATO exhibitors decided to screen *Kids* in mainstream theaters. Few in the industry budged; their cooperative and collusive commitment to the Incontestable R was steadfastly maintained. Despite losing the fight and going out unrated, *Kids* still grossed $7.4 million—a lot for an independent film—but it was primarily relegated to the art houses, reaffirming Hollywood's movies as a site of responsible entertainment.

After *Kids*, Miramax never again released an unrated or NC-17 film. The company only financed, distributed, and marketed low-to-medium-budget, adult-oriented films rated no higher than an R. Thus, as a major independent, Miramax effectively lost its autonomy and, with it, its ability to release pictures that challenged the boundaries of the R rating or were counterproductive to the interests of Disney. Films like *Malena* (2000) and *Kill Bill Vol. 1* (2003) were cut for sex and violence like all other films distributed by the MPAA signatories. Disney particularly exercised control over Miramax's output in two instances that challenged the parent company's conservative, patriotic brand. In 1997 the Weinsteins bought Kevin Smith's satire *Dogma*— a film about two fallen angels who try to sneak back into heaven through a religious loophole—from Disney after its corporate parent feared backlash from the Catholic Church. (The Weinsteins subsequently sold it to independent Lions Gate.) In 2004 the Weinsteins also bought the Michael Moore, anti–George Bush documentary *Fahrenheit 9/11* from Disney after chairperson Michael Eisner reportedly told the director that releasing the film would cost Disney tax breaks for its theme parks in Florida, where Bush's brother, Jeb, was governor.[83] (The Weinsteins subsequently codistributed the film under the name of the Fellowship Adventure Group along with Lions

Gate and IFC.) The Weinsteins parted ways with Disney in 2005 to start up a new distribution entity called simply the Weinstein Company.

The impact that corporate ownership had on provocative independent filmmaking in the late 1990s is also exemplified by the conduct of October Films, before and after its sale to Universal in the summer of 1997. A few years earlier October had weathered two rating battles: *When Night Is Falling*, discussed in chapter 4, and Pedro Almodóvar's *Kika* (1993; released in the United States in 1994), likely passed over by the newly acquired-by-Disney Miramax, who had profitably handled the director's last three films.[84]

At issue with *Kika,* a melodramatic satire about voyeurism, crime, and voluptuous women, had been the film's sexual explicitness and comedic tone toward rape, despite not having any frontal nudity, graphic violence, or drug use. One lovemaking scene contains a close-up of oral sex and a minute-long, three-quarter shot of sexual grinding; the nine-minute rape scene shows a rapist sticking an orange slice in Kika's vagina then swallowing it, followed by full shots of sexual grinding, then the rapist's masturbation off a balcony as we see his semen hit another woman in the face.[85] *Kika* undoubtedly was NC-17 based on the representational norms of responsible entertainment. "The sexuality of *[Kika]* was too explicit for us to give it an R," said Heffner.[86] October, however, expected a broader release for the film; it had already invested about $2 million in prints and advertising with the assumption that the film would be rated R and had signed a domestic rights deal for *Kika* that came attached with a clause prohibiting any cuts.[87] Without the option of cutting *Kika* down to an R and then losing its appeal, October had the choice to release the film with an NC-17 or unrated—an option only available to the company as an independent. As with *When Night Is Falling,* the company went with the latter.

Kika was the first film October ever submitted to the Rating Board for theatrical release, and the company quickly built its credibility on distributing risky material and protecting artists' visions. Life as a major independent under Universal, however, was not as sovereign as life as an independent. The *Hollywood Reporter* summarized the conundrum in a June 1998 headline: "Fourplay from October puts Uni in a Pickle."[88] The headline referred to the fact that October had four films on its release slate, all of which seemed destined to draw the dicey NC-17 rating. October's new corporate mind-set can easily be identified in a statement made by Dennis Rice, its president of worldwide marketing, in response to this possibility: "At the end of the day," he said, "it's the best tribute to the filmmaker if his work can be seen by as many people as it can. Of course, it's commercially more viable to have an R rating. It opens these films up to a wider audience and a broader range of

exhibitors."[89] Of the four films, only the Danish film *The Celebration* earned
an R on its first submission to the Rating Board. Another Danish film, *The
Idiots,* directed by Lars Von Trier, featured an image of hard-core sex, and its
unrated release was limited in the United States.[90] *Orgazmo,* written and
directed by *South Park*'s cocreator Trey Parker, lost its appeal and was released
with an NC-17. The raunchy spoof of the porn industry incurred no wrath
from Universal, however, probably because of the picture's frivolous and in-
offensive tone (quite the opposite of *Kika*), its extremely low production
value, and its complete lack of interest beyond that of the *South Park* fan
community.

The same cannot be said for Todd Solondz's *Happiness,* a disturbing
nihilistic comedy about the abnormal relationships of three sisters in sub-
urban New Jersey that touched on themes of masturbation, dismemberment,
and homosexual pedophilia. Despite the fact that the film won the International Critics' Prize for Best Film at Cannes in May 1998, it was never given
a chance (unlike *Orgazmo*) to be rated NC-17; Universal and its corporate
parent Seagram ordered October to drop *Happiness* from their release schedule prior to its submission to the Rating Board. "The reality is that there are
some elements in the film that thematically are inappropriate for our parent
company," remarked October partner John Schmidt about the decision, even
though his company had financed and produced the $2.5-million *Happiness*
themselves.[91] Having no choice in the matter, October sold *Happiness* to the
film's production company and international distributor, Good Machine,
which, in turn, formed a domestic arm specifically to release it. As Good
Machine's Bob Berney remarked after the sale, "I guess October thought they
had more internal freedom than they did."[92]

The outcome of *Happiness* reflects the relative autonomy of independent
filmmaking under the corporate umbrella. As a major independent, October
was powerless to prevent Universal from exercising a morality clause in its
contract for *Happiness* that allowed the MPAA signatory to escape its obligation to release the film. Before, as a genuine independent, October would
have fought the NC-17 and released *Happiness* unrated, if necessary, to protect the integrity of Solondz's work. Now, as a major independent, October
had to obey the wishes of its owner. Solondz understood Universal's lack of
support for the film: "If they thought my movie would gross $100 or $200
million, I think things would be different. But it's not worth all the flack and
controversy they anticipated from such a little speck of a movie as this."[93]

But what is the purpose of the major independent if not to finance and
distribute niche pictures like *Happiness* while reaping the benefits of their
owners' financial resources and economies of scale? "The implicit bargain

Figure 28. The relative autonomy of the major independent: pedophilia and *Happiness* (1998). Courtesy of the Academy of Motion Picture Arts and Sciences.

between the majors and independents was simple enough," wrote an anonymous critic in the *Economist* in 1998. "The big studios would provide cash and marketing in return for new talent and risky ideas."[94] As it turned out, however, the MPAA signatories would provide cash and marketing in return for new talent *only* if the ideas were not too risky, not too confrontational, or not too dissonant; in other words, they had to be "responsible entertainment."

Films that have the potential to repel reform groups, shareholders, and pay-ing audiences have rarely been welcome by the MPAA distributors—major independents or no major independents. Clearly, as Degen Pener stated in *Entertainment Weekly,* "[The independents] aren't as independent as they used to be."[95]

Solondz discovered this fact with his next project, *Storytelling* (2002), released by Fine Line—the specialty films division of New Line. An in-dependent distributor turned major independent, New Line was acquired by Turner Broadcasting System in 1994, which then merged with Time Warner in 1996. New Line had theatrically distributed a few NC-17 films under its Fine Line banner, but like other major independents, this hardly suggested a commitment to the adults-only rating. Zalman King's soft-core *Delta of Venus* (1995) barely got a theatrical release. The distribution of David Cronenberg's *Crash* (1996) was delayed almost a year after Time Warner vice chairperson Ted Turner objected to the sex and violence in the picture.[96] The only other NC-17 films released by New Line were directed by John Waters, the result of his thirty-year relationship with New Line chairperson Robert Shaye: *Pink Flamingos* (1972, rereleased in 1997), *Female Trouble* (1974, re-released in 1999), and *A Dirty Shame* (2004).[97]

In August 2001 *Storytelling* earned an NC-17 for an explicit interracial sex scene between a white graduate student, Vi (Selma Blair), and her black pro-fessor, Mr. Scott (Robert Wisdom). Composed in a graphic full shot, Mr. Scott has anal sex with Vi while demanding she repeatedly bait him with racist language: "Nigger, fuck me hard." Contractually obligated to deliver an R-rated picture to Fine Line, Solondz digitally inserted a red box over the sex act (as negotiated in his contract) with the racial epithet in order to lose the NC-17.[98] "I didn't want the Stanley Kubrick situation from *Eyes Wide Shut* (1999)," Solondz states, referring to a sixty-five-second orgy scene to which, in order to earn an R, Kubrick digitally inserted hooded and caped characters in three shots to hide the extras engaging in various sexual couplings.[99] The red box, Solondz cheekily adds, "is simply my way of informing adults that there are certain things they are not allowed to see in films made for adults."[100]

By the mid-2000s, the R-rated fate of *Storytelling* is typical of most "inde-pendent" films now distributed by MPAA signatories. Miramax and New Line, once the champions of the independent filmmaker and aesthetic, became their own nemeses. Besides these two companies, all other major independents have been phased out or absorbed under the majors' own art-house divisions, which rarely release NC-17 films. As Peter Bart put it, "These so-called indies are really mini-majors in drag, and they're governed by many of the same rules as the majors."[101] As of 2007 they include Universal Focus,

Figure 29. Robert Wisdom in *Storytelling* (2001).

Sony Pictures Classics, Warner Independent and Picturehouse (a partnership between New Line and HBO films), Paramount Vantage (née Paramount Classics), and Fox Searchlight. Sony Pictures Classics circulated *Broken English* (1997) in limited release with an NC-17 and two films in 2004: *Young Adam* (released in the UK in 2003) and Almodóvar's *Bad Education*. Fox Searchlight only released Bernardo Bertolucci's *The Dreamers* (2004; released in Italy in 2003) with an NC-17. And Universal Pictures (not Focus) released the documentary *Inside Deep Throat* (2005).

Despite this NC-17 blip in 2004 and 2005, *Variety* certainly misspoke in 1995 when it suggested that *Showgirls* "could enable other high powered film-makers to refuse to edit their films in order to obtain a more universally acceptable—or studio-required—R tag."[102] Cronenberg, Bertolucci, and Almodóvar are certainly world-renowned filmmakers, but in the United States their films (NC-17 or not) are still primarily considered art-house product for art-house theaters for art-house audiences. Only *Bad Education* made more than $5 million domestically ($5.2 million). With so few MPAA-signatory films rated NC-17, the situation after *Showgirls* is fundamentally the same as the situation before *Showgirls*.

Those leftover and newly formed independent distributors continue to test the adults-only waters with controversial pictures released NC-17 or unrated, but they have fared no better at the box office than the major in-

Figure 30. The *Village Voice* (April 17, 2001) ad for the unrated *The Center of the World* (2001).

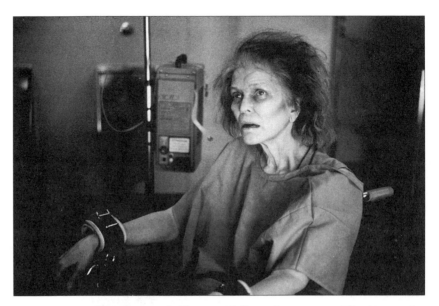

Figure 31. One of the most profitable unrated films of recent years: Ellen Burstyn in *Requiem for a Dream* (2000).

dependents. IFC's *Y tu mamá también* (2002) remains the gold standard of unrated films, crossing over into some mainstream NATO theaters on its way to $13.8 million, a record in the NC-17 era. Most others primarily remained in the art houses, doing far less business than they probably would have done with an R rating. They included Artisan's *Requiem for a Dream* (2000, $3.6 million) and *The Center of the World* (2001, $1.1 million), Lot 47's *L. I. E.* (2001, $1.1 million), Lions Gate's *Irreversible* (2002, $765,000), Kino International's *The Piano Teacher* (2002, $1 million), Palm Pictures' *Sex and Lucia* (2002, $1.5 million), Wellspring's *The Brown Bunny* (2004, $365,000) and *Palindromes* (2005, $550,000), Tartan's *Mysterious Skin* (2005, $713,000), and ThinkFilm's *Where the Truth Lies* (2005, $870,00) and *The Aristocrats* (2005, $6.3 million). (Well, maybe the obscenity-laden *The Aristocrats* would have fared worse.)

Without the financial backing and the distribution machinery of MPAA art-house divisions, these unaffiliated independent companies have great difficulty competing in the marketplace—NC-17, unrated, R, or otherwise. If producers have a highly sought-after independent film for sale, they often go to the MPAA signatories, who pay a higher price, offer a larger advertising budget, and provide vastly greater penetration in video and overseas markets. Block-booking arrangements between the MPAA distributors and NATO exhibitors prevent access to multiplex screens for independent product, and unaffiliated exhibitors are drawn to films with big stars and name directors working under the corporate umbrella.

What appears to be a textbook study in media synergy has, in effect, sharply reduced the number of unrated films released in this country over the last several years. Unrated films rarely account for more than 0.5 percent of the box-office total in a given year, regardless of the number of unrated films released that year.[103] The continuing market stigma of the NC-17 has effectively created a national cinema almost completely dependent on the formal and narrative elements of the Incontestable R. Unfortunately, it is difficult to know the number of compromises made by independent filmmakers in order to reap the benefits of distribution by an MPAA signatory. How many more R clauses have been included in a director's contract? How many screenplays have been rewritten to eliminate an "irresponsible" moment? How many films have been renegotiated after their initial submission to the Rating Board? The MPAA signatories have made a successful industry out of such agreements; the independents traditionally have not.

While there will never be a shortage of opportunistic filmmakers and independent distributors wanting to challenge the Incontestable R, the fact remains that the MPAA signatories are intent on preserving the commercial imperatives of responsible entertainment as much as the independents are intent on playing against them. The adults-only category is the battleground of these market forces, one that neither deliberately embraces the MPAA companies nor actively discriminates against the independents. It does operate, however, by a code of regulation invested in producing works of responsible entertainment, one created and stigmatized in the first place by the MPAA and NATO.

Conclusion

If you make a movie that a lot of people want to see, no rating will hurt you. But if you make a movie that few people want to see, no rating will help you.

—Jack Valenti, *Christian Science Monitor*, Sept. 22, 1995

If we return to the rating battles that began this book—the controversies over *Team America: World Police* and *The Cooler*—we can see that the line between the R and the NC-17 rating is about so much more than puppet sex and one and a half seconds of pubic hair. Boundary maintenance between these categories endows the Hollywood film industry with an affirmative cultural function in the classification era, what I have called "responsible entertainment." Negotiating the terrain of this boundary is the Rating Board of CARA, which calls for the arranging and filtering out of particular images, words, themes, and tones from NC-17 films to turn them into R-rated films.

The internal consistency of responsible R-rated entertainment at particular historical junctures—what I have called the Incontestable R—is inextricably linked to the stigmatization of the NC-17 by the MPAA and NATO. Their joint commitment to R-rated or lower films not only establishes the formal terms by which films get distributed and exhibited in the United States but safeguards the industry's economic and political interests. The Incontestable R preserves the MPAA's oligopoly, ensures NATO's participation in the rating system, and differentiates "Hollywood" films from the "independent" ones for moral reformers.

Although this book focuses solely on two rating categories from CARA— sex and nudity—I believe a similar study could be conducted on other Rating Board criteria, particularly violence. The work of Stephen Prince on the Production Code provides a point of entry into formulating the possible norms of screen violence in operation at a given time during the classification era.[1] Through his code of "substitutional poetics," expressed through various camera positionings, editing patterns, and sound/image relationships, Prince establishes a stylistic vocabulary for the depiction of screen violence in classical Hollywood, just as Lea Jacobs did for the representation of sexuality in the fallen woman film of that era. MPAA-member films released under CARA might exhibit similar codes, albeit of a more graphic nature, in a systematic way as well. This book has discussed many films edited for violence—*Cruising, Dressed to Kill, Basic Instinct,* and *Showgirls* (for video), for example—and several codes of representation may be shared among them that govern the thresholds of violence in the Incontestable R.

Prince's account of an interoffice memo prepared for Jack Valenti's congressional testimony before the National Commission on the Causes and Prevention of Violence in December 1968 reveals a preliminary philosophy of categorizing violence under CARA. The aggressor's emotional relationship to violence and the prolonging of violent acts are some of the variables used by examiners in assessing the rating for a film.[2] I caution those pursuing an aesthetic framework of violence under CARA, however, to keep in mind the chairperson of the Rating Board at the time of regulation. I have demonstrated that Stern and Heffner approached sex and violence in quite divergent ways that impacted representations of violence during their administrations. Stephen Farber's insider account of the rating system and Heffner's papers constitute valuable primary evidence for the Rating Board's activities that remain relatively unknown for Dougherty, Mosk, and Graves. The continued availability of unrated and R-rated versions of theatrical films on DVD sheds some light on the system of boundary maintenance currently in use, particularly in horror films such as *Saw* (2004), *Land of the Dead* (2005), and *Hostel* (2006).

Still, the unavailability of most internal CARA documents and the dearth of public discussion of its operations by its chairpersons after Heffner's departure in 1994 make any detailed analysis of the rating system extremely challenging. These obstacles, however, did not stop director Kirby Dick from exposing the secretive methods and practices of the current rating system in his 2006 documentary *This Film Is Not Yet Rated.* By weaving together an investigation into the identities of the Rating Board examiners, interviews with disgruntled filmmakers alongside clips of their films (Wayne Kramer [*The Cooler*], Matt Stone [*Team America: World Police*], Atom Erogan [*Where the Truth Lies*]), and his own journey through the rating process, Dick effectively unveils some of the same biases, hypocrisies, and prejudices consistently present in the rating system that I have discussed in this book: Valenti's contradictory statements and often blatant lies about rating policy, CARA's baseless and unscientific definition of the typical American parent (Judge

Ramos's "Average American Parent" standard), and the aesthetic boundaries of sexual grinding and pelvic thrusting of the R rating. Of considerable achievement in *This Film Is Not Yet Rated* is the revealing of the names and faces of the Rating Board examiners—many of who have served beyond their term limit or no longer have children under the age of eighteen—and the names of the Appeals Board members—whose membership still primarily consists of MPAA and NATO representatives. It should come as no surprise then that Dick lost his appeal for an R rating; *This Film Is Not Yet Rated* included the very clips that earned previous films an NC-17 and was released by IFC Films, an independent distributor. Like other films of its kind, *This Film Is Not Yet Rated* went out unrated rather than accept the NC-17 badge.

This Film Is Not Yet Rated soundly foregrounds CARA as a political and economic instrument of the MPAA signatories but only briefly acknowledges its place within a larger cooperative and collusive structure of industry self-regulation. For a more complete account of the rating system, one needs to consider NATO, the mass media, retail giants, politicians, and reform groups whose activities are often as secretive and erratic as the MPAA's. In fact, the Rating Board and the Appeals Board may play the least prominent role in the policing of responsible entertainment today, especially in light of the Incontestable R giving way to the "Indisputable PG-13" since the turn of the century. The distribution of R-rated films declined from 212 in 1999 to just 147 in 2004, with only four films making more than $100 million—*Collateral, Troy, The Passion of the Christ,* and *Fahrenheit 9/11.* That year, PG-13 films commanded a lion's share of the box office, grossing a combined $4.4 billion compared to PG films ($2.3 billion) and R films ($2.1 billion).[3] While R-rated moves are not becoming a "vanishing breed," as Russell Schwartz, now marketing head at New Line, suggests, they are playing a smaller role in the theatrical behavior of the MPAA signatories.[4]

A number of causes can explain this prodigious shift in the marketplace, most notably, the voluntary guidelines adopted by the MPAA and NATO after the Federal Trade Commission's (FTC) "Marketing Violent Entertainment to Children" report in 2000. Conducted in the wake of several high school shootings, including Columbine, in the late 1990s, the FTC study found the motion picture industry guilty of targeting R-rated films to minors as young as twelve years old through radio and television advertising, focus group research, and venues frequented by teenagers. The MPAA responded by restricting the marketing of R-rated films and dramatically reducing their output. NATO succeeded in tightening enforcement of its admission practices for R-rated pictures at its member theaters, which by 2004 comprised almost twenty-seven thousand of the approximately thirty-six thousand screens in the United States, representing twenty-three of the largest twenty-five chains.[5]

Other factors in the early 2000s likely led to the decline in production and box office of R-rated films as well. After 9/11 the industry curtailed the category's often graphic and realistic depiction of violence. Of 2005's top ten highest grossing films, only *Mr. and Mrs. Smith* could be said to contain any "real life" violence typical of blockbuster action films in the past. The others that are rated PG-13—*Star Wars: Episode III: Revenge of the Sith, Harry Potter and the Goblet of Fire, War of the Worlds, King Kong,* and *Batman Begins*—all take place in the realms of science fiction or fantasy.[6] Even horror films are being more and more trimmed to a PG-13, including the remakes of *The Grudge* (2004), *The Fog* (2005), and *When a Stranger Calls* (2006).

The decrease of theatrical R-rated movies can also be traced to the migration of explicit representations to the small screen. HBO's *The Sopranos* and Showtime's *The L Word* push the limits of violence and sex. Basic cable network FX feature shows like *Nip/Tuck* and *Rescue Me,* which air after 10 P.M. EST, contain material that likely would be considered R-rated if released into theaters. Comedy Central even runs uncut R-rated movies like *Clerks* or uncensored versions of their original programming like the *Roast of Pamela Anderson* (2005) after midnight. Additionally, with the DVD market rivaling and often exceeding the box-office returns for films, it became common practice by 2006 to release "unrated" or "uncut" versions of R-rated *and* PG-13-rated films on video. With an estimated 80 percent of total DVD sales coming from unrated editions of a title, the MPAA has simply transplanted a good portion of its audience from one media platform to another. Mass merchants like Blockbuster and Target will also carry unrated copies on a case-by-case basis, especially for films with added violence and language but not sex.[7]

The abandonment of cinematic sex by the MPAA, NATO, and the VSDA primarily leaves its NC-17 presentation up to the true independents. The marketing dollars and box-office clout of the majors' art-house divisions, however, predispose NATO exhibitors to commit fewer screens to independent product. Smaller box-office gross means fewer copies ordered by retailers. Throw an NC-17 into the mix, and these numbers increase exponentially. Despite NATO president John Fithian's claim that the stigma of the rating is unfounded and that his members would play the "right NC-17 in the right location,"[8] the fact remains that MPAA signatories are still not releasing films with the NC-17 rating.

As this book went to press in April 2007, MPAA head Dan Glickman and CARA chairperson Joan Graves announced a plan at the Sundance Film Festival to make the rating process more open and understandable for the public and filmmakers. These planned changes, undoubtedly a response to the outcry surrounding *This Film Is Not Yet Rated* a year earlier (the DVD would "coincidentally" be released the following week), included revealing the identities of the three senior examiners of the Rating Board and publishing the demographic information of the parents who serve on the Rating Board; expanding the membership of the Appeals Board to include film industry people from outside the MPAA and NATO; and allowing filmmakers to cite precedents in other films when challenging a rating at Appeals Board hearings.[9]

Unfortunately, these changes are almost entirely cosmetic, failing to address the same fundamental problems perennially leveled at the rating system: its veil of secrecy, its leniency on matters of violence over nudity and sexuality, and its representational boundaries between ratings. Unsurprisingly absent in the reforms to CARA was any modification to the NC-17 rating. Glickman only expressed that he would "like to see it used more" and vowed to speak with the Directors Guild of America and NATO.[10] A few months later at the ShoWest industry trade show, Glickman spoke to distributors and exhibitors about NC-17, urging the non-MPAA signatories to stop releasing unrated films and MPAA signatories to stop releasing unrated DVDs. He considered an unrated film "a slap in the face" to CARA and one that "challenges and flouts our ratings system."[11] Regardless of such entreaties and pronouncements, the fact remains that the age restrictions of the NC-17 will always limit its usage by the MPAA and NATO, whose members are committed to the appearance of responsible entertainment not only in the Incontestable R but across all rating categories. Until the Hollywood film industry changes the nature of its products, the NC-17 will be sparingly used and only in the least threatening of instances. And that's the naked truth.

Notes

INTRODUCTION

1. Nicole Sperling, "Reined-in Puppet Love Gets an R," *Hollywood Reporter,* Oct. 6, 2004.

2. Quoted in Rachel Abramowitz, "Puppet Sex Leads to Rating Rift," *Los Angeles Times,* Oct. 5, 2004.

3. Quoted in Scott Bowles, "Puppets Go Gunning for an Audience," *USA Today,* Oct. 12, 2004. Also see Anne Thompson, "Puppet Love: A Comedy with Strings Attached," *Washington Post,* Oct. 10, 2004.

4. For a full discussion of *The Cooler*'s rating woes see Patrick Goldstein, "Arguing Their Case against NC-17," *Los Angeles Times,* July 1, 2003; Wayne Kramer, "Will 'Cooler' Heads Prevail?" *Daily Variety,* Aug. 18, 2003.

5. Kim Masters, interview, *All Things Considered,* National Public Radio, Feb. 6, 2004.

6. Quoted in Steven Rosen, "Ratings System Has Macy on a Crusade," *Denver Post,* Oct. 17, 2003.

7. Kramer, "Will 'Cooler' Heads Prevail?"

8. Together with the MPAA and NATO, the IFIDA (International Film Importers and Distributors of America), a less-powerful and now defunct trade organization, was a founding partner in CARA, agreeing to abide by its rating designations for all of its products. According to the *IFIDA Film Directory* (1968–1969), its members included companies such as Adelphia Pictures, Allied Artists, American International Pictures, Avco Embassy, Cinemation, Distribix, Grove Press, Janus, Joseph Burstyn, Sherpix, and Silverstein International. The IFIDA went out of service in 1978.

9. This information is available on CARA's Web site at www.filmratings.com.

10. Although DreamWorks is not an official member of the MPAA, it does abide by the same policies as the other distributors. The mini-major was bought by NBC Universal in 2005. MGM bought United Artists in 1981 after the failure of *Heaven's Gate* (1980). Sony bought MGM in 2004.

11. United Artists Classics released Pier Paolo Pasolini's *Arabian Nights* and *The Canterbury Tales* with X ratings in 1979, the only adults-only releases from an MPAA signatory until 1990. In recent years the art-house divisions of the MPAA signatories have

offered NC-17 films in limited release; see, e.g., Fox Searchlight's (20th Century Fox) *The Dreamers* (2003; U.S. release 2004) and Sony Pictures Classics' *Bad Education* (2004).

12. See, e.g., two articles printed twenty-five years apart: Jack Valenti, "To Rate a Film Is Not to Censor It," *New York Times,* Dec. 9, 1973; "A Candid Interview with the Steely Head of the MPAA, Jack Valenti," E Online, Dec. 1998, http://www.eonline.com/Features/Specials/Ratings/Three/valenti.html.

13. Will H. Hays, *The Memoirs of Will H. Hays* (New York: Doubleday, 1955); Jack Vizzard, *See No Evil: Life Inside a Hollywood Censor* (New York: Simon and Schuster, 1971); James M. Wall, "Oral History with Geoffrey Shurlock," Louis B. Mayer Library, American Film Institute (Los Angeles: AFI, 1975); Raymond Moley, *The Hays Office* (New York: Bobbs-Merrill, 1945).

14. Garth Jowett, *Film: The Democratic Art* (Boston: Little, Brown, 1976); Robert Sklar, *Movie-Made America: A Cultural History of American Movies* (New York: Random House, 1975); Richard S. Randall, *Censorship of the Movies: The Social and Political Control of a Mass Medium* (Madison: University of Wisconsin Press, 1968); Ira Carmen, *Movies, Censorship, and the Law* (Ann Arbor: University of Michigan Press, 1966).

15. Richard Maltby, *Hollywood Cinema,* 2nd ed. (Malden, MA: Blackwell, 2003); Lea Jacobs, *The Wages of Sin: Censorship and the Fallen Woman Film, 1928–1942* (Madison: University of Wisconsin Press, 1991; repr. Berkeley: University of California Press, 1995); Gregory D. Black, *Hollywood Censored: Morality Codes, Catholics, and the Movies* (Cambridge, UK: Cambridge University Press, 1994); Gregory D. Black, *The Catholic Crusade against the Movies, 1940–1975* (Cambridge, UK: Cambridge University Press, 1997); Leonard J. Leff and Jerold L. Simmons, *The Dame in the Kimono: Hollywood, Censorship, and the Production Code from the 1920s to the 1960s* (New York: Grove Weidenfeld, 1990); Thomas Doherty, *Pre-Code Hollywood: Sex, Immorality, and Insurrection in American Cinema, 1930–1934* (New York: Columbia University Press, 1999); Ruth Vasey, *The World according to Hollywood, 1918–1939* (Madison: University of Wisconsin Press, 1997).

16. Stephen Prince, "Movies and Morality," in *A New Pot of Gold: Hollywood under the Electric Rainbow, 1980–1989* (Berkeley: University of California Press, 2000); Stephen Prince, "After the Deluge," in *Classical Film Violence: Designing and Regulating Brutality in Hollywood Cinema, 1930–1968* (New Brunswick, NJ: Rutgers University Press, 2003); Justin Wyatt, "The Stigma of the X: Adult Cinema and the Institution of the MPAA Ratings System," in *Controlling Hollywood: Censorship and Regulation in the Studio Era,* ed. Matthew Bernstein (New Brunswick, NJ: Rutgers University Press, 1999), 238–263; Jon Lewis, *Hollywood v. Hard Core: How the Struggle over Censorship Saved the Modern Film Industry* (New York: NYU Press, 2000).

17. Stephen Farber, *The Movie Rating Game* (Washington, D.C.: Public Affairs Press, 1972).

18. This oral history and related documents are housed in the Columbia University Oral History Collection in Butler Library, Columbia University.

19. Stephen Vaughn, *Freedom and Entertainment: Rating the Movies in an Age of New Media* (New York: Cambridge University Press, 2006).

20. Quoted in Patrick Goldstein, "For Teen Comedies, PG-13 Is In," *Los Angeles Times,* June 2, 1998.

21. See Gary Strauss, "Moore's 'Fahrenheit' to Keep Its R Rating," *USA Today,* June 23, 2004; Merissa Marr, "Moore's '9/11': What's Heat Worth," *Wall Street Journal,* June 23, 2004; and Gabriel Snyder, "The 'R' Stands for Resist," *Daily Variety,* June 22, 2004.

CHAPTER 1 — FILM REGULATION BEFORE THE RATING SYSTEM

1. Thomas Frank, *One Market under God: Extreme Capitalism, Market Populism, and the End of Economic Democracy* (New York: Random House, 2000), xvi.

2. Ibid., 29.

3. Robert W. McChesney, *Rich Media, Poor Democracy: Communication Politics in Dubious Times* (New York: New Press, 2000), 17. Originally published in hardcover by the University of Illinois Press in 1999. Page citations are to the New Press edition.

4. Ibid., 2.

5. Ruth Vasey, *The World according to Hollywood, 1918–1939* (Madison: University of Wisconsin Press, 1997), 157.

6. Richard Maltby, *Harmless Entertainment: Hollywood and the Ideology of Consensus* (Metuchen, NJ: Scarecrow, 1983), 102.

7. Stephen Farber, *The Movie Rating Game* (Washington, D.C.: Public Affairs Press, 1972), 2.

8. Raymond Moley, *The Hays Office* (New York: Bobbs-Merrill, 1945), 7. Before 1986 only Raymond Moley had access to primary materials of the PCA. His book is compromised, however, by his affiliation with the MPPDA. See Lea Jacobs's summary and criticism of Moley's work in *The Wages of Sin: Censorship and the Fallen Woman Film, 1928–1942* (Berkeley: University of California Press, 1995), 18–20.

9. Gerald Gardner, *The Censorship Papers: Movie Censorship Letters from the Hays Office, 1934–1968* (New York: Dodd, Mead, 1987), xi–xiii.

10. Gregory D. Black, *Hollywood Censored: Morality Codes, Catholics, and the Movies* (Cambridge, UK: Cambridge University Press, 1994), 6; Gregory D. Black, *The Catholic Crusade against the Movies, 1940–1975* (Cambridge, UK: Cambridge University Press, 1997), 2.

11 Francis G. Couvares, ed., *Movie Censorship and American Culture* (Washington, D.C.: Smithsonian Institution Press, 1996); Matthew Bernstein, ed., *Controlling Hollywood: Censorship and Regulation in the Studio Era* (New Brunswick, NJ: Rutgers University Press, 1999). Couvares's article, as well as many other pieces in his collection, first appeared in the December 1992 issue of *American Quarterly*.

12. Matthew Bernstein, introduction to *Controlling Hollywood*, 4.

13. See Lea Jacobs, "Industry Self-Regulation and the Problem of Textual Determination," *Velvet Light Trap* 23 (spring 1989): 4–15; reprinted in Bernstein's *Controlling Hollywood*, 87–101; see chapter 1 of Annette Kuhn's *Cinema, Censorship, and Sexuality, 1909–1925* (London: Routledge, 1988). Janet Staiger labels the model originally described by Kuhn as the eventualization/diagnosis model:

> This model stresses an account of "the conditions of operation and effectivity of film censorship," of "processes and practices" (the eventualization). Instead of seeing a law or a shot edited out of a final product as a static object, this model considers the activity of censoring to be determined and causal (the diagnosis). The model promotes the recognition of censorship as operating within broader social contexts than the specific institutions most obviously involved in prohibition. The object of inquiry consequently is not any specific board of censorship (such as the National Board of Censorship in the 1910s or the Breen Office of the 1930s) but the wider social and cultural ideologies determining those groups' activities. (*Bad Women: Regulating Sexuality in Early American Cinema* [Minneapolis: University of Minnesota Press, 1995], 14)

14. Jacobs, *The Wages of Sin*, 21–23.

15 Kuhn, *Cinema, Censorship, and Sexuality*, 127.

16. Ibid., 6; Sue Curry Jansen, *Censorship: The Knot That Binds Power and Knowledge* (New York: Oxford University Press, 1991), 25.

17. Curry Jansen, *Censorship*, 16.

18. Jon Lewis, *Hollywood v. Hard Core: How the Struggle over Censorship Saved the Modern Film Industry* (New York: NYU Press, 2000), 7.

19. Leonard J. Leff and Jerold L. Simmons, *The Dame in the Kimono: Hollywood, Censorship, and the Production Code from the 1920s to the 1960s* (New York: Grove Weidenfeld, 1990), 266; Thomas Doherty, *Pre-Code Hollywood: Sex, Immorality, and Insurrection in American Cinema, 1930–1934* (New York: Columbia University Press, 1999), 1.

20. Richard S. Randall, *Censorship of the Movies: The Social and Political Control of a Mass Medium* (Madison: University of Wisconsin Press, 1968), 6.

21. I borrow the phrase "political energy" from ibid., 5.

22. Quoted in the documentary *Hollywood Mavericks* (dir. Florence Dauman and Gale Ann Stieber, 1990).

23. Maltby, *Harmless Entertainment*, 10; see also chap. 1 of Richard Maltby, *Hollywood Cinema*, 2nd ed. (Oxford: Blackwell, 2003).

24. *Mutual Film Corp. v. Ohio Industrial Commission*, 236 U.S., 230 Supreme Court, 1915. The last remaining municipal regulatory board, the Dallas Motion Picture Classification Board, ceased its operations on Aug. 16, 1993.

25. Maltby, *Harmless Entertainment*, 96.

26. Ibid., 53–56; Maltby, *Hollywood Cinema*, 61.

27. Vasey, *The World according to Hollywood, 1918–1939*, 5–7.

28. The following accounts of self-regulation prior to the Production Code Administration are primarily drawn from Garth Jowett, *Film, the Democratic Art* (Boston: Focal Press, 1976); and Richard Maltby, "The Production Code and the Hays Office," in *Grand Design: Hollywood as a Modern Business Enterprise, 1930–1939*, ed. Tino Balio (Berkeley: University of California Press, 1993).

29. "The Motion Picture Production Code (as published 31 March, 1930)," reprinted in Maltby, *Hollywood Cinema*, 593–597. "Moral Obligations" is listed in all caps in the 1930 Production Code document, as are such words as *entertainment, helpful, harmful, moral importance, art, product, thing*, and *effect*. These capitalized terms affirmed the cultural and social function of movies as entertainment for the masses and not as an informative or destructive vehicle in the name of art.

30. James Wingate replaced Jason Joy as director of the SRC after Joy accepted an executive position at Fox in June 1932. In August 1933 Joy returned to the SRC after Will Hays persuaded Fox to let the MPPDA borrow him for a year. Wingate continued to direct the SRC, but Joseph Breen was, in effect, responsible for its operations. Shortly thereafter, Breen replaced Wingate as director when the MPPDA renamed the SRC the Production Code Administration in June 1934. See Frank Walsh, *Sin and Censorship: The Catholic Church and the Motion Picture Industry* (New Haven, CT: Yale University Press, 1996), 66–74.

31. Albert E. Van Schmus (PCA staff member), interview by Barbara Hall, Academy of Motion Picture Arts and Sciences Oral History Program (1992), 101, 156.

32. Jacobs describes the fallen woman genre: "These films concern a woman who commits a sexual transgression such as adultery or premarital sex. In traditional versions of the plot, she is expelled from the domestic space of the family and undergoes a pro-

tracted decline. Alone on the streets, she becomes an outcast—often a prostitute—suffering various humiliations which usually culminate in her death. There are other variants of the story, however, in which the movement away from the family does not lead to a decline in class. Instead, the heroine, a stereotypical 'kept woman' or 'gold digger,' uses men to become rich" (Jacobs, *The Wages of Sin*, x).

33. Ibid., 115.

34. Ibid., 64–81, 116–131.

35. Ibid., 122.

36. Ibid., 124–130. Jacobs also discusses how Garbo's star charisma and the use of close-ups could actually work against the PCA's strategies for condemning adultery.

37. Mary Beth Haralovich, "The Proletarian Woman's Film of the 1930s: Contending with Censorship and Entertainment," *Screen* 31, no. 2 (summer 1990): 172–187.

38. See Matthew Bernstein, "A Tale of Three Cities: The Banning of *Scarlet Street*," in Bernstein, *Controlling Hollywood*, 157–185.

39. Ibid., 175.

40. Ellen Draper, " 'Controversy Has Probably Destroyed the Context': *The Miracle* and Movie Censorship in America in the 1950s," in Bernstein, *Controlling Hollywood*, 194.

41. Maltby, *Hollywood Cinema*, 161.

42. Lewis Jacobs, *The Rise of the American Film: A Critical History* (New York: Teachers College Press, 1967), 292. First published 1939 by Harcourt, Brace.

43. Maltby, *Hollywood Cinema*, 120–121.

44. Jowett, *Film, the Democratic Art*, 276.

45. See Douglas Gomery, *Shared Pleasures: A History of Movie Presentation in the United States* (Madison: University of Wisconsin Press, 1992), 66–67.

46. The *Paramount* decision amended an unsuccessful consent decree between the government and the industry in 1940 that called for a halt to unfair trade practices but failed to demand the end of vertical integration. See Jowett, *Film, the Democratic Art*, 277–279.

47. Quoted in "The Morality Crisis," *Newsweek*, April 19, 1965, n.p.

48. Quoted in Randall, *Censorship of the Movies*, 23.

49. Roberto Rossellini's *The Miracle* was one film in the trilogy *Ways of Love* (1950). The other two films were Jean Renoir's *A Day in the Country* and Marcel Pagnol's *Jofroi*. Lillian Gerard, the managing director of the Paris Theatre, which showed *The Miracle*, provides a firsthand account of the controversy and eventual landmark ruling in two articles: " 'Withdraw the Picture!' the Commissioner Ordered," *American Film*, June 1977, 26–32; and "*The Miracle* in Court," *American Film*, July-August 1977, 26–32.

50. See Edward de Grazia and Roger K. Newman, *Banned Films: Movies, Censors, and the First Amendment* (New York: R. R. Bowker, 1982), 81–86.

51. Barbara Wilinsky, *Sure Seaters: The Emergence of Art House Cinema* (Minneapolis: University of Minnesota Press, 2001), 87–89.

52. For more details on *The Moon Is Blue* see Lewis, *Hollywood v. Hard Core*, 105–108.

53. Leff and Simmons, *The Dame in the Kimono*, 203.

54. For more information see Tino Balio, *United Artists: The Company That Changed the Film Industry* (Madison: University of Wisconsin Press, 1987), 71–72.

55. The MPAA also made minor revisions to the Production Code in 1938, 1939, 1946, 1947, 1951, and 1954. See John Sargent's self-regulation chart in Jowett, *Film, the Democratic Art,* 420.

56. James Gilbert, *A Cycle of Outrage: America's Reaction to the Juvenile Delinquent in the 1950s* (New York: Oxford University Press, 1986), 144.

57. Lewis, *Hollywood v. Hard Core,* 109–110.

58. Gilbert, *A Cycle of Outrage,* 175–178, 159. The 1956 Code is printed in full in Murray Schumach, *The Face on the Cutting Room Floor: The Story of Movie and Television Censorship* (New York: William Morrow, 1964).

59. For a discussion of these films' negotiations with the Legion of Decency see Walsh, *Sin and Censorship,* 282–306.

60. Jowett, *Film, the Democratic Art,* 430.

61. The Legion of Decency changed its name to the National Catholic Office for Motion Pictures (NCOMP) on July 8, 1965.

62. Schumach, *The Face on the Cutting Room Floor,* 258–259.

63. Leff and Simmons, *The Dame in the Kimono,* 237.

64. Schumach, *The Face on the Cutting Room Floor,* 259.

65. See, e.g., the end of chapter 10 and all of chapter 11 in Leff and Simmons, *The Dame in the Kimono;* Van Schmus, interview, 192; and Jack Vizzard, *See No Evil: Life Inside a Hollywood Censor* (New York: Simon and Schuster, 1970), 159–171.

66. Vizzard, *See No Evil,* 162.

67. Paul Monaco, *The Sixties: 1960–1969* (Berkeley: University of California Press, 2001), 58.

68. Jowett, *Film, the Democratic Art,* 439.

69. Lewis, *Hollywood v. Hard Core,* 127.

70. Ibid., 129.

71. Schumach, *The Face on the Cutting Room Floor,* 260.

72. These statistics are provided by Randall, *Censorship of the Movies,* 208.

73. Lewis, *Hollywood v. Hard Core,* 136.

74. See Leff and Simmons, *The Dame in the Kimono,* 252–253.

75. Lewis, *Hollywood v. Hard Core,* 139.

76. Leff and Simmons, *The Dame in the Kimono,* 265.

77. Quoted in Nora Ephron, "New Film Code: Parents to Direct," *New York Post,* Sep. 21, 1966.

78. All references come from a fifteen-page pamphlet entitled "Code of Self-Regulation" published by the Motion Picture Association of America in 1966.

79. Van Schmus, interview, 294–297.

80. Richard S. Randall, "Censorship: From *The Miracle* to *Deep Throat,*" in *The American Film Industry,* ed. Tino Balio, rev. ed. (Madison: University of Wisconsin Press, 1985), 510–536.

81. Richard S. Randall cites a *Variety* article that states that a proposal to eliminate the practice of MPAA-member studios releasing films through a subsidiary was voted down during deliberations over the draft of the 1966 Code. See Randall, *Censorship of the Movies,* 204.

82. Quoted in Robert Windeler, "As Nation's Standards Change, So Do Movies," *New York Times,* Oct. 8, 1968.

83. Robert Windeler, "Hollywood Is Preparing a Broad Film Classification System," *New York Times,* Sep. 21, 1968; Lewis, *Hollywood v. Hard Core,* 146.

84. Julian S. Rifkin, "Now Is the Time," *NATO News,* July 15, 1968, 1.

85 . *Ginsberg v. New York,* 390 U.S. 629 (1968); *Interstate Circuit, Inc. v. Dallas,* 390 U.S. 676 (1968).

86. MPAA, *A Year in Review,* June 1968, 23.

87. Only one major theater group, the Walter Reade Organization, refused to support classification because it believed the rating system was unconstitutional and would lead to government censorship. See Julian C. Burroughs Jr., "X Plus 2: The MPAA Classification System during Its First Two Years," *Journal of the University Film Association* 23, no. 2 (1971): 45–46.

CHAPTER 2 — CARA AND THE EMERGENCE
OF RESPONSIBLE ENTERTAINMENT

1. Jon Lewis, *Hollywood v. Hard Core: How the Struggle over Censorship Saved the Modern Film Industry* (New York: NYU Press, 2000), 135.

2. MPAA, Personal Statement of Jack Valenti, President, Motion Picture Association of America, in Connection with Announcement of New National Voluntary Film Rating System, Oct. 7, 1968; Jack Valenti, "The Movie Rating System," *Daily Variety,* 42nd Anniversary Issue, Oct. 28, 1975; MPAA, The Voluntary Movie Rating System: How It Began, Its Purpose, the Public Reaction, 1991; MPAA, Voluntary Movie Rating System Celebrates 30 Years of Providing Information to America's Parents, press release, Oct. 27, 1998.

3. Valenti, "The Movie Rating System."

4. Bruce A. Austin, "Making Sense of Movie Rating Statistics," *Box Office,* Oct. 1991, 45.

5 Charles Champlin, "What Will H. Hays Begat: Fifty Years of the Production Code," *American Film* 6, no. 1 (Oct. 1990): 42–46, 86, 88.

6. Stephen Vaughn, *Freedom and Entertainment: Rating the Movies in an Age of New Media* (Cambridge, UK: Cambridge University Press, 2006), 29.

7. Albert E. Van Schmus, interview by Barbara Hall, Academy of Motion Picture Arts and Sciences Oral History Program (1992), 102.

8. Quoted in "Movies—G, M, R, X," *Newsweek,* Oct. 21, 1968, 98.

9. MPAA, *Motion Picture Production Code and Rating Program: A System of Self-Regulation,* Motion Picture Association of America, 1968 (my emphasis).

10. MPAA, Personal Statement of Jack Valenti (my emphasis).

11. Quoted in Kim Masters, "Rating Game," *Premiere* (U.S.), Sep. 1988, 64.

12. *Movie Ratings and the Independent Producer: Hearings before the Subcommittee on Special Small Business Problems of the Committee on Small Business,* 95th Cong., 1st sess. March 24, April 14, May 12, June 15, and July 21, 1977. H. Rep. 90-916, 3–4.

13. The International Film Importers and Distributors of America was a less-powerful and now defunct trade organization, going out of service in 1978. According to the IFIDA Film Directory, 1968–1969, its members included Adelphia Pictures, Allied Artists, American International Pictures, Avco Embassy, Cinemation, Distribix, Grove Press, Janus, Joseph Burstyn, Sherpix, and Silverstein International, to name a few.

14. MPAA, *Motion Picture Production Code and Rating Program* (my emphasis).

15. Lewis, *Hollywood v. Hard Core,* 153.

16. Justin Wyatt, "The Stigma of the X: Adult Cinema and the Institution of the MPAA Ratings System," in *Controlling Hollywood: Censorship and Regulation in the Studio Era,* ed. Matthew Bernstein (New Brunswick, NJ: Rutgers University Press, 1999), 250–251.

17. Jack Valenti, "The Movie Rating System."

18. Wyatt, "The Stigma of the X," 241, quoting from Glenn Collins, "Film Ratings: Guidance or Censorship?" *New York Times,* April 9, 1990.

19. These statistics are not based on *Variety*'s rating tabulation that charts a year from November to October. These numbers are based on the actual year and come from "X-Rated Films, 1968–1973," *Hollywood Reporter,* 43rd Anniversary Edition, Nov. 1973. If we include Allied Artists and Avco Embassy, the smallest and short-lived of the MPAA signatories, who released a slate of legitimate and soft-core products, domestic and foreign, X-rated and otherwise, these statistics would look as follows: 1968: 4; 1969: 10; 1970: 11; 1971: 7; 1972: 1; and 1973: 2.

20. In 1970, only a year later, Paramount won an appeal against the X rating for *Medium Cool,* obtaining an R rating for the film.

21. Quoted in Vincent Canby, "For Better or Worse, Film Industry Begins Ratings," *New York Times,* Nov. 1, 1968.

22. "X Marks the Spot," *Newsweek,* Feb. 24, 1969, 101.

23. Bob Lardine, "Movie Industry Is on a Spot Marked X," *New York Sunday News,* July 20, 1969.

24. *Riot* eventually was awarded an M and was criticized for its mindless violence and homosexual candor.

25. "X Marks the Spot," 101.

26. Lewis, *Hollywood v. Hard Core,* 153. United Artists self-imposed the X on *Midnight Cowboy* rather than officially being awarded the rating from CARA.

27. Quotation ("By now"), in Stephen Farber, *The Movie Rating Game* (Washington, D.C.: Public Affairs Press, 1972), 49, 50–51, 66–67. At this time scripts were still vetted by CARA, just as in the days of the PCA, but only in regard to the rating that it may receive on completion of the film.

28. Quoted in Farber, *The Movie Rating Game,* 51.

29. A. D. Murphy, "$-Sign over MPAA Alphabet, Distribs Wanna Shun Risky 'R,'" *Variety,* Nov. 25, 1970, 5. Even though the M (later the GP then PG) category was frequently a site of contestation in the early years of CARA, I hardly believe that films of X caliber found their way into this rating. *Variety* does not provide any evidence for this assertion.

30. Wyatt, "The Stigma of the X," 244; Lewis, *Hollywood v. Hard Core,* 188. These statistics are drawn from data in *Variety,* which counts the MPAA calendar year as November to October since CARA was established on November 1, 1968.

31. See Julian C. Burroughs Jr., "X Plus 2: The MPAA Classification System during Its First Two Years," *Journal of the University Film Association* 23, no. 2 (1971): 53.

32. Aubrey quoted in Associated Press, "X-Rated Films Shunned," *Christian Science Monitor,* April 13, 1971; Fox source quoted in Jack Langguth, "Doctor X," *Saturday Review,* Dec. 2, 1972; Arkoff and Rugoff quoted in "Rating the Rating System," *Time,* May 31, 1971, 73.

33. Wyatt, "The Stigma of the X," 239.

34. Canby, "For Better or Worse."

35. "Film Rating System Announced: Four Ratings Geared to Protect Children," *NATO News*, Oct. 1968, 1, 4.

36. See Lardine, "Movie Industry Is on a Spot Marked X," 10.

37. See Vincent Canby, "Why Do They Laugh at 'G' Movies," *New York Times*, Nov. 2, 1969.

38. Charlie Poorman, "Survival Booking . . . in the Days of G, M, R, and X," *Motion Picture Herald*, July 16, 1969.

39. See "Young NATO Polls Theatres," *NATO News*, Dec. 1969, 8–9. Young NATO suspected that the percentage of theater owners avoiding X-rated films decreased since the time of survey.

40. Wyatt, "The Stigma of the X," 249–250.

41. "'Protecting Public' vs. 'Censorship,'" *Variety*, Feb. 25, 1970, 7; "Newspaper Rating Problems Grow," *NATO News*, Sep. 1969, 13.

42. Burroughs, "X Plus 2," 48. Cited from *New York Times*, Nov. 28, 1969; Leonard Gross, "What's Blue at the Movies?" *Los Angeles Times West Magazine*, July 16, 1972, 20; Vincent Canby, "The Ratings Are Wrong," *New York Times*, June 4, 1972.

43. MPAA, *Statement by Jack Valenti, President, MPAA, before Subcommittee No. 3 of the Committee on the Judiciary House of Representatives*, Jan. 28, 1970.

44. Quoted in Gene Arneel, "Valenti Raps Loew's 'Stitch' Booking; Can't Be Voyeur & Respectable Biz," *Variety*, Jan. 28, 1970, 4.

45. "Harris Sues MPAA, TOA, Par Alleging Conspiracy and 'Trade Libel' vs. 'Stitch,'" *Variety*, Feb. 11, 1970, 4. The suit also states that Paramount was upset that the $15-million *Paint Your Wagon* playing at Loew's State II was making much less money than the $1-million *Without a Stitch*, which shared the same building; "Clagett Tidying MPAA's New Bills; 39 Wanna Tax X," *Variety*, March 25, 1970, 5; Gene Arneel, "Censor Threats Haunt MPAA; Just Too Much, if Mostly Silly," *Variety*, March 18, 1970, 5.

46. Thomas Schatz, "The New Hollywood," in *Film Theory Goes to the Movies*, ed. Jim Collins, Hilary Radner, and Ava Preacher Collins (New York: Routledge, 1993), 16.

47. Again, I am not counting the smaller distributor, Avco Embassy, which released the relatively unknown exploitation film *A Place Called Today* with an X in 1972.

48. A. D. Murphy, "Code in Perspective over 4 Yrs.: Measure Indie Production Flood; U.S. Makers Seek G and PG Ratings," *Variety*, Nov. 8, 1972, 19. The trade paper also added that the possibility of a new adults-only rating to cover "quality" films had been severely undermined after Stanley Kubrick pulled *A Clockwork Orange* out of release in August for sixty days in order to qualify for a lower rating after cutting two scenes.

49. *Miller v. California*, 423 U.S. 15 (1973); *Paris Adult Theater I v. Slaton*, 423 U.S. 49 (1973). In *Miller* the Court did offer some examples of what a statute could regulate as obscenity: (a) patently offensive representations or descriptions of ultimate sexual acts, normal or perverted, actual or simulated; and (b) patently offensive representations or descriptions of masturbation, excretory functions, and lewd exhibition of the genitals.

50. *Jenkins v. Georgia*, 418 U.S. 153 (1973).

51. Lewis, *Hollywood v. Hard Core*, 262.

52. Stephen Farber and Estelle Changas, "What Has the Court Saved Us From?" *New York Times*, Dec. 9, 1973. See also, "Has the Supreme Court Saved Us from Obscenity?" *New York Times*, Aug. 5, 1973.

53. Jack Valenti, "To Rate a Film Is Not to Censor It," *New York Times,* Dec. 9, 1973. See also Jack Valenti, "'Censorship Is Deadly,'" *New York Times,* Aug. 5, 1973; Jack Valenti, "Editorial," *New York Times,* Feb. 24, 1974.

54. Jack Valenti, "Ratings Are for Parents, Not Critics," *New York Times,* June 18, 1972.

55. Vaughn, *Freedom and Entertainment,* 32. Vaughn quotes from Farber and Changas, "Insiders Rate Film Code Board as 'Unreformed,'" *Los Angeles Times,* Aug. 8, 1971, Calendar sec.

56. Stern quoted in "The War between 'Censors' and Producers (Rated R)," *Los Angeles Herald Examiner,* July 16, 1972. Also see "Stern Quitting as Code Chief," *Daily Variety,* Dec. 3, 1973; Will Tusher, "Stern to C.P.I.; Hunter Tops Brut; Netter Out," *Hollywood Reporter,* Dec. 3, 1973.

57. Robert Landry, "If You Make an X, Take an X," *Variety,* Sep. 9, 1970, 1, 24; Valenti quoted in Moira Hodgson, "Move Ratings—Do They Serve Hollywood or the Public?" *New York Times,* May 24, 1981.

58. A. D. Murphy, "Code Ratings Analysis since '68; Self-Imposed X's Outside Record," *Variety,* Nov. 6, 1974.

59. Schatz, "The New Hollywood," 17.

60. *Emmanuelle* was released in Dec. 1974, making it a 1974–1975 release, according to the MPAA's November-to-October accounting schedule.

61. Lea Jacobs. *The Wages of Sin: Censorship and the Fallen Woman Film, 1928–1942* (Madison: University of Wisconsin Press, 1991), xi.

62. Quotation ("reflect"), in Richard Heffner, interview by author, New York City, July 11, 2006; quotation ("power"), in Richard Heffner, *Reminiscences of Richard D. Heffner,* 2:81, Oral History Collection of Columbia University (hereafter cited as Heffner, *Reminiscences*).

63. Dale Pollock, "R-Rated 'Cruising': The MPAA Seal of Disapproval," *Los Angeles Times,* May 4, 1980, Calendar sec.; Jack Garner, "Ratings: Do They Tell Moviegoers as Much as They Should?" *Rochester (NY) Democrat and Chronicle,* Sep. 14, 1980.

64. James Har. [Harwood], review of *Cruising, Variety,* Feb. 12, 1980. Perhaps one explanation for *Variety*'s condemning review was that *Cruising* producer Jerry Weintraub barred its reporter from the film's press screening. Weintraub said he based his decision on a matter of policy to bar any reviews from appearing too early before a film's release. Most people believed, however, that the timing of his action was intended to keep at bay critical opinion of the film in order to bring General Cinemas and other defecting chains back into the fold of theaters screening *Cruising* and to prevent the "escape" of others. See Stephen Klain, "Weintraub to Media: 'Fan Dispute, But Hold Your Critics,'" *Variety,* Feb. 6, 1980, 4, 38.

65. Richard D. Heffner, "RDH Pre-Oral History Memorandum to Chuck Champlin for the Year 1980," Oral History Collection of Columbia University, 3 (hereafter cited as Heffner, "Pre-Oral History Memo," followed by the year). The film was originally optioned then dropped by *French Connection* (1971) producer Philip D'Antoni in the wake of the *Miller* decision. See Farber and Changas, "What Has the Court Saved Us From?"

66. For more detailed information on these protests see Charles Lyons, *The New Censors: Movies and the Culture Wars* (Philadelphia: Temple University Press, 1997), 117–122; Stephen Prince, "Movies and Morality," in *A New Pot of Gold: Hollywood under the Electronic Rainbow, 1980–1989* (Berkeley: University of California Press, 2000), 343–348;

Edward Guthmann, "The *Cruising* Controversy: William Friedkin and the Gay Community," *Cineaste* 10, no. 3 (summer 1980): 2–8; and Thomas D. Clagett, *William Friedkin: Films of Aberration, Obsession, and Reality*, expanded and updated 2nd ed. (Los Angeles: Silman-James, 2003), 237–262.

67. Arthur Bell, "Bell Tells," *Village Voice*, July 16, 1979.

68. Charles Campbell, supervising sound editor of *Cruising*, said that 80 percent of the film was "looped"—the actors' dialogue rerecorded—as a result of harassment by demonstrators during filming. See Clagett, *William Friedkin*, 250–251.

69. Vito Russo, *The Celluloid Closet: Homosexuality in the Movies*, rev. ed. (New York: Harper and Row, 1987), 259.

70. "Largest Theater Chain Rejects Film 'Cruising,'" *Los Angeles Herald Examiner*, Jan. 31, 1980; Martin Gould, "'Cruising' to Be Rescreened by General Cinema," *Hollywood Reporter*, Feb. 5, 1980; GCC quoted in Aljean Harmetz, "How 'Cruising' Received Its 'R' Rating," *New York Times*, Feb. 16, 1980.

71. Prince, "Movies and Morality," 346.

72. "2nd Look Nix by GCC: 'Cruising' an X Pic," *Variety*, Feb. 13, 1980, 5, 219; Whitman quoted in Harmetz, "How 'Cruising' Received Its 'R' Rating."

73. See "Hub Rues Sack Use of Cinema 57 for 'Cruising' Pic," *Variety*, Feb. 20, 1980; "Hassanien Screens 'Cruising'; UATC Dates to Stand," *Hollywood Reporter*, Feb. 5, 1980.

74. See Tino Balio, *United Artists: The Company That Changed the Film Industry* (Madison: University of Wisconsin Press, 1987), 132.

75. "UATC Posts Warning at Windows: 'Cruising' Is X Film in R Clothing," *Variety*, Feb. 20, 1980. UATC similarly notified its patrons with the showing of Columbia's *Hardcore* in 1979.

76. Jonna Jeffries, "'Cruising' Sparks Booker Apologies, Patron Complaints," *Box Office*, March 10, 1980, 1.

77. Dale Pollock, "*Cruising* Tails Off," *Los Angeles Times*, March 16, 1980, Calendar sec.; Pollock, "R-Rated 'Cruising.'"

78. Quotation ("worst thing"), in Heffner, "Pre-Oral History Memo 1980," 8; Weintraub's comments from Heffner papers, "RDH Summary of Major Events Relating to *Cruising*," July 7, 1980, doc. 80-2, in the Oral History Collection of Columbia University (hereafter cited as Heffner papers, followed by title of memo, date, and document number); quotation ("intensity"), in Heffner papers, Heffner to Valenti, Dec. 31, 1979, doc. 80-6; quotation ("treatment"), in Heffner, "Pre-Oral History Memo 1980," 11; quotation ("never"), in Heffner, "Pre-Oral History Memo 1980," 53 (*responsibly* is my emphasis).

79. Mark Kermode, "William Friedkin" (interview), *Guardian*, Oct. 22, 1998.

80. Richard Heffner, email correspondence with author, July 31, 2006; Heffner, "Pre-Oral History Memo 1980," 8. Steven Ginsberg, "Friedkin and Weintraub Defend 'Cruising' against MPAA's Rating Charges," *Variety*, June 18, 1980, 6; Kermode, "William Friedkin."

81. Quoted in Harmetz, "How 'Cruising' Received Its 'R' Rating."

82. Heffner, "Pre-Oral History Memo 1980," 15–16.

83. Prince, "Movies and Morality," 358. For further information see Pollock, "R-Rated 'Cruising'"; "'Cruising' in New Ratings Rumpus; 'R' Taken, Given," *Variety*, June 11, 1980, 4, 30; and "Did 'Cruising' Respect Rulings?" *Variety*, June 25, 1980, 4, 37.

84. Quoted in Pollock, "R-Rated 'Cruising.'" Also at the time Valenti said, "The board has rated over 5,500 films, and two out of 5,500 [the other being an obscure 1975

independent film, *Abduction*] have had this happen so it's a pretty good record. Everyone makes mistakes and the system is not without mistakes. But this disagreement has not abused or torched the system" ("Did 'Cruising' Respect Rulings?" 37).

85. See, e.g., Heffner papers, "RDH Summary of Major Events Relating to *Cruising*," July 7, 1980, doc. 80-2; Heffner papers, Heffner to Valenti, Feb. 27, 1980, doc. 80-7.

86. The most detailed accounts of the editing of the film appear in Clagett, *William Friedkin*, 253–256; and in Laurent Bouzereau, *The Cutting Room Floor* (New York: Citadel, 1994), 171–173. Bud Smith recalls: "We had to cut out a lot from the scene that takes place in a gay bar. There was a guy lying in a bathtub, and another one was pissing on him. There was a scene of copulation as you're panning from Al Pacino's point of view; you basically saw guys giving each other blow jobs. Way in the back, there was a guy up in a strap, a leather sling, and someone else reaches out and puts some gel on his forearm and sticks it up his rectum. All this was in the original dailies." Quoted in Bouzereau, *The Cutting Room Floor*, 171–172; also see Harmetz, "How 'Cruising' Received Its 'R' Rating."

87. Vincent Canby, "Screen: Pacino Stars in Friedkin's 'Cruising,'" review, *New York Times,* Feb. 15, 1980; Heffner, quoted in Harmetz, "How 'Cruising' Received Its 'R' Rating."

88. Jack Valenti, "Editorial" (see note 54 above). According to Friedkin he did visit Aaron Stern at CARA during production on *The Exorcist* to ask him how to film the scene in which Regan masturbates with a crucifix. See Ronald Gold, "Ask MPAA Drop X, 'Fight Censorship'; Valenti Sees no 'Libertarian' Trends," *Variety,* June 21, 1972, 6.

89. See David A. Cook, "Genres I: Revision, Transformation, and Revival," in *Lost Illusions: American Cinema in the Shadow of Watergate and Vietnam, 1970–1979* (Berkeley: University of California Press, 2000), 226; Dawn B. Sova, *Forbidden Films* (New York: Checkmark, 2001), 121–124; Bouzereau, *The Cutting Room Floor*, 157–161.

90. Peter Wood says this percentage is about one-third, though Heffner corrects this number in his first draft of a letter to the editor of the *New York Times* in response to Wood's article. See Peter Wood, "'Dressed to Kill'—How a Film Changes from 'X' to 'R,'" *New York Times,* July 20, 1980; Richard D. Heffner, "In Defense of Film Rating Practices," *New York Times,* Aug. 24, 1980. See also Heffner, "Pre-Oral History Memo 1980," 13.

91. Quoted in Heffner, "Pre-Oral History Memo 1980," 53.

91. Laurence F. Knapp, introduction to *Brian De Palma: Interviews,* ed. Laurence F. Knapp (Jackson: University Press of Mississippi, 2003), ix.

93. Lewis, *Hollywood v. Hard Core*, 277; Lyons, *The New Censors*, 69–71.

94. Quoted in Wood, "'Dressed to Kill.'"

95. For more of the exact nature of these cuts see Bouzereau, *The Cutting Room Floor,* 137–140.

96. Heffner, "In Defense of Film Rating Practices," 15. In his oral history Heffner reflects on these erroneous press accounts: "Maybe that was the toughest part of my years there, having to deal with what the press did in picking up the attacks that were irrational, unfair, and to deal with the fact that the press seldom come to get a response, and I guess, to some large extent, because Jack Valenti frightened them off" (Heffner, *Reminiscences,* 24:1510).

97. See Lyons, *The New Censors*, 68–80; Lewis, *Hollywood v. Hard Core*, 277–280; Prince, "Movies and Morality," 353–355; and Sova, *Forbidden Films*, 112–114.

98. Judy Stone, "Interview: Brian De Palma," *Newsday*, Aug. 17, 1980. Quoted in Lyons, *The New Censors*, 73–74, 79.

99. See, e.g., Jay Ducassi, "Rewrite or Be Banned, 'Scarface' Producer Told," *Miami Herald*, Aug. 21, 1982; "'Scarface' to L.A.," *Variety*, Sep. 1, 1982; Ana Veciana-Suarez, "'Scarface' Producers Come to Make Scenes," *Miami Herald*, April 13, 1983.

100. Quotation ("fix"), in Heffner, *Reminiscences*, 17:1054; Rehme quoted in "De Palma's 'Scarface' in Ratings Battle," *Boston Globe*, Oct. 27, 1983. Also see "Scarface Gets an X Rating," *Miami Herald*, Nov. 5, 1983; De Palma quoted in "'Scarface' Gets an X Rating"; Bregman quoted in Joe Starita, "'Scarface' Rating Will End Up in Eye of Beholder," *Miami Herald*, Nov. 27, 1983; Gary Arnold, "'Scarface': X Mars the Movie," *Washington Post*, Nov. 8, 1983.

101. De Palma quotation ("excessively"), in David Gritten, "The Battle to Avoid the X Rating," *Los Angeles Herald Examiner*, Dec. 9, 1983; quotation ("accumulation"), in Stephen Farber, "'Scarface' and the Onus of the X Rating," *New York Daily News*, Nov. 20, 1983, Leisure sec.; Heffner, *Reminiscences*, 17:1051.

102. Quoted in Gritten, "The Battle to Avoid the X Rating." De Palma found his attempts to be futile in appeasing the Rating Board: "The board never tells you what to do. They simply address themselves to certain areas. When you fix those, they say they have trouble with other things in your movie. Eventually, they've recut your movie for you." Quoted in Aljean Harmetz, "Movie 'Scarface' Gets X Rating," *New York Times*, Oct. 30, 1983.

103. See Stephen Vaughn's account of these appeals in *Freedom and Entertainment*, in which Vaughn also draws from Heffner's papers. In a personal email to me Heffner said, "But remember that before [Valenti] could say or do anything concerning [*All the President's Men*'s] final rating, I had gotten up to indicate to the Appeals Board that were the Rating Board not literally bound by the so-called 'language rule' we would have given the film a PG rating . . . and, most importantly, that WE urged the Appeals Board TO DO JUST THAT, EVEN IF WE COULDN'T!" (Aug. 1, 2006).

104. David Chute, "For De Palma, Violence's Just a Slice of Life," *Los Angeles Herald Examiner*, Dec. 8, 1983. Lois Romano, "'Scarface' Reprieve," *Washington Post*, Nov. 9, 1983. Some reports say that this was the second cut of the film.

105. Heffner initially wanted to bring New York governor Mario Cuomo's wife, Matilda, to the proceeding to testify for *Scarface*'s X. He ultimately dismissed that idea, knowing it could alienate MPAA executives to a point that could lead to the demise of the rating system. See Vaughn, *Freedom and Entertainment*, 112.

106. For Heffner's account of the hearing see *Reminiscences*, 17:1055–18:1064. Also see Romano, "'Scarface' Reprieve"; Starita, "'Scarface' Rating Will End Up in Eye of Beholder."

107. Heffner papers, "Statement by Richard Heffner, Chairman, Classification and Rating Administration, to the Appeals Board on the Occasion of the Appeal of CARA's X Rating for 'Scarface,'" Nov. 8, 1983, doc. 83-5.

108. Gritten, "The Battle to Avoid the X Rating."

109. Heffner often cited the following Tocquevillean concerns as informing his views on self-regulation: "If one satisfied the needs, just sufficiently satisfied the needs of the majority, then this system could prevent the will of the majority from turning into the tyranny of the majority and we could avoid censorship" (*Reminiscences*, 2:42).

110. Quoted in Lynn Hirschberg, "Brian De Palma's Death Wish," *Esquire*, Jan. 1984, 79–83.

111. Vaughn, *Freedom and Entertainment,* 114.

112. Lyons, *The New Censors,* 79.

CHAPTER 3 — FROM X TO NC-17

1. See Charles Lyons, *The New Censors: Movies and the Culture Wars* (Philadelphia: Temple University Press, 1997).

2. The British Board of Film Classification has an "18" rating for "artistic" films (restricted to adults eighteen and over) and an "R18" for explicit works containing sex between consenting adults (also restricted to adults eighteen and over).

3. Jack Mathews, "Is It Time to Change the Ratings System for Movies?" *Los Angeles Times,* April 12, 1990, Calendar sec.; Charles Champlin, "Commentary; Dropping the X," *Los Angeles Times,* June 17, 1990, Calendar sec.

4. Quoted in Glenn Collins, "Guidance or Censorship? New Debate on Rating Films," *New York Times,* April 9, 1990.

5. "NATO Unit Asks 'AO' (Adults Only) to Escape Stigmatizing Via 'X,'" *Variety,* March 25, 1970, 5.

6. See Ronald Gold, "Ask MPAA Drop X, 'Fight Censorship'; Valenti Sees No 'Libertarian' Trends," *Variety,* June 21, 1972, 6.

7. Gene Shalit, "The Rating Game," *Look,* Nov. 3, 1970, 83.

8. "N.Y. Critics Vote Condemns Code; Valenti Cites Risks of Retreat; Sez 'Dailies Now the Censors,'" *Variety,* May 10, 1972.

9. The *Miami Herald,* the *San Diego Union,* the *Houston Chronicle,* and the *Fort Worth Star-Telegram* restricted the amount of space given to advertisers of X-rated films. See Stephen Grover, "Banning Ads for Dirty Movies," *Wall Street Journal,* May 15, 1972.

10. "N.Y. Critics Vote Condemns Code."

11. Arthur Knight, "Knight at the Movies," *Hollywood Reporter,* May 15, 1972.

12. Judith Crist to Jack Valenti, May 18, 1972, New York Public Library clippings file. Crist cc'd the letter to William Wolf, chairman of the New York Film Critics Circle, and Ronald Gold, a writer at *Variety.*

13. See Jack Langguth, "Doctor X," *Saturday Review,* Dec. 2, 1972, 10; and David A. Cook, "The Auteur Cinema: Directors and Directions in the Hollywood Renaissance," in *Lost Illusions: American Cinema in the Shadow of Watergate and Vietnam, 1970–1979* (Berkeley: University of California Press, 2000), 77.

14. A. D. Murphy, "Over 50% 'Restricted' Ratings in U.S.," *Variety,* Nov. 5, 1975, 7.

15. Aljean Harmetz, "How 'Cruising' Received Its 'R' Rating," *New York Times,* Feb. 16, 1980.

16. By 1979 the G rating amounted to only 7 percent of the majors' output, whereas it had first commanded 32 percent. See "Rated Major Pix Up 21% from Last Year, Per MPAA," *Variety,* Nov. 7, 1979, 24, 32.

17. Quoted in Aljean Harmetz, "Movie Ratings—Too Much of a Mystery?" *New York Times,* May 3, 1978.

18. Quoted in ibid.

19. See Richard Heffner, *Reminiscences of Richard D. Heffner,* 4:186, Oral History Collection of Columbia University (hereafter cited as Heffner, *Reminiscences*); also see Stephen Vaughn, *Freedom and Entertainment: Rating the Movies in an Age of New Media* (New York: Cambridge University Press, 2006), 50; Harmetz, "Movie Ratings—Too

Much of a Mystery?"; Dale Pollock, "Ratings Struggle to Stay Abreast," *Los Angeles Times,* May 5, 1980; Charles Champlin, "What Will H. Hays Begat," *American Film* 6, no. 1 (Oct. 1980): 42–46, 86, 88.

20. Quoted in Gerald Jonas, "The Man Who Gave an X Rating to Violence," *New York Times,* May 11, 1975.

21. Richard Heffner, interview by author, New York City, July 11, 2006.

22. Heffner papers, Valenti memo, Feb. 18, 1977; Heffner to Valenti, Feb. 24, 1977; and Heffner to Valenti, March 7, 1977 (docs. are all 84-9).

23. See Heffner papers, Heffner to Valenti, April 11, 1977, doc. 80-38; Heffner to Valenti, March 24, 1980, doc. 80-38; Heffner to Valenti, Feb. 23, 1981, doc. 81-1; Heffner to Valenti, May 12, 1982, doc. 82-24; Heffner to Valenti, Dec. 13, 1983, doc. 83-14.

24. See, e.g., Heffner papers, Heffner to Barry Diller, March 17, 1980, doc. 80-35; Heffner to Lew Wasserman, Oct. 10, 1980, doc. 80-J.

25. Heffner papers, Richard Orear to Jack Valenti, Jan. 25, 1981, doc. 82-16. Also see Heffner to Valenti, Nov. 11, 1981, doc. 90-1.

26. Heffner papers, interoffice memo to Heffner, May 8, 1981, doc. 81-6; Heffner to Valenti, May 11, 1981, doc. 81-6; Heffner to Valenti, May 18, 1981, doc. 81-7; Valenti to Heffner, May 22, 1981, doc. 81-8.

27. Heffner, "Pre-Oral History Memo 1980," 80. See Vaughn, *Freedom and Entertainment,* 116, for a more detailed description of this experiment.

28. Heffner papers, Orear to Heffner, Jan. 5, 1982, doc. 82-17. Orear would later insist, however, that Valenti's poll was inaccurate and that the public did clamor for more descriptive explanations to a film's rating. See Will Tusher, "Valenti Doesn't Convince Orear on Ratings," *Daily Variety,* Nov. 1, 1983.

29. Heffner, "Pre-Oral History Memo 1980," 82–83.

30. For a local account of these events see Jane Myers, "A Curious Spectacle at the Movies This Summer," *Ann Arbor News,* Sep. 14, 1980.

31. William Paul, *Laughing Screaming: Modern Hollywood Horror and Comedy* (New York: Columbia University Press, 1994).

32. See Will Tusher, "NATO Push for Relaxed R-Rating, Legal Panel Highlight Conclave Biz," *Variety,* Oct. 26, 1983, 7, 374; "Ratings Change Delays Irking NATO Members," *Daily Variety,* Oct. 31, 1983.

33. With *Jaws* all of the Rating Board examiners had initially rated the film R and called Heffner in to see it. But before he arrived, the Rating Board reconsidered the rating and awarded the film a PG in a five-to-two vote. Heffner still got some edits made to the film, but more than likely Valenti intervened on behalf of Wasserman. See Heffner, *Reminiscences,* 5:277.

34. Richard Heffner, interview by author, New York City, July 11, 2006. For more information on the *Poltergeist* case see Vaughn, *Freedom and Entertainment,* 114–115.

35. Heffner papers, William Nix to Valenti, May 6, 1982, doc. 82-1; James M. Wall to Jack Valenti, June 14, 1982, doc. 82-5.

36. Richard Heffner, interview by author, New York City, July 11, 2006; Heffner papers, Heffner to Steven Spielberg, July 23, 1982, doc. 82-2.

37. "Just What Makes a Movie PG-13?" *San Francisco Chronicle,* July 4, 1984.

38. See Leslie Bennetts, "Debate over Film Ratings Widening," *New York Times,* June 23, 1984; Richard Zoglin, "Gremlins in the Rating System," *Newsweek,* June 25, 1984; Gail

Bronson and Steve Hawkins, "Movie Violence Getting Out of Hand," *U.S. News and World Report,* June 18, 1984; Vincent Canby, "As a Rating, PG Says Less Than Meets the Eye," *New York Times,* June 10, 1984.

39. See Aljean Harmetz, "Hollywood Plans New Rating to Protect Children under 13," *New York Times,* June 20, 1984; David Sterritt, "The Proposed PG-13 Film Rating," *Christian Science Monitor,* June 28, 1984.

40. See Vincent Canby, "Are the Ratings Just Alphabet Soup?" *New York Times,* April 20, 1986.

41. Heffner papers, Valenti to Heffner, June 7, 1984, doc. 84-10-C.

42. Heffner, *Reminiscences,* 19:1192.

43. Richard Heffner, email correspondence with author, Aug. 4, 2006.

44. Heffner, *Reminiscences,* 19:1193–1194.

45. See Heffner papers, William F. Fore to Valenti, July 13, 1984; William F. Fore to Barry Diller, July 13, 1984; William F. Fore to Julian Rifkin, July 13, 1984 (docs. are all 84-10-Q). Also see Aljean Harmetz, "Some Groups Unhappy with PG-13 Film Rating," *New York Times,* Aug. 13, 1984. Heffner says that the initial concerns with the PG-13 had to do with the first three films carrying that rating in 1984: *The Woman in Red, Red Dawn,* and *Dreamscape.* Heffner awarded these films a PG-13 with the understanding that the category was restrictive. Had he known Valenti would change the classification warning, he would have given them each an R. In time, though, Heffner thought the PG-13 did effectively distinguish between stronger and softer unrestricted films. See Heffner, *Reminiscences,* 19:1189–1192.

46. Aljean Harmetz, "X Rating for 'Angel Heart' Is Upheld," *New York Times,* Feb. 14, 1987. The film *9½ Weeks* also added ninety seconds to its home video version, but the additional material was still not enough to warrant anything beyond the R rating given to its theatrical release.

47. "Appeals Board Upholds 'Angel Heart' X Rating," *New York Times,* Feb. 21, 1987.

48. Quoted in Anne Thompson, "Selling a Rating Alphabet War Pits Creativity vs. the Box Office," *Chicago Tribune,* March 8, 1987.

49. See Andrew Sarris, "Sex Is Over-Rated," *Village Voice,* April 7, 1987.

50. Aljean Harmetz, "Video of 'Angel Heart' Restores Edited Scene," *New York Times,* July 23, 1987.

51. Jack Mathews, "Motion Picture Assn.: Raters of the Lost Art?" *Los Angeles Times,* March 6, 1987, Calendar sec.; Roger Ebert, "Artful Adult Films Should Rate 'A,' " *Chicago Sun-Times,* March 1, 1987; Vincent Canby, "Anatomy of an R Rating," *New York Times,* March 8, 1987.

52. Jack Valenti, "Film Rating: From A to X," *Los Angeles Times,* Feb. 28, 1987.

53. Quoted in Aljean Harmetz, "New Debate on Rating for Movies," *New York Times,* March 5, 1987.

54. *Dark Obsession* was eventually released in June 1991 with an NC-17. *The Killer* was released without a rating.

55. Quoted in Jill Abramson, "Burying the X," *Premiere* (U.S.), Jan. 1991, 30.

56. Described in *Maljack Productions, Inc. v. Motion Picture Association of America, Inc.,* United States Court of Appeals, District of Columbia Court, no. 93-7244.

57. Elaine Dutka, "The Horrors of Filmmaking," *Los Angeles Times,* Sep. 1, 1991, Calendar sec.

58. Quotation ("disturbing"), in "*Henry* Takes Tortuous Path to Screen," *Hollywood Reporter,* April 20, 1990; McNaughton quoted in Peter Bates, "Lost and Found," *Cineaste* 17, no. 4 (1990): 56. Also see the production notes in the press kit for *Henry: Portrait of a Serial Killer;* and Heffner, *Reminiscences,* 24:1513.

59. Heffner, *Reminiscences,* 4:224.

60. Even though Triumph Releasing was a division of Sony, it was treated as an independent distributor by the trade journals.

61. See Janet Maslin, "G, PG, R, and X: Make the Letter Reflect the Spirit," *New York Times,* April 29, 1990; Charles Champlin, "Commentary; Dropping the X," *Los Angeles Times,* June 17, 1990, Calendar sec.; Hal Hinson, "Smash the Ratings System!" *Washington Post,* April 29, 1990; Richard Corliss, "X Marks the Top," *Time,* April 9, 1990, 95; Jack Mathews, "Is It Time to Change the Ratings System for Movies?" *Los Angeles Times,* April 12, 1990.

62. Mathews, "Is It Time to Change the Ratings System for Movies?"

63. Quoted in Hinson, "Smash the Ratings System!"

64. Justin Wyatt, "The Formation of the 'Major Independent': Miramax, New Line, and the New Hollywood," in *Contemporary Hollywood Cinema,* ed. Steve Neale and Murray Smith (London: Routledge, 1998), 80.

65. Bart Mills and Nina J. Easton, "'Scandal' Faces Another Shock—an X-Rating," *Los Angeles Times,* March 16, 1989, Calendar sec.

66. Heffner, *Reminiscences,* 25:1562–1563.

67. Quoted in Daniel Cerone, "'Scandal' to Make New Bid for R Rating," *Los Angeles Times,* April 8, 1989, Calendar sec.; "Movie Rating Board Sticks to X-Rating for 'Scandal' Flick," Associated Press, April 7, 1989.

68. Heffner, *Reminiscences,* 25:1561–1562

69. Quoted in Collins, "Guidance or Censorship?"

70. Quoted in Michael Blowen, "'The Cook, the Thief . . .' and the Rating Issue," *Boston Globe,* April 1, 1990. The film was eventually released on video in an R-rated version.

71. Quoted in Collins, "Guidance or Censorship?"

72. Ibid.

73. Susan Wloszczyna, "'Cook' Fills Theaters Despite Ratings Flap," *USA Today,* April 20, 1990.

74. Hinson, "Smash the Ratings System!"

75. Quoted in Michael Fleming, "Rating Rift Reaches Majors: Will Studio Make A OK?" *Variety,* June 20, 1990, 22.

76. Richard Heffner, interview by author, New York City, July 12, 2006; Heffner *Reminiscences,* 26:1622–1623.

77. See Steve Weinstein, "Pedro Almodóvar: Living under the X," *Los Angeles Times,* May 6, 1990, Calendar sec.; Glenn Collins, "Almodóvar Film's X Stands," *New York Times,* April 25, 1990.

78. Quoted in Jay Carr, "Almodóvar Decries Creeping Censorship in United States," *Boston Globe,* May 20, 1990.

79. "Almodóvar Appeals X Given to His New Film," *New York Times,* April 23, 1990; also see Weinstein, "Pedro Almodóvar: Living under the X."

80. Richard Heffner, email correspondence with author, Aug. 4, 2006.

81. Andrew L. Yarrow, "Almodóvar's Film's X Rating Is Challenged in Lawsuit," *New York Times*, May 24, 1990.

82. Richard Huff, "Suit Charges MPAA Ratings Unfair," *Daily Variety*, May 18, 1990.

83. See Gene Arneel, "Says 'X' Kills Pic; Sues Code," *Variety*, Dec. 1, 1971.

84. Maljack's suit was eventually dismissed by a Washington, D.C., Federal Court judge in March 1992 who ruled that the X rating for *Henry* "was not done unfairly or in bad faith." See "Court Throws Out Maljack Ratings Suit against MPAA," *Daily Variety*, March 23, 1992. They appealed the case in *Maljack Productions, Inc. v. Motion Picture Association of America, Inc.*, United States Court of Appeals, District of Columbia Court, no. 93-7244.

85. *Miramax Films Corp. v. MPAA*, 560 New York Supplement, 2nd ed., 730 (1990). Each of the following quotes is taken from this opinion. The prosecution prepared a nine-minute tape of sexual scenes from *The Postman Always Rings Twice* (1981), *Blue Velvet* (1986), *9½ Weeks* (1986), *Fatal Attraction* (1987), and *The Accused* (1988) that they believed were more sexual than *Tie Me Up! Tie Me Down!*

86. William Kunstler with Sheila Isenberg, *My Life as a Radical Lawyer* (New York: Birch Lane Press, 1994), 366.

87. Heffner claims that Ramos needed a case to improve his public image after the *New York Daily News* ran a story about his discrimination against women. Heffner believes his ruling in the Miramax case suggesting that experts instead of parents should be judging films on whether they discriminated against women and minorities reflected this front-page story. See Heffner, *Reminiscences*, 26:1625–1626.

88. See Will Tusher, "Up Loses Fights; Judge Comes Down on MPAA," *Variety*, July 25, 1990, 20; Glenn Collins, "Judge Upholds X Rating for Almodóvar Film," *New York Times*, July 20, 1990; Vicki Sabatini, "Directors Blast X Ratings; Valenti Says Ruling 'Idiotic,'" *Hollywood Reporter*, July 23, 1990; Jack Mathews, "A Rational Look at an Irrational System," *Los Angeles Times*, July 21, 1990, Calendar sec.

89. Quoted in Collins, "Judge Upholds X Rating for Almodóvar Film." Notably absent was any reference to ex-CARA chairperson Aaron Stern, who was fired in 1974 for those very reasons.

90. Quoted in Sabatini, "Directors Blast X Ratings."

91. Quoted in Mathews, "A Rational Look at an Irrational System."

92. Valenti, however, did meet with executives of the MPAA-member companies a few weeks before the court decision to discuss dropping the X altogether if the case went against the MPAA. See Will Tusher, "Valenti: No Dice on No Children Rating," *Variety*, July 25, 1990, 20; Collins, "Judge Upholds X Rating for Almodóvar Film."

93. Quoted in David J. Fox, "Rating System Faces Challenges on Two Fronts," *Los Angeles Times*, July 21, 1990, Calendar sec.

94. The Film Advisory Board offered six ratings: C for Children, F for Family, M for Mature, VM for Very Mature, EM for Extremely Mature, and AO for Adults Only. PD (Parental Discretion) later replaced M, and PD-M (Parental Discretion–Mature) replaced the VM. How these ratings would be more helpful to a parent than the MPAA ratings befuddles the author. See FAB's Web site, www.filmadvisoryboard.org.

95. "Rating Service Competition Heats Up as X-Ratings, Prices Become Issues," *Video Marketing Newsletter*, July 9, 1990.

96. See "Still More X-citement: 'Cold,' 'King,' Branded," *Variety*, July 25, 1990, 20; "X-Rating on 'Hardware' Thriller Film Appealed," United Press International, July 19, 1990;

Fox, "Rating System Faces Challenges on Two Fronts"; John Horn, "Filmmakers Seek to Nix X Rating," Associated Press, July 27, 1990. *King of New York* was released with an R.

97. *Hardware* was later trimmed to an R. A scene of a character being caught and killed in a mechanical door was edited by removing thirty-eight frames of film, amounting to 1.5 seconds of running time. See David J. Fox, "Trade Group Seeks Rating Modifications," *Los Angeles Times,* Aug. 20, 1990, Calendar sec. Also, *In the Cold of the Night* was trimmed by thirty-six seconds to earn an R. See Steve Pond, "Ratings: A Matter of Seconds," *Washington Post,* Aug. 24, 1990.

98. Quoted in Alex Patterson, "Let X = X," *Village Voice,* July 31, 1990, 59.

99. Quoted in Sabatini, "Directors Blast X Ratings."

100. Jack Mathews, "Top Directors Join New Drive to Overhaul X," *Los Angeles Times,* July 5, 1990, Calendar sec.

101. The "biggest point of contention," said Mark Lipsky, president of Silverlight, was a scene where a character peruses a porn magazine featuring pregnant women, called "Poppin' Mamas." See Vicki Sabatini, "Silverlight Might Use Own 'A' Rating for Wang's 'Life,'" *Hollywood Reporter,* Weekly International Edition, July 24, 1990, 1, 65. Another reason reported for the X was a scene depicting a character eating a candy bar extricated from a mound of dog feces.

102. "An Open Letter to Jack Valenti," *Hollywood Reporter,* July 25, 1990.

103. The National Society of Film Critics at the time was composed of forty-two members from national, general-interest publications with Peter Rainer at its helm. In response to his letter Heffner told him that CARA could not have a rating for "good" films and "bad" films: "Whatever letter or number or symbol is used for the purpose, only one rating should legitimately signal 'not for kids' . . . and it mustn't be denied to people we disdain. Then YOU do the rest. The Rating Board must not become the Critics' Corner!" See Jay Carr, "Critics Urge a New Rating," *Boston Globe,* June 17, 1990; Gary Arnold, "Films Escape X, but Battle over Ratings Continues," *Washington Times,* Aug. 9, 1990.

104. Quoted in David Fox, "Distributor Rejects X Rating, Gives Its Adult Film an A," *Los Angeles Times,* July 25, 1990, Calendar sec. In advertising copy submitted to newspapers, a disclaimer read, "This film contains adult themes or images that may not be appropriate for viewers under 18 years of age. This film does not carry a rating issued by the MPAA. Many leading filmmakers believe the MPAA's current rating system promotes censorship and does not serve the best interests of the public." Shapiro-Glickenhaus also released *Frankenhooker* with an A rating.

105. The phrase "crisis of confidence" comes from Charles Champlin, "MPAA Ratings: A Crisis of Confidence," *Los Angeles Times,* July 24, 1990, Calendar sec.

106. Heffner, *Reminiscences,* 26:1597.

107. Quoted in Sean Mitchell, "The X Rating Gets Its Day in Court," *Los Angeles Times,* June 21, 1990, Calendar sec.

108. Quoted in Arnold, "Films Escape X, but Battle over Ratings Continues."

109. Joan Graves, "Rating Board Replies," *Los Angeles Times,* June 30, 1990, Calendar sec.

110. See Fleming, "Rating Rift Reaches Majors," 1, 22; Roger Ebert, "Scorsese, Lynch May Force Change in Movie Ratings," *Chicago Sun-Times,* May 17, 1990.

111. Quoted in Anne Thompson, "Censorship Debate Where X Still Marks the Unmarketable Spot," *San Francisco Chronicle,* June 17, 1990.

112. Quoted in Jeanine Williams, "Lynch Going 'Wild' about Movie Ratings," *USA Today,* May 22, 1990. Lynch only had to edit one shot in *Wild at Heart.* He applied a smoke effect over the sight of Willem Dafoe's head rolling on the ground after being blown off by a shotgun. See Jay Carr, "'Wild at Heart' Altered to Get R," *Boston Globe,* July 29, 1990.

113. Quoted in Carla Hall, "Directors, MPAA Chief Meet on Film Ratings," *Washington Post,* Aug. 10, 1990.

114. Quoted in Matthew Gilbert, "Scorsese Tackles the Mob," *Boston Globe,* Sep. 16, 1990. In this article Scorsese also said *Taxi Driver* improved after cutting it down to an R rating. "The worst problem I've had was with *Taxi Driver,*" he says. "Eventually, I tinted down the shoot-out sequence and printed it high contrast. And actually it looked better—it was the *Daily News.*"

115. Heffner, *Reminiscences,* 26:1628.

116. Quoted in Jeanine Williams, "Scorsese Minds His P's and Q's and Gets an R," *USA Today,* June 28, 1990.

117. See Jack Mathews, "David Lynch's 'Wild at Heart' Wows Cannes," *Los Angeles Times,* May 21, 1990, Calendar sec.

118. Quoted in David J. Fox, "Jack Valenti Says Change Possible for Film Ratings," *Los Angeles Times,* Aug. 10, 1990, Calendar sec. Also see David J. Fox, "Writers Guild Urges Changes in MPAA Rating System," *Los Angeles Times,* Aug. 6, 1990, Calendar sec.; and Will Tusher, "Helmers Apparently Satisfied with Film Ratings Roundtable," *Variety,* Aug. 15, 1990, 3, 24. The people who attended the meeting were Brian Walton, executive director of the Writers Guild of America; Glenn Gumpel, national executive director of the Directors Guild of America; and Phil Alden Robinson, Barry Levinson, John Landis, Walter Hill, Edward Zwick, Menahem Golan, Mark Lester, and Harold Becker.

119. Quoted in Tessa Horan, "The X Effect: Distributors Challenge MPAA Ratings," *Independent Film and Video Monthly,* Nov. 1990, 4–5. See also Tusher, "Helmers Apparently Satisfied with Film Ratings Roundtable," 3, 24; and Martin Kasindorf, "Future of X-Rating Debated," *Newsday,* Aug. 9, 1990.

120. As late as September 26, the very day the X was scrapped and replaced with an NC-17, Valenti was quoted as saying, "I have always been opposed to [creating an adults rating]. It's not even being considered." See Jack Mathews, "MPAA May Adopt New Rating by End of Week," *Los Angeles Times,* Sep. 26, 1990, Calendar sec. A day earlier, Valenti had said, "I have no problem with a new rating, but not one that's adult only, between X and R." See Charles Fleming and David Kissinger, "Film Critics Put Weight behind Adults-Only Rating," *Daily Variety,* Sep. 25, 1990.

121. Heffner papers, Heffner to Valenti, May 25, 1990, doc. 90-1.

122. Heffner papers, Heffner to Valenti, Aug. 1, 1990, doc. 90-3.

123. Fox, "Trade Group Seeks Rating Modifications."

124. Parents' Rating Service, "New Movie Rating System Takes Effect; PRS Accuses MPAA of Abuse of Trust," press release, Aug. 28, 1990.

125. Even after the X changed to an NC-17, proposals for a new motion picture rating system did not stop. See Carole Lieberman's editorial on MIND—Movies Influence Neuropsychological Development—and its three rating categories (Child-Safe, Teen-Safe, and Adult-Only) in "Counterpunch: A Psychological Approach to Rating Movies," *Los Angeles Times,* Oct. 1, 1990.

126. Stephen Farber, "A Major Studio Plans to Test the Rating System," *New York Times,* Sep. 4, 1990.

127. Jack Kroll, "X Marks the Trouble Spot," *Newsweek,* Sep. 17, 1990, 58.

128. *The Right Stuff* was nominated for eight Academy Awards and won four; *The Unbearable Lightness of Being* won best film and best director awards from the National Society of Film Critics.

129. Farber, "A Major Studio Plans to Test the Rating System."

130. David Kissinger, "X-Rated 'June' Could Ignite Major Revolt against MPAA," *Variety,* Sep. 10, 1990, 3.

131. Quoted in Farber, "A Major Studio Plans to Test the Rating System."

132. Quoted in Richard Corliss, "It's Great! Don't Show It! A Misguided Rating System Slaps an X on a Discreetly Erotic Film," *Time,* Sep. 17, 1990, 70; quoted in Michael Sragow, "X Rating Threatens Henry Miller Film," *San Francisco Examiner,* Aug. 27, 1990.

133. Quoted in Farber, "A Major Studio Plans to Test the Rating System."

134. See Jon Lewis, *Hollywood v. Hard Core: How the Struggle over Censorship Saved the Modern Film Industry* (New York: NYU Press, 2000), 105–108.

135. Quoted in Jack Mathews, "Oct. 3 Marks the Spot for Movie Showdown," *Los Angeles Times,* Sep. 15, 1990, Calendar sec.

136. MPAA, "Major Changes for Motion Picture Rating System," press release, Sep. 27, 1990.

137. See, e.g., David J. Fox, "X Film Rating Dropped and Replaced by NC-17," *Los Angeles Times,* Sep. 27, 1990.

138. Two years later, in July 1993, the MPAA added explanatory statements for the PG and PG-13 as well.

139. Heffner papers, Heffner to Valenti, July 18, 1990, doc. 90-2.

140. Quoted in Kroll, "X Marks the Trouble Spot," 58.

141. See Mathews, "Oct. 3 Marks the Spot for Movie Showdown"; Larry Rohter, "A 'No Children' Category to Replace the X Rating," *New York Times,* Sep. 27, 1990. Also see Heffner papers, *Reminiscences,* 26:1598–1600.

142. Mathews, "Oct. 3 Marks the Spot for Movie Showdown."

143. MPAA, "Major Changes for Motion Picture Rating System."

144. William Kartozian, "A Change and a Challenge," *NATO News,* Nov. 1990, 2.

145. John Voland, "NC-17 Winning Acceptance as Part of American Moviegoing," *Hollywood Reporter,* Oct. 26, 1990.

146. Janet Maslin, "Is the NC-17 an X in a Clean Raincoat?" *New York Times,* Oct. 21, 1990.

147. Quoted in Jay Carr, "X No Longer Marks the Spot," *Boston Globe,* Sep. 30, 1990.

148. Hal Lipper, "At Last, an Adult Decision," *St. Petersburg Times,* Sep. 29, 1990.

149. Martin A. Grove, "Hollywood Report," *Hollywood Reporter,* Oct. 10, 1990.

150. Quoted in Hal Hinson, "Film Industry Revises Rating System," *Washington Post,* Sep. 27, 1990.

151. Jack Mathews, "What Change in Film Rating System Means," *Los Angeles Times,* Sep. 27, 1990, Calendar sec.

152. Quoted in Richard Gold, "X Gets the Ax but Exhibitors, Papers May Not Buy NC-17," *Variety,* Oct. 1, 1998, 3, 103.

153. Quoted in Hinson, "Film Industry Revises Rating System."

154. Grove, "Hollywood Report," 5.

155. Fox, "The First Impact of the New Movie Rating."

156. See Gold, "X Gets the Ax," 3, 103.

157. See Will Tusher, "Town Fathers Force Withdrawal of NC-17-Rated 'Henry & June,'" *Variety,* Oct. 8, 1998, 5; and David J. Fox, "'Henry and June' Ban Called an 'Isolated Situation,'" *Los Angeles Times,* Oct. 6, 1990, Calendar sec. The Dedham Board of Selectmen soon after adopted a hands-off policy on the showing of NC-17 films after being threatened with legal action by Philip Kaufman and high-profile attorney Alan Dershowitz. See Will Tusher, "Dedham Decision Hailed, but 'June' Still Shut Out," *Daily Variety,* Oct. 11, 1990.

158. Catherine Gewertz, "Movie Rated NC-17 Creates Scuffle Outside," *Los Angeles Times,* Orange County ed., Oct. 6, 1990.

159. Quoted in Jack Mathews, "Sell-Out Crowds for 'Henry & June,'" *Los Angeles Times,* Oct. 8, 1990, Calendar sec.

160. See "Florida Town Mulls NC-17 Ordinance," *Los Angeles Times,* Nov. 15, 1990, Calendar sec.; David J. Fox, "Building Controversy over NC-17," *Los Angeles Times,* Nov. 20, 1990, Calendar sec.; David J. Fox, "NC-17 Movie Rating Law Defeated in Florida," *Los Angeles Times,* Nov. 22, 1990, Calendar sec.; and Will Tusher, "Kissimmee Kisses NC-17 Law Goodbye," *Daily Variety,* Nov. 21, 1990.

161. Larry Rohter, "Resistance to NC-17 Rating Develops," *New York Times,* Oct. 13, 1990. The broadcast television networks similarly vetted NC-17 films. NBC would review commercials on a case-by-case basis (never to air before 11:30 p.m.), and CBS and NBC would air ads after 10 p.m. See David J. Fox, "The First Impact of the New Movie Rating," *Los Angeles Times,* Sep. 28, 1990, Calendar sec.; and David J. Fox, "Ads for NC-17 Film Find Acceptance," *Los Angeles Times,* Oct. 5, 1990, Calendar sec.

162. John Voland, "Alabama Paper Refuses 'Henry' Ad," *Hollywood Reporter,* Oct. 10, 1990.

163. Quoted in "NC-17 Rating Hits a Snag as Newspapers Reject Ads," *Orange County Register,* Oct. 17, 1990.

164. Quoted in Will Tusher, "Porn Scorn Looms as NC-17 Threat," *Daily Variety,* Oct. 16, 1990.

165. Quoted in Fox, "Building Controversy over NC-17."

166. Kartozian, "A Change and a Challenge," 2.

167. Will Tusher, "Question of Porn Nags NC-17," *Daily Variety,* Nov. 13, 1990.

168. Quoted in David J. Fox, "Distributor of Sexually Explicit Film May Seek NC-17," *Los Angeles Times,* Nov. 7, 1990, Calendar sec. Parker had already released an edited, softcore version of *Blonde Emanuelle in 3-D* with an NC-17, but after poor earnings and complaints from audiences attending the show at the Nuart Theater in Los Angeles, he decided to resubmit the hard-core version.

169. Steve Pond, "Ratings and the Porn Purveyors," *Washington Post,* Nov. 9, 1990.

170. See Fox, "Building Controversy over NC-17."

171. See Joseph McBride, "Two Religious Orgs Protest NC-17 Rating," *Daily Variety,* Sep. 28, 1990; "2 Church Groups Condemn NC-17 Rating," *Los Angeles Times,* Sep. 29, 1990, Calendar sec.; M. S. Mason, "Revamped Film Rating System: Why It Changed, How It Works," *Christian Science Monitor,* Oct. 3, 1990; and Ari L. Goldman, "Religion Notes," *New York Times,* Oct. 6, 1990.

172. For an exchange of letters between Valenti and Reverend Edward J. O'Donnell of the United States Catholic Conference after the NC-17's announcement, see Heffner papers, doc. 90-6.

173. After the Dallas Motion Picture Classification Board was declared unconstitutional by the U.S. Supreme Court in *Interstate Circuit v. Dallas* in 1968, the city rewrote its ordinance under constitutional law. The board ceased its operation on Aug. 16, 1993, after twenty-seven years of service. For a history of the Dallas board see Michael Phillips, "Not Suitable in Dallas," *Los Angeles Times,* Sep. 18, 1990, Calendar sec.

174. Quoted in John Voland, "Religious, Right-Wing Groups Seek Return of Local Film Boards," *Hollywood Reporter,* Nov. 1, 1990.

175. In response to the NCTV proposal Valenti said the plan "is not only wrong, but it would create chaos for moviegoers. Imagine a patchwork of dozens or hundreds of rating boards, all with their own special attitudes. It would be a confusing mess to moviegoers and to theaters." See Dennis Wharton, "Conservatives Call for Local Rating Boards," *Variety,* Nov. 19, 1990.

176. In a packet to its members an AFA letter read: "The MPAA recently did away with the X rating for hardcore pornographic movies. They changed the X to an NC-17 rating. Don't be fooled. It is still an X-rated film. It just has a new and misleading rating. By removing the stigma of the X rating, Hollywood is hoping that your local theaters and videostores will begin to book and rent pornographic movies." Blockbuster, of course, denies that its anti-NC-17 stance has anything to do with the American Family Association. The company voiced the same denial in 1989 when it refused to carry *The Last Temptation of Christ.* See John Voland, "Blockbuster Blasted over NC-17 Video Ban," *Hollywood Reporter,* Jan. 15, 1991; "Blockbuster Video Refuses to Carry NC-17," *Entertainment Litigation Reporter,* Jan. 28, 1991.

177. Quoted in David J. Fox, "Blockbuster Video Rates NC-17 Films Unsuitable for All," *Los Angeles Times,* Jan. 14, 1991, Calendar sec.

178. Quoted in Voland, "Blockbuster Blasted over NC-17 Video Ban."

179. "NC-17 Rating Gets Mixed Reviews from Vid Dealers," *Daily Variety,* Jan. 23, 1991.

180. Quoted in Fox, "Blockbuster Video Rates NC-17 Films Unsuitable for All."

181. See Will Tusher, "MPAA Opens Fire in War on 350 Obscenity Bills," *Daily Variety,* Nov. 15, 1990.

182. Vaughn, *Freedom and Entertainment,* 27. These statistics come from CARA's *Annual Report, 1969–1999.*

CHAPTER 4 — THE INCONTESTIBLE R AS A CODE OF PRODUCTION

1. Richard Heffner, email correspondence with author, Aug. 4, 2006.

2. Richard Heffner, *Reminiscences of Richard D. Heffner,* 26:1620, Oral History Collection of Columbia University (hereafter cited as Heffner, *Reminiscences*).

3. Lea Jacobs, *The Wages of Sin: Censorship and the Fallen Woman Film, 1928–1942* (Berkeley: University of California Press, 1995), 22–26.

4. Information about the Rating Board's day-to-day operations can mainly be extracted from speeches, government records, and media remarks made by ex-MPAA president Jack Valenti and current head Dan Glickman (who became president in September 2004), as well as CARA chairpersons Eugene Dougherty, Aaron Stern, Richard Heffner, Richard Mosk, and Joan Graves. This summary of CARA is compiled from a number of sources, including MPAA, *The Voluntary Movie Rating System: How It Began, Its Purpose, the Public Reaction* (1991); Jack Valenti, "The Movie Rating System," *Daily Variety,* 42nd Anniversary Issue, Oct. 28, 1975; *Everything You Always Wanted to Know about the Movie Rating System,* MPAA and NATO pamphlet, late 1990s; National

Association of Theatre Owners, "The Movie Rating System," in *1994–1995 Encyclopedia of Exhibition,* 333–339; and Lynn Elber, "Movie Ratings Board Invites Scrutiny of Process, Intent," Associated Press, Jan. 25, 2006. Also see Stephen Vaughn's description in *Freedom and Entertainment: Rating the Movies in an Age of New Media* (New York: Cambridge University Press, 2006), 26–41; and, of course, Heffner's papers and oral history in the Oral History Collection of Columbia University.

5. As a point of contrast, in 1975 the member companies of the MPAA were Allied Artists, Avco-Embassy, Columbia, 20th Century–Fox, Paramount, United Artists, MCA-Universal, and Warner Bros.

6. See David Geffner, "Double Standard," *Filmmaker,* summer 1998, 22; Timothy M. Gray, "The Nuts and Bolts of Movie Rating," *Daily Variety,* July 12, 1994; and Sam Frank, "The CARA Board," *Box Office,* Oct. 1990, 44.

7. CEO Dan Glickman splits MPAA duties with Bob Pisano, who is the organization's president and chief operating officer. See Dave McNary, "Split Decision for MPAA," *Daily Variety,* Sep. 23, 2005.

8. In Oct. 1990, Frank says, the Rating Board consisted of ten parents: seven of whom were mothers aged forty-three to forty-nine; two were fathers, ages thirty-five and forty-five; and a seventy-year-old grandfather who also happens to be an assistant film director. This is one of the rare instances where the composition of the Rating Board is actually printed. Frank, "The CARA Board," 44. Also see Moira Hodgson, "Movie Ratings—Do They Serve Hollywood or the Public?" *New York Times,* May 24, 1981. Hodgson's article reads: "The current contingent includes three women—a black, Barbara Murray; a Mexican-American, Mona Elkin (both PTA mothers); and a children's book author, Lola Minz. The men are Timothy Joyce, a young newspaperman, and John Bloch, a teacher and film writer associated with the American Film Institute." A brief background description of the Rating Board's membership, minus names, is given in Hal Hinson, "The People Who Rate the Films," *Newsday,* Nov. 12, 1988, 3. In addition *Variety* reported that the California State Parent Teachers Association is permitted to nominate a candidate for a seat on the rating board. See "Ratings Bd. Reveals It Recruits Members from California PTA," *Variety,* March 6, 1985, 8.

9. Gray, "The Nuts and Bolts of Movie Rating."

10. Heffner papers, green ballots for *Tie Me Up! Tie Me Down!* March 23, 1990, doc. 90.

11. Jack Valenti, "Movie Ratings Are for Parents, Not Profits," *Daily Variety,* Aug. 23, 1994.

12. This description comes from the *1994–1995 Encyclopedia of Exhibition;* Heffner, phone interview by author, July 27, 2006. Also see Geffner, "Double Standard," 22; Frank, "The CARA Board," 44.

13. Elber, "Movie Ratings Board Invites Scrutiny of Process, Intent."

14. Quotation ("nine"), in Gray, "The Nuts and Bolts of Movie Rating"; quotation ("offended"), in Pamela McClintock, "Retiring MPAA Marketing Arbiter Has Seen It All," *Video Business,* Feb. 5, 2003.

15. Quotation ("parents"), in Alan Mirabella, "MPAA's Man of Letters," *Los Angeles Daily News,* Aug. 26, 1990; quotation ("dos and don'ts"), in Richard Harrington, "A Tale of Two Pictures: Should Hollywood Be Rated R, for Racist?" *Washington Post,* Feb. 2, 1992; quotation ("underlying"), in Elber, "Movie Ratings Board Invites Scrutiny of Process, Intent"; quotation ("American parents"), in "Egoyan Film Receives U.S. Slap," *Toronto Star,* Aug. 25, 2005.

16. Quotation ("f[uck]"), in Benjamin Svetkey, "Why Movie Ratings Don't Work," *Entertainment Weekly,* Nov. 25, 1994, 30; quotation ("If you say"), in Leonard J. Leff and Jerold L. Simmons, *The Dame in the Kimono* (New York: Grove Weidenfeld, 1990), 279.

17. Quoted in Brooks Boliek, "3 Decades Later, Valenti Works on Ratings Sequel," *Hollywood Reporter,* Nov. 15–17, 1996.

18. William Paul, *Laughing Screaming: Modern Hollywood Horror and Comedy* (New York: Columbia University Press, 1994), 11–12.

19. Quotation ("incest"), in Arthur Knight, "'G' as in Good Entertainment," *Saturday Review,* March 1, 1969, 40; quotation ("double standards"), in Sam Frank, "Counterpunch: Ratings Boards an Affront to First Amendment," *Los Angeles Times,* May 31, 1993, Calendar sec.; quotation ("eroticism"), in Jill Abramson, "Burying the X," *Premiere* (U.S.), Jan. 1991, 30; quotation ("lenient"), in Bruce Feld, "*Sliver* Deliverer Phillip [*sic*] Noyce," *Drama-Logue,* May 27, 1993–June 2, 1993; quotation ("breast"), in Hal Lipper, "Again, X Marks a Sore Spot," *St. Petersburg Times,* Sep. 24, 1990; quotation ("chopped off"), in Stephen Schaefer, "Director Annaud Hates Rating Game," *USA Today,* Nov. 17, 1992.

20. Heffner said he was always tougher on violence than sex compared to the other members of the Rating Board. He was often referred to as the "dirty old man," he said in a personal interview with author, July 11, 2006.

21. Quotation ("Puritan ethic"), in R. M. Townsend, "An Interview with Movie Boss Jack Valenti," *Mainliner,* Feb. 1974, 24; quotation ("intensity"), in "Jack Valenti Defends Feature Ratings," *American Cinemeditor,* fall 1987, 11.

22. Quoted in Richard Natale, "CARA Mia, Why?" *LA Weekly,* July 9, 1993, n.p.

23. Quoted in Peter Wood, "'Dressed to Kill'—How a Film Changes from X to R," *New York Times,* July 20, 1980.

24. Ratings information available at www.mpaa.org.

25. The last word after "engaged" I cannot make out from the form. The numbers refer to the reel and feet of film. See Heffner papers, green ballots for *Tie Me Up! Tie Me Down!* March 23, 1990, examiner 2, doc. 90.

26. "Jack Valenti Defends Feature Ratings."

27. Heffner, interview by author, July 12, 2006.

28. See Stephen Prince, *Classical Film Violence: Designing and Regulating Brutality in Hollywood Cinema, 1930–1968* (New Brunswick, NJ: Rutgers University Press, 2003).

29. Quotation ("force"), in Glenn Collins, "Guidance or Censorship? New Debate on Rating Films," *New York Times,* April 9, 1990; quotation ("producer"), in Vincent Canby, "Film View: Anatomy of an R Rating," *New York Times,* March 8, 1987.

30. Quoted in Collins, "Guidance or Censorship?"

31. Quoted in Laurent Bouzereau, *The Cutting Room Floor* (New York: Citadel Press, 1994), 207.

32. Robert W. Welkos provides a summary of the film: "*Basic Instinct* is a police thriller about a San Francisco detective's (Douglas) investigation into the murder of a local club owner and promoter. The prime suspect is a rich bisexual writer (Stone), whose most recent mystery novel includes a crime that closely resembles the club owner's murder. The two become involved while the detective investigates both the crime and the woman's bisexual past." See "Director Trims 'Basic Instinct' to Get R Rating," *Los Angeles Times,* Feb. 11, 1992, Calendar sec.

33. See Nina J. Easton, "Eszterhas vs. Verhoeven," *Los Angeles Times,* Aug. 23, 1990, Calendar sec. Heffner also references this article in "Pre-Oral History Memo 1992," 21–22.

34. Charles Lyons, *The New Censors: Movies and the Culture Wars* (Philadelphia: Temple University Press, 1997), 107–145; Vaughn, *Freedom and Entertainment,* 210–212.

35. Quotation ("how far"), in director's commentary from *Basic Instinct,* Pioneer Special Edition, laser disc; quotation ("anyone"), in Richard Corliss, "What Ever Became of the NC-17?" *Time,* Jan. 27, 1992, 64.

36. Heffner, "Pre-Oral History Memo 1992," 26 (my emphasis).

37. Paul Verhoeven actually approached Linda Fiorentino for the Tripplehorn role, but she wanted Stone's role. Verhoeven solicited Fiorentino by demonstrating to her what, I believe, is the "date rape" scene. According to Fiorentino, "Paul said, 'but Linda, there's all this nudity and all these sex scenes and'—he actually got up out of his chair and was hanging over the table—'and you're hanging over somebody and you're making love to them, and there would be nothing hanging down.' He didn't mean to insult me. It was funny. I thought, is this conversation about my tits? Because if it is, it's over! I literally did not get a part because of my breasts. Well, you win some, you lose some, I guess." Quoted in Holly Millea, "If Linda Fiorentino Were a Movie, She'd Be Rated NC-17," *Premiere* (U.S), Dec. 1994, 84–88.

38. See Heffner papers, "Ratings Pending Week of January 31, 1992," doc. 92-5; Heffner, "Pre-Oral History Memo 1992," 25–26; Trish Deitch Rohrer, Jeffrey Wells, and Juliann Garey, "Adventures in the Skin Trade: Michael Douglas Courts Scandal with Kinky Hit Thriller 'Basic Instinct,'" *Entertainment Weekly,* April 3, 1992; and Bouzereau, *The Cutting Room Floor,* 191.

39. Quoted in Bouzereau, *The Cutting Room Floor,* 210–211.

40. See, e.g., Corliss, "What Ever Became of the NC-17?"; and Heffner's remarks about the article in "Pre-Oral History Memo 1992," 22–23.

41. Director's commentary from *Basic Instinct,* Pioneer Special Edition, laser disc.

42. Heffner said that the senior examiners of CARA prepared these reports for him so he could keep up to date on all pending rating cases. See Heffner papers, "Ratings Pending Week of January 31, 1992," doc. 92-5; Heffner, "Pre-Oral History Memo 1992," 24.

43. As he did with other big-budget limit texts from MPAA signatories, Valenti hounded Heffner with calls that an NC-17 rating for *Basic Instinct* would sink Carolco and Michael Douglas financially, who presumably had millions of dollars riding on the film. This would explain the somewhat hands-on approach of the Rating Board with this film. See, e.g., Heffner, *Reminiscences,* 28:1734.

44. In addition to the weekly ratings-pending report, these comparisons are derived from four sources: a viewing of the unrated laser disc version of the film; Deitch Rohrer, Wells, and Garey, "Adventures in the Skin Trade"; Bouzereau, *The Cutting Room Floor,* 180–216; and David Morrell, "*Basic Instinct*—Director's Cut," review of laser disc, *Perfect Vision,* fall 1993, 152–155.

45. Verhoeven said the graphic nature of this scene was in response to the anger he felt from all the activists demonstrating against his film: "I was so annoyed that I shot the date-rape scene between Nick and Beth so that there was very little leeway—only to show how far you can go as a film-maker before it becomes banal. The script only touches on that meeting—but I thought, 'If they want to take offence at something that much, then I'll give them something to take offence at!' . . . Very brave of Michael Douglas to play that so explicitly, because at that moment he did not say, as so many

stars in Hollywood would have done, 'This is too risky, I have to think of my audience, I mustn't alienate them.'" Quoted in Rob van Scheers, *Paul Verhoeven,* trans. Aletta Stevens (London: Faber and Faber, 1997), 249.

46. Paul Verhoeven, *Showgirls: Portrait of a Film* (New York: Newmarket Press, 1995), 13.

47. Bouzereau, *The Cutting Room Floor,* 202–203.

48. Quoted in van Scheers, *Paul Verhoeven,* 253.

49. David Ansen, "Kiss Kiss Slash Slash," *Newsweek,* March 23, 1992, 54; John Hartl, "NC-17 Can Stir Up Controversy—As Well as the Box Office," *Seattle Times,* Jan. 17, 1993.

50. Heffner, "Pre-Oral History Memo 1992," 34–35.

51. Heffner is extremely critical of Maslin's comments. He says rating a film on its "overall tenor" showed great ignorance on her part about the rating system. Janet Maslin, "Sure, She May Be Mean, But Is She a Murderer?" *New York Times,* March 20, 1993. Richard Heffner to Charles Champlin, in Heffner, "Pre-Oral History Memo 1992," 32–33.

52. *Oxford English Dictionary Online,* www.oed.com (accessible by subscription only).

53. Jacobs, *The Wages of Sin,* 112–115.

54. Heffner, "Pre-Oral History Memo 1992," 30.

55. Heffner papers, "Ratings Pending Week of January 31, 1992," doc. 92-5.

56. Yorozu was the spokesperson for the Department of General Administration in Washington State, commenting after Secretary of State Ralph Munro had opposed the use of the State Capitol Building for the filming of *Body of Evidence* on account of Madonna and the movie's subject matter.

57. See, e.g., William Grimes, "NC-17 Rating Declares a Film Is . . . What?" *New York Times,* Nov. 30, 1992; David J. Fox, "R vs. NC-17—What's the Difference? Filmmakers, Exhibitors, Are Bewildered by Inconsistent Ratings," *Los Angeles Times,* Jan. 18, 1993, Calendar sec.; Mark Harris, "Abridged Too Far?" *Entertainment Weekly,* Jan. 15, 1993.

58. For clarity I will refer to any non-R-rated version as the NC-17 version, although the film may have only received a tentative NC-17 from the Rating Board and been released unrated on video.

59. *Body of Evidence*'s similarity to *Basic Instinct* is remarkable. Both begin with female-dominant sex leading to murder; "One has his heart stopped by an ice pick, the other by a drug- and exercise-induced thrombosis." The plots involve a sexually aggressive woman who seduces the lawman investigating those deaths. They also contain a mysterious "other woman" with a hidden agenda. Both films also have plenty of graphic and nontraditional sex scenes as their showpieces. See Jack Mathews, "The 'Evidence' Seems Instinctive," *Newsday,* Oct. 18, 1992.

60. Quotation ("understand"), in David J. Fox, "Madonna Set to Push Limits Once More with NC-17 Movie," *Los Angeles Times,* Aug. 31, 1992; quotation ("difference"), in Kirk Honeycutt, "Madonna's 'Body' Film May Try NC-17 Release," *Hollywood Reporter,* Aug. 31, 1992; quotation ("explosive"), in Judy Brennan, "MGM Planning No Appeal as 'Body' Is Rated NC-17," *Daily Variety,* Aug. 31, 1992.

61. Quoted in David J. Fox, "Madonna Movie Will Be Edited for 'R.'" *Los Angeles Times,* Oct. 30, 1992, Calendar sec.

62. See Doris Toumarkine, "MGM Weighs NC-17 Release of 'Evidence,'" *Hollywood Reporter,* Jan. 12, 1993.

63. Quotation ("totally removed"), in "'Body' Checks," *BPI Entertainment News Wire*, Nov. 24, 1992; quotation ("minor portions"), in Fox, "Madonna Movie Will Be Edited for 'R'"; and John Horn, "Fear of Adults-Only Rating Prompts Changes in Madonna Movie," *Associated Press*, Oct. 30, 1992.

64. See Kathy Tyrer, "Rules of 'Evidence'; Pundits Cast Marketing as Central in Film's Flop," *Adweek*, Feb. 1, 1993. Tyrer says that "research showed that the demographics of the Madonna audience are far from that needed for a major feature film. 'From a movie marketing standpoint, the project came with built-in problems,' said a source involved with the research. 'It was a fairly narrow, young, female and also homosexual following.'"

65. Doris Toumarkine, "MGM Tug-of-War over Hot 'Body,'" *Hollywood Reporter*, Feb. 19, 1993. When the NC-17 version of *Body of Evidence* finally made its appearance on video on June 16, 1993, dealers could purchase the film, along with *The Lover* and a "passion pack," for a special price. The "passion pack" included a *Body of Evidence* champagne bottle bubble bath, a champagne glass, an eight-inch candle, a lead crystal candlestick holder, and a pair of handcuffs. *Last Tango in Paris* and the unrated *9½ Weeks* were also thrown in for free with the deal. See "Passion Pack Offer," *June 1993 Videocassette Preview*, MGM/UA home video.

66. Quotation ("stigma"), in Kirk Honeycutt, "Stigma of NC-17 Label Driving Away Filmmakers; Malle's 'Damage,' and Madonna's 'Body' Dodge," *Hollywood Reporter*, Nov. 1, 1992; quotation ("aesthetic myopia"), in Bernard Weinraub, "Louis Malle Cuts a Film and Grows Indignant," *New York Times*, Dec. 22, 1992; as well as in John Evan Frook, "Malle Charges MPAA with 'Aesthetic Myopia,'" *Daily Variety*, Dec. 16, 1992; and "Malle: MPAA Ratings 'Aesthetic Myopia,'" *Hollywood Reporter*, Dec. 16, 1992; quotation ("stunned"), in Horn, "Fear of Adults-Only Rating Prompts Changes in Madonna Movie."

67. Martin A. Grove, "*Damage* Didn't Deserve an NC-17," *Hollywood Reporter*, Dec. 7, 1992.

68. Quoted in William Grimes, "Reviewing the NC-17 Rating: Clear Guide or an X by a New Name?" *New York Times*, Nov. 30, 1992.

69. Quoted in Honeycutt, "Stigma of NC-17 Label Driving Away Filmmakers."

70. New Line Cinema press release, *New Line Cinema to Appeal MPAA's NC-17 of Louis Malle's Damage*, Oct. 29, 1992.

71. During the appeal Malle was recuperating in Los Angeles following heart surgery. He arranged for a videotaped statement to be played for the Appeals Board. New Line president and CEO Michael Lynne and director Mike Nichols attended the hearing. Richard Heffner discusses *Damage*'s appeal at length in his oral history. See Heffner, "Pre-Oral History Memo 1992," 68–75; Heffner, *Reminiscences*, 28:1747–1750; also see Andy Marx, "'Damage' Appeals Don't Sway MPAA; Even after Star-Studded Pleas, NC-17 Sticks to Malle's Pic," *Daily Variety*, Nov. 13, 1992.

72. It appears from press reports that New Line had hoped the film would win its appeal and be rerated R without cuts. When this did not happen, however, the company's public declarations about artistic expression and respecting the work of an international filmmaker turned out to be all marketing. Malle, knowing New Line needed an R and that he was contractually obligated to deliver one, reedited *Damage*, however reluctantly, for wide release in the United States. See Chris McGowan, "Voyager Looks to Reap Spoils from 'Damage' Laser Exclusive," *Billboard*, July 10, 1993; and Harris, "Abridged Too Far," *Entertainment Weekly*, Jan. 15, 1993.

73. Other reports vary, claiming the deleted portions range from four to nine seconds. In my comparison of the two versions on DVD, however, I found that the total difference is around three seconds.

74. Lynne quoted in Frook, "Malle Charges MPAA with 'Aesthetic Myopia.'"

75. See Heffner, "Pre-Oral History Memo 1992," 71.

76. Quotation ("My friends"), in Harris, "Abridged Too Far"; Heffner, "Pre-Oral History Memo 1992," 84; quotation ("bad situation"), in "Video Interview with Malle," *Damage* laser disc, Criterion Collection; quotation ("reeling"), in Fox, "R vs. NC-17—What's the Difference?"

77. The film did not open until April 16, 1993. *Wide Sargasso Sea* was released on video in both NC-17 and R versions.

78. Quoted in Grimes, "Reviewing the NC-17 Rating."

79. John Hartl, "'Wide Sargasso Sea' Sexy but Not Satisfying," review, *Seattle Times,* May 7, 1993; Kenneth Turan, "'Wide Sargasso Sea' Implausible but Atmospheric," review, *Los Angeles Times,* April 23, 1993, Calendar sec.; Steve Murray, "Cruisin' with Karina: Model-Turned-Actress Lombard Sails from Steamy Role in 'Sargasso Sea' to Big-League Thrills in 'The Firm,'" *Atlanta Journal and Constitution,* May 24, 1993; Mick LaSalle, "Highfalutin' Hots on the 'Wide Sargasso Sea,'" review, *San Francisco Chronicle,* May 14, 1993; quotation ("sidling"), in Suzanna Andrews, "She's Bare. He's Covered. Is There a Problem?" *New York Times,* Nov. 1, 1992.

80. Vincent Canby, "Mrs. Rochester No. 1, Long before 'Jane Eyre,'" *New York Times,* April 16, 1993; Lawrence Cohn, "'Wide Sargasso Sea,'" review, *Daily Variety,* April 14, 1993.

81. Quoted in Lawrence Cohn, "Aries to Release NC-17 'Lieutenant,'" *Daily Variety,* Aug. 3, 1992.

82. Quoted in Doris Toumarkine, "NC-17 Doesn't Bust 'Lieutenant,'" *Hollywood Reporter,* Dec. 4, 1992.

83. Quoted in Chris Willman, "Off Centerpiece: Abel Ferrara: Lights! Camera! Anguish!" *Los Angeles Times,* Jan. 3, 1993, Calendar sec.

84. Heffner, "Pre-Oral History Memo 1992," 16.

85. Judy Brennan, "'Lover' Director in Cutting Mood." *Daily Variety,* June 23, 1992.

86. My historical understanding of the situation is pulled from the following sources: Brennan, "'Lover' Director in Cutting Mood"; Steve Pond, "Editing for Effect; Drastic Cut of 'The Lover' was Director's," *Washington Post,* June 26, 1992; Joseph McBride, "'Lover' Embraces R Rating after MPAA Dumps NC-17," *Daily Variety,* July 17, 1992; Colin Waters, "'Lover' Second Time Around; If Not Lovelier, Franker Telling Is Still Masterful," *Washington Times,* Oct. 25, 1992; Jane Galbraith, "Steam from Saigon," *Los Angeles Times,* Oct. 30, 1992, Calendar sec.; Stephen Schaefer, "Director Annaud Hates Rating Game," *USA Today,* Nov. 17, 1992.

87. Quotation ("graphic sex"), in Brennan, "'Lover' Director in Cutting Mood"; quotation ("sexually"), in Heffner, "Pre-Oral History Memo 1992," 65.

88. Quotation "terrible mistake," in "Pre-Oral History Memo 1992," 65; quotation ("lovemaking and lesbianism"), in William Grimes, "Reviewing the NC-17 Rating: Clear Guide or an X by a New Name?" *New York Times,* Nov. 30, 1992; quotation ("rough violent"), in Harris, "Abridged Too Far?"

89. The *New York Times* identified this person incorrectly as Lenore Rosenman. See Andrews, "She's Bare. He's Covered. Is There a Problem?"

90. See Heffner "Pre-Oral History Memo 1992," 65–69; Heffner, *Reminiscences,* 28:1741–1744 and 31:1834–1837.

91. One report states the Rating Board demanded this cut, but another report suggests Annaud chose to do it himself. Heffner vehemently says the Rating Board played no role. See Schaefer, "Director Annaud Hates Rating Game"; and Mitchell Fink, "The Hand That Robs the Cradle," *People,* Nov. 9, 1992, 43.

92. The unrated European version of *The Lover,* never submitted to CARA, contains around twenty-five more seconds of sexual movement in its first three love scenes, while the fourth love scene includes an additional seventy-second sequence where March makes love astride Leung. In the unrated version, a brief shot of his penis can even be seen entering her. March and Annaud both deny that she and Leung actually made love on the set, but this shot does look pretty real.

93. Heffner was still in office when this first cut was viewed by the Rating Board. Also, Rush suffered a heart attack after the firing because of stress. See Claudia Eller, "Who's Got the Right to 'Color' Final Cut?" *Los Angeles Times,* April 23, 1994, Calendar sec.

94. Anita M. Busch, "H'w'd Pix Greenlights NC-17 'Color' Release," *Daily Variety,* July 18, 1994; quotation ("female nude form"), in *CNN Showbiz Today,* Aug. 17, 1994, transcript no. 606-3; Jane Galbraith, "Rating 'Color of Night,'" *Newsday,* Aug. 18, 1994; Stephen Schaefer, "Gate Beats 'Art' as Willis Flick Goes for the 'R,'" *Boston Herald,* Aug. 17, 1994.

95. See, e.g., Donald La Badie, "Director Errors Shatter 'Night,' Video to Show Willis in Buff," *Memphis Commercial Appeal,* Aug. 20, 1994; Larry Light and Julie Tisner, "A Full-Frontal Assault on Sexism," *Business Week,* Aug. 29, 1994, 4; Bruce Westbrook, "Artistic Concerns Rule for 'Color,'" *Houston Chronicle,* Aug. 26, 1994; Frank Bruni, "Exposing the Nudity Ratings," *Pittsburgh Post-Gazette,* Oct. 1, 1994.

96. Marcy Magiera, "'Color of Night' Set for Video as Director's Cut," *Video Business,* Dec. 9, 1994. George Cosmatos, director of *Tombstone* (1993), came in to shoot new scenes for the picture after Rush was fired. Primarily, a new ending was shot by Cosmatos, but the footage was never used in either the theatrical or video version of *Color of Night.* See Kirk Honeycutt, "For Rush, Two Shades of 'Color,'" *Hollywood Reporter,* Aug. 8, 1994.

97. Richard Rush said, "My version is longer, darker, denser, more erotic. But every scene in [Cinergi topper] Andy Vajna's version I developed, shot, cast and am extremely fond of. They have shortened and juggled scenes. Theirs is a simpler movie to watch; mine is a denser and more convoluted movie." Quoted in Honeycutt, "For Rush, Two Shades of 'Color.'"

98. Quoted in Dennis Hunt, "A Sexier 'Night' Video Doesn't Bare All," *Los Angeles Times,* Feb. 3, 1995, Calendar sec.

99. A Disney executive attested to this fact when he stated, "Let's just say there was some creative use of dissolves" to earn an R rating. Quoted in Galbraith, "Rating 'Color of Night.'"

100. See Magiera, "'Color of Night' Set for Video as Director's Cut"; and Hunt, "A Sexier 'Night' Video Doesn't Bare All."

101. Oddly, the European video version with the additional ten seconds is not Rush's extended director's cut as reported in the U.S. press. It is the theatrical European release (117 minutes) with added footage from the U.S. theatrical release. This version of *Color of Night* has never been released on video in the United States.

102. Quoted in Meredith Berkman, "Close, but No Cigar," *Entertainment Weekly,* Sep. 9, 1994, 59.

103. Quoted in John Brodie, "Marketers Turn Ratings Battle into Positive Publicity; Sex! Controversy! PR!" *Variety,* Aug. 29, 1994, 7.

104. Quotation ("strong belief,"), in Greg Evans, "October to Appeal NC-17 'Night' Rate," *Variety,* Oct. 2, 1995, 3; quotation ("strong message"), in GLAAD press release, *GLAAD Objects to MPAA NC-17 Rating on Lesbian Film,* Oct. 31, 1995; Greg Evans, "MPAA Taking 2nd Look at 'Night,' " *Daily Variety,* Oct. 31, 1995.

105. Gary Dretzka, "The Sky Is Falling on Film's R Rating," *Chicago Tribune,* Nov. 6, 1995. The film's ad also caused problems for the *Toronto Globe and Mail.* See "Globe Confirms Boss Queried Lesbian Kiss Ad," *Toronto Star,* May 9, 1995.

106. Kirk Honeycutt, "MPAA Keeps 'Night's' NC-17," *Hollywood Reporter,* Nov. 3, 1995.

107. Quotation ("misunderstanding"), in Edward Guthmann, "Director Finds Gender Does Matter," *San Francisco Chronicle,* Nov. 25, 1995; quotation ("homophobia"), in Robert Koehler, " 'Night Is Falling' Rekindles the Ratings Controversy," *Los Angeles Times,* Nov. 20, 1995, Calendar sec. (Rozema's emphasis). Also see Karen Cook, "The Nipple Effect," *Village Voice,* Nov. 21, 1995, 24; and Claudia Isé, "The Underneath," *Los Angeles View,* Nov. 17–23, 1995, 17; quotation ("degree"), in Koehler, " 'Night Is Falling' Rekindles the Ratings Controversy"; quotation ("decision"), in Kirk Honeycutt, "NC-17 Won't Fall at 'Night,' " *Hollywood Reporter,* Nov. 9, 1995.

108. Heffner, interview by author, July 12, 2006.

109. Graves quoted in Elber, "Movie Ratings Board Invites Scrutiny of Process, Intent" (see note 4 above).

110. Quoted in Peter Stack, "Sensual 'Kama Sutra' Arouses Censors' Ire," *San Francisco Chronicle,* March 2, 1997.

111. Quoted in "Writer/Director Gregor Nichols on Appealing the Film's NC-17 Rating," www.sonypictures.com/classics/broken/nc-17.html.

112. Leslie Rubinkowski, "Sex and Violence," review of *Broken English, Pittsburgh Post-Gazette,* July 18, 1997.

113. Janet Maslin, "A Freedom Fighter for Love," *New York Times,* May 2, 1997.

114. Gary Levin, "Ads' Basic Instinct: Show-It-All and Sell," *Variety,* Sep. 11, 1995.

115. This R scene also contains an unmotivated zoom of the man's buttocks thrusting that appeared in the unrated version. As a result, what was once a full shot of sexual movement in the frame is now a close-up of the actors' faces.

116. A close-up, however, of Fiorentino's stiletto heel pressing into her lover's groin area, revealing his pubic hair, is kept in the R version.

117. Margy Rochlin, "Beauty, Brains, and a Knack for Giving Censors Pause," *New York Times,* April 12, 1998.

118. Quotation ("sweatload"), in Peter Bart, "Ratings Game Gets Gamier," *Variety,* Oct. 13, 1997, 4; quotation ("ass humping"), in "Boogie Man: Roughcut Q & A," www.ptanderson.com; Paul Thomas Anderson, interview by David Rensin, *Playboy,* Feb. 1998. In the Rensin article Anderson says only forty seconds were cut for the R. Quotation ("Nina Hartley"), in *Fresh Air with Terry Gross,* National Public Radio, Oct. 30, 1997. Available at www.ptanderson.com. Also see Gary Susman, "Boogie Man," *Village Voice,* Oct. 14, 1997.

119. The remaining sexual footage led porn scholar Peter Lehman to remark, "*Boogie Nights* represents porn by not representing its most notorious ingredient." See "Will the Real Dirk Diggler Please Stand Up?" *Jump Cut* 42 (1998): 34.

120. Wahlberg also masturbates in a truck before he gets beat up, but all hand movement takes place offscreen.

121. Bart, "Ratings Game Gets Gamier," 4.

122. Todd McCarthy, "'Two Girls and a Guy,'" review, *Variety*, Sep. 1, 1997.

123. "MPAA Ratings," *Daily Variety*, Nov. 5, 1997.

124. See Amy Wallace, "Rated O (for Obsessed)," *Los Angeles Times*, Nov. 12, 1997, Calendar sec.; Gary Dretzka, "'Two Girls' and a Sex Scene," *Chicago Tribune*, April 26, 1998.

125. Dretzka, "'Two Girls' and a Sex Scene."

126. Quotation ("Average American"), in Barry Koltnow, "If You Can't Lick 'Em, Behead 'Em," *Bergen County (NJ) Record*, April 19, 1998; quotation ("blockheaded"), in Jeff Gordinier, "Dirty Movie," *Entertainment Weekly*, April 24, 1998; quotation ("beyond"), in Robin DeRosa, "No NC-17, Please," *USA Today*, Oct. 21, 1997; quotation ("anyone"), in Wallace, "Rated O (for Obsessed)."

127. Quoted in Dretzka, "'Two Girls' and a Sex Scene."

CHAPTER 5 — *SHOWGIRLS:* THE FEASIBILITY AND FATE OF THE NC-17 RATING

1. Peter Rainer, "Was It Really the Last Tango?" *Los Angeles Times*, Dec. 15, 1991, Calendar sec.

2. Richard Maltby, *Hollywood Cinema*, 2nd ed. (London: Blackwell, 2003), 57.

3. Verhoeven also made sexually provocative films in his native Holland. The Rating Board also gave his film *Turkish Delight* (1973) the adults-only rating.

4. According to *Variety*, "*Showgirls* was acquired by an affiliate of media and textile conglomerate Chargeurs in a deal that refunded all production costs on *Showgirls*, freeing up Carolco's funds for its big-budget *Cutthroat Island* (1995). As part of the agreement, Carolco has an option to buy back 50% of the picture within a certain amount of time." See Anita M. Busch, "'Showgirls' to MGM/UA," *Daily Variety*, Nov. 4, 1994.

5. Reportedly, when *Showgirls* was being shopped around, Universal offered Verhoeven and Eszterhas $30 million if it was made to fit an R or $12 million if it ended up with an NC-17. See Claudia Puig, "'Showgirls' May Help Give NC-17 Releases a Leg Up," *Los Angeles Times*, Oct. 10, 1995, Calendar sec.

6. William Grimes, "In the Wings: A Movie with Few Clothes and No Regrets," *New York Times*, Feb. 12, 1995.

7. Catherine Jordan, "'Showgirls' Has Studios Shy of NC-17 Exposure," *Hollywood Reporter*, Oct. 5, 1995.

8. Christopher Goodwin, "Naked Ambition," *Sunday Times* (London), Sep. 10, 1995.

9. Joshua Mooney, "Nice Tits, Shame about the Film," *Empire* (London), Feb. 1996, 65.

10. Quoted in Claudia Puig, "MGM Embraces NC-17 Rating for 'Showgirls,'" *Los Angeles Times*, July 21, 1995. John Calley, president of UA, echoed Mancuso's words when he said, "It's a fairly reasonable business risk." Quoted in Marshall Fine, "NC-17 'Showgirls' Is Risque Business," *USA Today*, Feb. 7, 1995.

11. Quoted in Puig, "MGM Embraces NC-17 Rating for 'Showgirls.'"

12. Grimes, "In the Wings." Conflicting accounts place Eszterhas's fee for the script between $3 million and $3.7 million.

13. Kevin Goldman, "Selling of 'Showgirls' Draws Keen Interest," *Wall Street Journal*, Sep. 8, 1995. According to the article the trailer was not being shown with R-rated films that attracted the teenage audience, such as *Dangerous Minds*.

14. Mike Caruso, a spokesman for Blockbuster, said, "We don't feel that families coming in our stores should be subjected to what most of society considers to be unacceptable material for public consumption." Quoted in David Holstrom, "'Showgirls': Does New Film Peddle Pornography?" *Christian Science Monitor,* Sep. 22, 1995.

15. According to Mike Dampier, who managed Tower Video on Sunset Boulevard in West Hollywood, "The first day we put [the video] out they all rented out really fast and we were completely out for two, three days." Quoted in Claudia Puig, "'Showgirls' Nets Fans with Hot Spot on Web," *Los Angeles Times,* Sep. 20, 1995, Calendar sec.

16. Quoted in Claudia Puig, "'Showgirls' and NC-17: Grin and Bare It," Sep. 16, 1995, *Los Angeles Times,* Calendar sec.

17. Stephen Galloway, "'Showgirls' Will Dance with an NC-17," *Hollywood Reporter,* July 21, 1995.

18. In regard to the ad for *Showgirls* a spokesperson for the MPAA said, "We thought long and hard about that because we've been such sticklers about nudity [in newspaper ads]. But we felt ultimately that it was tasteful." Quoted in Jack Mathews, "Sensual Film Ad Passes Test," *Pittsburgh Post-Gazette,* Aug. 12, 1995.

19. This artwork is borrowed from a similar image used on a 1992 book jacket by photographer Tono Sano.

20. Goldman, "Selling of 'Showgirls' Draws Keen Interest"; Gary Levin, "Ads' Basic Instinct: Show-It-All and Sell," *Variety,* Sep. 11, 1995, 17–18.

21. After showing an eight-minute teaser trailer to exhibitors, Verhoeven said: "I certainly tried to pull out all the stops. I think they were intrigued, and unless they're forbidden by law, exhibitors will try to play the film. I don't want to put myself in a bad position with the MPAA, but I think it will be difficult to give this an R. Maybe impossible, I think, but you never know." Quoted in Michael Fleming, "Verhoeven Shopping Big Budget Fare to Studios," *Variety,* May 22, 1995, 2.

22. John Horn, "The Naked Truth: 'Showgirls' to Open with NC-17 Rating," *Entertainment Today,* Sep. 15, 1995.

23. Quotation ("hard-core porn movie"), in Horn, "The Naked Truth"; quotation ("times change"), in "Hollywood Tries an Extra Dose of Sex," *U.S. News and World Report,* Sep. 18, 1995, 28; quotation ("easier"), in Fine, "NC-17 'Showgirls' Is Risque Business."

24. Holstrom, "'Showgirls': Does New Film Peddle Pornography?"

25. Lewis Beale, "Nude Bomb or Bonanza?" *New York Daily News,* Aug. 7, 1995.

26. Michael Williams, "Chargeurs Engages in Risque Pic Business," *Variety,* Oct. 9, 1995, 9.

27. John Brodie and Anita M. Busch, "'Girls' Nails NC-17; MGM/UA Standing Behind Pic," *Daily Variety,* July 21, 1995.

28. Benjamin Svetkey, "Girls, Girls, Girls: Hollywood Catches Flesh-Dance Fever with 'Showgirls,'" *Entertainment Weekly,* Sep. 29, 1995, 31.

29. The press release, dated Sep. 20, 1995, read:

Showgirls, rated NC-17, opens Friday, Sept. 22, on 1300 screens. It is a concentrated effort by director Paul Verhoeven, screenwriter Joe Eszterhas and distributor MGM/UA to make X-rated, raunchy movies mainstream and acceptable to the American public. To achieve this end, the movie has been heavily advertised on TV, in print, posters, on the Internet, and in video stores. Eszterhas said, "I'd like to advise teenagers: don't let anyone stop you from seeing this movie." Jack Valenti, champion of the ratings system, said Eszterhas "needs medical attention." The Christian Film and Television Commission and Movieguide urges all moral Americans to boycott this movie. Refuse to attend and encourage others not to attend. With the detrimental effects of pornography well documented, all Americans would be foolish to give their money to MGM/UA.

30. Puig, "'Showgirls' Nets Fans with Hot Spot on Web."

31. Andy Seiler, "Hollywood's NC-17 Faces True Test Today," *USA Today*, Sep. 22, 1995.

32. Quoted on *CNN Showbiz Today*, Sep. 20, 1995, transcript no. 905.

33. Quoted in Puig, "'Showgirls' and NC-17." Eszterhas said, "It's a chauvinistic position to [advertise] this on the sports pages, because of its more sensational aspects. I want young women to see this movie because young women will respond to this movie in the same ways that they responded to [the Eszterhas-scripted] *Flashdance*." In Eszterhas's autobiography his wife says in a journal that Joe deliberately told the ID story to every reporter despite pleas to stop from MGM/UA. See Joe Eszterhas, *Hollywood Animal* (New York: Knopf, 2004), 589.

34. Katherine Stalter, "'Showgirls' Site Sets Web on Fire," *Variety*, Sep. 18, 1995, 5–6.

35. Quoted in Horn, "The Naked Truth."

36. Quoted in John Leland, "Base Instinct," *Newsweek*, Sep. 25, 1995, 88.

37. Dana Kennedy quoted on *CNN Showbiz Today*, Sep. 22, 1995, transcript no. 906-2.

38. Janet Maslin, "$40 Million Worth of Voyeurism," *New York Times*, Sep. 22, 1995; Kenneth Turan, "The Naked Truth about 'Showgirls,'" *Los Angeles Times*, Sep. 22, 1995, Calendar sec.; William Cash, "See What Nomi Is Doing to the Movies," *Daily Telegraph* (London), Sep. 23, 1995; Anthony Lane, "Starkness Visible," *New Yorker*, Oct. 9, 1995; Richard Corliss, "Valley of the Dulls," *Time*, Oct. 2, 1995, 74.

39. As Maltby observes, "Part of Hollywood's appeal to its audiences lies in 'a sympathetic character overcom[ing] a series of obstacles to achieve his or her desire.'" Thus a portion of the blame for *Showgirls*' box-office failure must be placed on its unlikable protagonists. See Maltby, *Hollywood Cinema*, 21.

40. Quotation ("anyone else"), in Levin, "Ads' Basic Instinct," 18; Leland, "Base Instinct," 89; Tom Shone, "Just a Couple of Dumb Blondes, *Times* (London), Jan. 14, 1996; quotation ("perception problem"), in Chrissy Iley, "Limping over the Shock Barrier," *Sunday Times* (London), Jan. 7, 1996, sec. 3.

41. Puig, "'Showgirls' Nets Fans with Hot Spot on Web."

42. Susan King, "'Showgirls' Racking Up the Orders," *Los Angeles Times*, Dec. 21, 1995, Calendar sec.

43. "No Show," *Video Software Magazine*, Oct. 1995, 13.

44. Verhoeven said:

The first time I read Joe's script for *Showgirls*, I knew that I could not make this film in a way to satisfy myself, ethically and artistically, and at the same time satisfy the normal studio requirement that a director must meet the MPAA Rating Board minimum standards for an "R" rating. We knew rather early in the development of this movie that sexuality and sexual power would be one of the core dramatic issues, but we didn't think in terms of ratings. The emerging prospect of trying to direct an adult movie that deals with naked dancers within the arbitrary "R" strictures of the Rating Board made me very unhappy. (Paul Verhoeven, *Showgirls: Portrait of a Film* [New York: Newmarket Press, 1995], 14)

45. The R-rated movie's video box cuts the image off at Berkley's cleavage. See Galloway, "'Showgirls' Will Dance with an NC-17"; Scott Hettrick, "'Showgirls' Makes

MPAA's Cuts," *Hollywood Reporter,* Dec. 4, 1995; and Peter M. Nichols, "By Dropping a Minute or So, a Studio Hopes to Widen the Home Audience for 'Showgirls,'" *New York Times,* Dec. 8, 1995.

46. Quoted in Puig, "'Showgirls' May Help Give NC-17 Releases a Leg Up."

47. Ibid.

48. Stephen Battaglio, "THR Poll: NC-17 Can Strip Away Quarter of B.O.," *Hollywood Reporter,* Dec. 5, 1995.

49. Quoted in "Topless Bottoms Out," *People,* Oct. 23, 1995, 18; quoted in Jordan, "'Showgirls' Has Studios Shy of NC-17 Exposure."

50. See Kenneth Heard, "'Naughty' Movie Forced from Town," *Memphis Commercial Appeal,* Sep. 27, 1995; "Pampa Theater Cancels 'Showgirls,'" United Press International, Sep. 30, 1995; Andy Seiler, "'Showgirls' Stripped from Screens in Some Cities," *USA Today,* Sep. 27, 1995; Joe Mahr, "Protestors Say It Should Be Curtains for 'Showgirls,'" *Springfield (IL) State Journal Register,* Oct. 13, 1995; "Williston Ministers, Theater Owners Feuding," *Bismarck (ND) Tribune,* Oct. 5, 1995.

51. Quoted in Puig, "'Showgirls' May Help Give NC-17 Releases a Leg Up."

52. Battaglio, "THR Poll."

53. Quoted in Steve Daly, "Let's Balk about Sex," *Entertainment Weekly,* Oct. 6, 1995, 41.

54. Quoted in Jordan, "'Showgirls' Has Studios Shy of NC-17 Exposure."

55. Quoted in Sheila Benson, "Despite Oscar's '93 Salute to Women, Actresses Face the Same Old Obstacles," *Variety,* Jan. 1, 1996, 54.

56. Alyssa Katz, "'Lolita,'" *Nation,* Aug. 24, 1998, 35.

57. Andrew Hindes, "'Showgirls' Aside, Erotica Grinds On," *Variety,* Oct. 30, 1995, M26.

58. See Chris Nashawaty, "Is T & A DOA?" *Entertainment Weekly,* Nov. 10, 1995, 6–7.

59. Katz, "'Lolita,'" 35.

60. Buckley said, "The movie's so over the top I thought the filmmakers had to know what they were doing. Finally I concluded it was drug damage and they had no idea."

61. Trip Gabriel, "'Showgirls' Crawls Back as High Camp at Midnight," *New York Times,* March 31, 1996; Josh Young, "*Showgirls*' Remarkable Return," *Sunday Telegraph* (London), April 21, 1996.

62. Jessica Shaw, "Party Girls," *Entertainment Weekly,* March 22, 1996, 21.

63. "'Showgirls' Sweeps in Awards for 1995's Worst Movies," Associated Press, March 25, 1996. The record was subsequently broken the following year by another stripper movie, *Striptease* (1996). *Showgirls* also was awarded the Golden Raspberry in 1999 for "Worst Picture of the Decade" and "Worst Actress of the Century" for Elizabeth Berkley, but it lost to *Battlefield Earth* in the 2004 awards for "Worst 'Drama' of Our First 25 Years."

64. Quoted in Young, "*Showgirls*' Remarkable Return."

65. The NC-17 video states 131 minutes and the R version states 128 minutes, but the latter's running time actually hovers around 130 minutes.

66. Quoted in Nichols, "By Dropping a Minute or So."

67. See King, "'Showgirls' Racking Up the Orders"; Nichols, "By Dropping a Minute or So."

68. Linda Ruth Williams, "Nothing to Find," *Sight and Sound,* Jan. 1996, 30. Also see her book, *The Erotic Thriller in Contemporary Cinema* (Bloomington: Indiana University Press, 2005).

69. Jon Lewis, *Hollywood v. Hard Core: How the Struggle over Censorship Saved the Modern Film Industry* (New York: NYU Press, 2000), 8.

70. Eric Schaefer, *"Bold! Daring! Shocking! True!": A History of Exploitation Films, 1919–1959* (Durham, NC: Duke University Press, 1999), 153–154. Schaefer also states that "Hays attempted to extract pledges from exhibitor chain members not to play the [exploitation] movies and went further by instructing distributors not to supply any house with regular films once it had opened its screen to 'the obnoxious sex film'" (148).

71. Ibid., 145, 410–411.

72. Gavin Smith, "Sundance 'Kids.' Entries to the Sundance Film Festival 1995, Park City UT," *Film Comment*, March 1995; Greg Evans and Todd McCarthy, "Will 'Kids' Be Too Hot for Harvey?" *Variety*, Feb. 6, 1995.

73. See Justin Wyatt, "The Formation of the 'Major Independent': Miramax, New Line and the New Hollywood," in *Contemporary Hollywood Cinema*, ed. Steve Neale and Murray Smith (London: Routledge, 1998), 74–90.

74. Quoted in Kirk Honeycutt, "Dis Denies Input in 'Crazy' Move," *Hollywood Reporter*, March 30, 1994.

75. Quoted in Bernard Weinraub, "Miramax Turns Over Film on Outspoken Comedian," *New York Times*, March 30, 1994.

76. According to Degen Pener, Miramax trimmed an explicit male-male sex scene before releasing *Priest*. Whether this was done before or after its submission to CARA is not known. See "What Price 'Happiness'?" *Entertainment Weekly*, Oct. 30, 1998.

77. Greg Evans, "Disney Stays at Arm's Length from 'Priest,'" *Variety*, April 10, 1995.

78. Quoted in Charles Fleming, "Are They Happy Together?" *Newsweek*, April 10, 1995, 44.

79. Quoted in Dan Cox, "Valenti: 'Kids' Can't Make R Cut," *Daily Variety*, May 30, 1995.

80. Quoted in Elaine Dutka, "Miramax Circumvents 'Kids' Controversy," *Los Angeles Times*, June 29, 1995.

81. Quotation ("our opinion), in Louis B. Parks, "Ratings Ruckus; Miramax Battles Movie Board over Giving 'Kids' an NC-17," *Houston Chronicle*, July 14, 1995; quotation ("rating system fails"), in Kirk Honeycutt, "'Kids' Appeal Denied; to Be Released without Rating," *Hollywood Reporter*, July 13, 1995; quotation ("forum"), in Honeycutt, "'Kids' Appeal Denied"; quotation ("grateful"), in Paul F. Young, "Excalibur to Appeal NC-17 of 'Kids,'" *Variety*, July 10, 1995, 17; quotation ("If ever a movie"), in Kirk Honeycutt, "Valenti Blasts Dershowitz for 'Kids' Rating Comments," *Hollywood Reporter*, July 14, 1995.

82. Honeycutt, "'Kids' Appeal Denied."

83. See Jim Rutenberg, "Disney Is Blocking Distribution of Film Critical of Bush," *New York Times*, May 5, 2004.

84. Shawn Levy, "Almodóvar's *Kika*; You Can't Keep a Good Woman Down," *Film Comment*, May-June 1994, 59–62.

85. Ibid. Levy perfectly describes the both disturbing and humorous nature of the rape scene:

It begins as a news flash: porn star-turned-rapist Paul Bazzo has escaped from prison by using the self-flagellating ritual practiced on his hometown saint's day as a ruse. Having whipped blood from his back, he arrives in Madrid to visit his sister, Kika's taciturn maid. Juana is willing to let him steal, to let him tie her to a chair, to let him beat her, to let him violate her twice, but he cannot resist having his way with her mistress, first—and most jaw-slackeningly—with a segment of an orange, then with himself. A peeping Tom (whose absurdly makeshift telephoto lens kids both Hitchcock and Powell) phones in the crime-in-progress to the police, who laze over the apartment, assuming it's a crank call. One cop is strictly killing the morning with the visit, but his partner is suddenly possessed with the spirit of the Public Good: he crashes through doors, frees the maid, and leaps into the bedroom, where the rapist is straining toward his successive orgasm.

It would be the dramatic climax of an American film, but Almodóvar pushes it all so far it becomes farce. The cops cannot stop the rapist's insane thrusts, even when they put a gun to his head and threaten to use it; a grotesque melee ensues, bodies tangling, cops straddling Kika, the rapist fleeing to the balcony; he masturbates into the street and leaps to safety, leaving the apartment and Kika's illusions of domestic tranquility (she has been engaged for all of a day) in ruins.

86. Quoted in Kirk Honeycutt, "October Plans Appeal over 'Kika's' NC-17," *Hollywood Reporter,* April 21, 1994.

87. Leonard Klady, "'Kika' NC-17 Appealed to Pix Ratings Board," *Daily Variety,* April 20, 1994; Doris Toumarkine, "Almodóvar, Garbus Join in 'Kika' Appeal," *Hollywood Reporter,* April 21, 1994.

88. Thom Geier, "Fourplay from October Puts Uni in a Pickle," *Hollywood Reporter,* June 3, 1998.

89. Ibid.

90. In *Entertainment Weekly* Degen Pener wrote that October was requiring Von Trier to deliver an R cut of *The Idiots.* Von Trier's assistant said the director was not too keen on cutting the film and was "considering putting a black box with the word censorship on it that will be moving as [the characters] have intercourse." See "What Price 'Happiness'?" The film has never been available domestically on DVD or VHS.

91. Quoted in Dan Cox, "'Happiness' Over at October Films," *Daily Variety,* July 2, 1998. Also see Thom Geier and Josh Chetwynd, "'Happiness' Too Hot for October Owner Seagram," *Hollywood Reporter,* July 2, 1998.

92. Quoted in Degen Pener, "What Price 'Happiness'?"

93. Quoted in Renee Graham, "The Dark Side of 'Happiness,'" *Boston Globe,* Oct. 18, 1998.

94. "Tales of Hollywood. Hate the Sin, Hate the Sinner," *Economist,* Oct. 10, 1998, 92.

95. Pener, "What Price 'Happiness'?"

96. On the other hand, Samuel Goldwyn, who became a major independent after MGM bought Metromedia, its parent company, in July 1997, did release the controversial *Bent* under the Goldwyn Entertainment banner but only in a few theaters. This may perhaps be attributed to the fact that, in the past, MGM has always been more willing to take chances on risky product (*Last Tango in Paris, Showgirls*) than other MPAA signatories.

97. As a subsidiary of Time Warner at the time, New Line had to obtain a rating for the rerelease of these films per its membership in the MPAA. John Waters loved that New Line actually asked for an NC-17 for *Pink Flamingos,* even though it was released in 1972 without a rating. "I loved the idea of the ratings board having to sit down to watch it. Talk about an endless screening! It's as rude as it ever was, maybe ruder because of the political correctness issue." Quoted in Richard Harrington, "Revenge of the Gross-Out King! John Waters's 'Pink Flamingos' Enjoys a 25th-Year Revival," *Washington Post,* April 6, 1997.

98. Todd Solondz discusses his contract negotiations with Fine Line in depth in John Clark's "Bard of Suburbia," *Los Angeles Times,* Jan. 13, 2002, Calendar sec.

99. Quoted in Scott Timberg, "Revenge of the Nerd," *New Times Los Angeles,* Jan. 24, 2002. According to *Eyes Wide Shut* producer Jan Harlan, she warned Kubrick during shooting that the orgy sequence was too explicit for an R rating. Pat Kingsley, the publicity agent for Tom Cruise and Nicole Kidman, agrees: "He thought he could get away with an R. Then he realized he couldn't do it." It was during editing that Kubrick himself suggested the placement of computer-generated figures in front of couples engaged in sexual activity. See Bernard Weinraub, "Kubrick, Edited," *New York Times,* July 16, 1999; Andy Seiler, "Covering Up to Get an R Rating," *USA Today,* July 16, 1999.

100. Quoted in Terry Lawson, "Todd Solondz Tells Controversial Stories," *Toronto Star,* Feb. 8, 2002. MTV also felt there were "certain things" in *Storytelling* its "young adult" audience should not be allowed to see despite the film's R rating. After reviewing a tape of *Storytelling,* the network cancelled Selma Blair's appearance on its most popular teenage show, *Total Request Live,* issuing a statement that "the film's content was not appropriate for TRL's audience." See Rebecca Traister, "Blair Ditch Project," *New York Observer,* Feb. 4, 2002.

101. From *Sunday Morning Shootout,* American Movie Classics (AMC), airdate July 25, 2004.

102. Quoted in Brodie and Busch, " 'Girls' Nails NC-17" (see note 27 above).

103. Anthony D'Allesandro of *Variety* provided me with these figures calculated using EDI data.

CONCLUSION

1. Stephen Prince, *Classical Film Violence: Designing and Regulating Brutality in Hollywood Cinema, 1930–1968* (New Brunswick, NJ: Rutgers University Press, 2003).

2. Ibid., 255–263.

3. Gabriel Snyder, "Don't Give Me an 'R,' " *Variety,* Feb. 21, 2005, 8.

4. Quoted in Dade Hayes and Jonathan Bing, "H'wood: R Kind of Town," *Variety,* March 31, 2003, 1+.

5. Carl Diorio, "FTC Says Fewer Teens Get into R-Rated Films," *Daily Variety,* Oct. 15, 2003; John Fithian, email correspondence with author, Aug. 16, 2004.

6. See Motion Picture Association, "2005 Theatrical Market Statistics," www.mpaa.org/researchstatistics.asp.

7. Susanne Ault, "Indies Rave Over Unrated; As Chains Shy Away," *Video Business,* April 18, 2005.

8. John Fithian, email correspondence with author, Aug. 16, 2004.

9. For example, see Pamela McClintock, "Updating Ratings," *Daily Variety,* Jan. 17, 2007; David M. Halbfinger, "Hollywood Rethinks Its Ratings Process," *New York Times,* Jan. 18, 2007; and Gregg Kilday, "Raters to Offer Full Disclosure," *Hollywood Reporter,* Jan. 17, 2007. See also Kirby Dick's criticism of the MPAA's announcement in "Bad Ratings," *Los Angeles Times,* Jan. 24, 2007.

10. Quoted in "Revisit NC-17 Rating, MPAA Chief Says," United Press International, Jan.23, 2007.

11. Quoted in Michael Speier and Ian Mohr, "Good Times at ShoWest," *Daily Variety,* Mar. 14, 2007.

Index

Author's note: Due to the extraordinary number of appearances throughout the book, I have left out the following terms from the index: CARA, Incontestable R, PCA, Production Code, MPAA, rating system, and responsible entertainment.

Page numbers in italics indicate illustrations.

About the Author

Kevin S. Sandler is an assistant professor of media arts at the University of Arizona, where he teaches in the Producing Program. He specializes in U.S. contemporary media, censorship, and animation and has published in a wide range of journals and anthologies, including *Cinema Journal* and *Animation Journal*. He is the editor of *Reading the Rabbit: Explorations in Warner Bros. Animation* (New Brunswick, NJ: Rutgers University Press, 1998); coeditor of *Titanic: Anatomy of a Blockbuster* (New Brunswick, NJ: Rutgers University Press, 1999), and author of *Scooby Doo* (Duke University Press, forthcoming).